THE

LANCASHIRE

LIBRARY

TITLE

A comedy of errors or, The Marriage
records of England and Wales, 1837-1899.

"A Comedy of Errors"

or

THE MARRIAGE RECORDS OF ENGLAND AND WALES 1837 - 1899

MICHAEL WHITFIELD FOSTER

WELLINGTON, NEW ZEALAND

1998

*Throwing light for the first
time on the story of the
GRO records of the 19th century*

i

ISBN   0-473-05581-3

Published by

Michael W Foster
19 Khouri Avenue
Wellington 6005
New Zealand

07752257
Printed by   PPR

Lithoprint Limited
19-21 Hopper Street
Te Aro
Wellington
New Zealand

First Edition 1998

The elegance of Smedley Hydro

Smedley Hydro, Southport, home of the General Register Office

Smedley Hydro, Certificate Services, "a working office"

Microfilm cassettes of birth records

Contents

Abbreviations

BDM	Births, deaths and marriages
CD-ROM	Compact disk - read only memory
GRO	General Register Office (part of ONS)
IGI	International Genealogical Index (of the LDS)
LDS	Latter-day Saints (the Mormon church)
OCR	Optical character recognition (of digitised text)
ONS	Office for National Statistics (formerly OPCS)
OPCS	Office of Population, Censuses & Surveys
Q1	The March quarter (January, February, March)
Q2	The June quarter (April, May, June)
Q3	The September quarter (July, August, September)
Q4	The December quarter (October, November, December)
RG	The Registrar General
TSR	Taunton Superintendent Registrar

Photographs

Front cover The author's grandparents on their wedding day, Alfred Robert Evans and Hannah Edith Kirtland, September 1896

Back cover Signing the registers, the author and his wife, Joyce Margaret Munford, August 1960

Behind title page

a)	Smedley Hydro, Southport, home of the General Register Office
b)	The elegance of Smedley Hydro
c)	Certificate Services, "a working office"
d)	Microfilm cassettes, births

FOREWORD

An author should whenever possible avoid writing his own foreword, partly because he has written quite enough already and partly because the reader feels a little more confidence in an author who is prepared to trust his reputation and fortunes to the opnion of someone other than himself.

The Deputy Registrar General of England and Wales has written that if she contributed a foreword it would be along the lines of :

> "The incompleteness and inaccuracies of the GRO indexes, particularly of the 1800 records, has long been known but Michael's research and the results contained in this book provide evidence of the extent of the problem.
>
> Whilst the solutions he suggests in Chapter 9 are not implementable because of the resource implications for the Registration Service, his work serves as a useful reminder of the effort required to put things right. It also emphasises the need to take into account the quality of the indexes when considering a computerised solution to access to records."

I feel that this research is a big step along the way towards the redevelopment of the system because it opens up knowledge of the system for public discussion as never before. Michael Armstrong of Family Tree Magazine has spoken of groups such as the Federation of Family History Societies and the Society of Genealogists giving their opinions on possible future options on behalf of genealogists. I have no doubt that this research will provide those groups, and genealogists in general, with a new view of the current system.

Until a way to correct the problems can be found (which probably implies funds and well organised voluntary effort), this book will be a valuable guide and background for all those using the current system.

I have not discussed ways and means of ordering certificates, something that is well covered elsewhere.

WELLINGTON, SOMERSET 1844/Q4
750a Robert Trenchard, Elizabeth Forbear, James Lewis, *Sarah Sparks*, *Thomas Walker*, Catharine Masey, *Joseph King*, Betsey Nation
Of the four marriages on this page of the marriage record, the four names in italics are missing from the index. How do we know ? Read on and you will find out.

Chapter 1   What it is all about

This book comes from nearly six years' work on the marriage records of England and Wales, from the beginning of civil registration in 1837. These records are a mainstay of family research for people of British stock (using the term British somewhat loosely). The indexes to the records as microfiche or film are in constant use by dedicated genealogical researchers round the world, in libraries and various family history centres. The indexes, for births deaths and marriages separately, are the key to the records of events and the means of ordering copies of official certificates.

My work hasn't been aimed at personal research. Instead it has aimed at exploring the structure of the records and errors in the indexes (inevitable when you consider the size of the task and the conditions and equipment at the time). There is much to be learned about the records, their characteristics and their peculiarities. The more I look, the more I seem to find. The book is really a story, the story of a journey of discovery (as I have subtitled chapter 4), an exciting journey despite the long and tedious work along the way. It describes the structures of the system and explains the many ways in which errors were able to develop.

I will try to share these findings in the hope that they will help your research and make it more interesting. It is emphatically *not* a rehash of anything written before. It is based on new research and the story is a new one. I hope that even those well used to the system will be surprised by what they learn. Beyond these immediate aims, the greatest hope is that the findings will affect the future of the records themselves.

The index of marriages, as many readers will know, is an index to the records of marriages in England and Wales since civil registration began in 1837 (Chapter 2 describes the 1836 legislation establishing the system). The index is organised by year and by quarter. Within each quarter the brides and grooms are listed in alphabetical order, together with a reference to the volume and page by which the entry can be found in the actual records of the marriages. The same method applies to births and deaths. They are all national indexes, combining names countrywide, unlike some other record systems where each county may need to be searched separately. (Chapter 3 takes a look at some examples from the marriage index). The marriage index was my chosen field because it yields a more complex and informative picture. It is underlaid by an interesting parish structure.

If you have used the index of marriages, have you ever noticed that there are far more references to pages with odd numbers than to pages with even numbers ? Have you puzzled over a faint or illegible reference and wished there was something to help you decide what it ought to be ? Have you pored through the marriage index looking for a bride to match the reference details for the bridegroom you have found ? Have you perhaps had the later disappointment of finding that the supposed partners were wrong after all and that you have done additional research to no avail ? Have you been unlucky enough to order a marriage certificate only to find that the reference was "wrong", yet you could read it clearly enough ? Have you simply been unable to find an index entry for someone you know was married ? This book will throw light on all these questions and tell you far more besides. The story of the marriage records is a fascinating detective story.

My years of research, even with the help of worldwide friends, have only covered a little over one per cent of the 1837-1899 material but this is an unprecedented sample. The work has gathered over 250,000 name entries for selected sections of the marriage index into computer files. This has revealed the structure of the primary record system and its changes over time, and exposed errors and omissions in the index and the underlying records.

Be aware, however, that the book can only describe the tip of the iceberg. As I shall point out later, out of the files of one per cent of the index entries for the 1800s only about a tenth have been checked in the research you will read about. Nor can I describe all the discoveries that have been made.

I saw, as this material built up, that it was becoming a unique way to assess the quality and completeness of the indexing process. Thanks to its form as an exact parallel of the marriage records, it had become a tool to make a direct and efficient check on the index and on the primary records.

My proposal to do this, at the same time contributing towards this book, was accepted by the Registrar General and led to several weeks of work within the ONS organisation, checking well over 20000 of my index entries against the films of marriage records. Six months would not have sufficed to check all my material. This work has taken the exploration back from the index to the marriage records, and back beyond those records to throw some light on the

2

marriage registers and the indexes of the district registrars. The extent of the errors and omissions has grown far beyond the original expectations.

Thus, as I have said, the book is a story of a journey of discovery as well as a description of errors and omissions found along the way.

It is important to stress that the basis for my acceptance by the Registrar General was not academic prominence, nor genealogical seniority, nor access for personal research, nor any sort of commercial objective, but simply the hard work of six years in creating a computer resource unequalled in the world and specifically designed for this task. Those other reasons would not have qualified. This unprecedented study can't be seen as a "toe in the door". It has been a unique basis for access to the marriage records and I hope its results will be of real value to the ONS organisation and of interest to the genealogical community at large. I also hope my proposals for an overhaul of the early records will be well received.

The major step of going half way round the world to work in the General Register Office was a leap into the unknown. How could I be sure that such research would actually produce any of the results I was looking for ? Would the project prove too hard, perhaps for reasons of legibility of the records or because the GRO's internal organisation might be unsuitable in some way ? Had I built up expectations and hopes in isolation from the "real world" that I was going to visit ? Might my picture of the project prove to be a mirage ?

At Southport it quickly became clear that the concerns were unnecessary. Access to the records was excellent, rack upon rack of records in microfilm cassettes. Despite the many staff accessing the records continuously, there was no problem at all in using any of the films as needed. Legibility, of course, is a problem (as later chapters will show) but it wasn't a problem in pursuing this research. Even a few days' work were enough to start building up a big collection of data on differences between the records and the indexes, unindexed marriage partners, copying errors, apparent copying omissions. No amount of staring at the marriage index or even at the marriage records would by itself reveal these problems. I quickly saw that my checking process was unique and that the whole organisation and direction of my research had proved exactly right.

The biggest problem in this sort of work is always the tedium of winding monotonously through film after film, checking item after item without finding anything out of the ordinary. It is important to break up the work in any way possible and to devise side issues to maintain concentration and interest. Conversely I felt the need to cover as much ground as possible.

Ironically it is probably much the same feeling of tedium that led to many of the errors in the record system in the first place. Concentration and interest are essential in tasks such as copying, indexing and typing.

This book is *not* directly about the often-voiced question of freer access to the records. Its concern is mainly descriptive. If anything, however, through what it tells about some of the characteristics of the system, it could well suggest a very different approach to questions of that sort. There are factors generally unknown, as will emerge from this book, that could well lead to some rethinking. The conclusions and proposals for radical changes are outlined in Chapter 9, together with suggestions for two further investigations into the quality of the early records.

As I have said, this is by no means the full story of the 19th century marriage records, let alone of the other vital records. The full story will probably never be told because checking all or most of the records will never happen.

I have not included any research into the 19th century registers now in County Record Offices, though noting Anthony Camp's comment in 1993 that over 90% of them are now in various of them. The time frame of my research visit to Southport was not wide enough to let me get to County Record Offices nor was there time for a second visit within the time frame for producing this book. The entire purpose of the research visit was to compare the GRO indexes against the GRO marriage films. Suffice it to say that my sorted computer files of GRO indexes that you will soon meet are as ideal for efficient checks against registers in county offices as for the work with the GRO marriage records on film in Southport. Such a project would be almost as valuable as my proposals in Chapter 9 for comparative work in the offices of Superintendent Registrars though it could be less comprehensive.

Let me pause and digress here for a moment. Henry Fielding, as the very first line of his novel "Joseph Andrews", writes "It is a trite but true observation, that examples work more forcibly on the mind than precepts ..." and I have felt the need to adopt that principle for this book. It very soon became clear that although the *writer* can draw on a mental picture of the material under discussion, that same picture isn't available to a *reader*. Hence a liberal use of examples to illustrate the workings of the record system and also its imperfections. In common with many other novels of the 1700s, "Joseph Andrews" ends with the revelation that some of the characters are not who we (and they) thought they were. The marriage records of the 1800s can be every bit as surprising, with some situations that might have given Henry Fielding a store of new ideas.

4

This now seems the right place to record thanks to people round the world who have contributed to the huge task of collecting the data, people such as Annette Easton, Janice Freeman, Barbara Kolle, Tom Miller, Frances Stewart, Iris Tolley. Also to two friends who added invaluably to the quality of the data by checking some of the entries most illegible on film and fiche by look-ups in the indexes at St Catherine's House and later Myddelton House in London, namely Derek Griffis and Alan Merryweather, and to John Harnden in Hereford for some valued insights and encouragement and for providing evidence unearthed in the County of Herefordshire District Council records office. All have helped to speed the task and improve its results and potential, and have been a great source of encouragement. Others who gave valuable encouragement at a very early stage in my efforts were Ron Jones of Auckland and the late Ted Wildy, whose work in the field of indexing led me into taking the same path when retirement gave me time. I have also had the benefit of the excellent working conditions and facilities in the family history section of the New Zealand National Library in Wellington.

Lastly, and crucial to the final research, thanks go to ONS on behalf of the genealogical community at large for allowing the research to be taken to its logical conclusion and for the hospitable welcome that made it satisfying, enjoyable and productive. The book will show that this access opened new pathways to discoveries not foreseen. I hope ONS will be well repaid by the findings and my reports and will use them in improving the system.

I should like to dedicate this book to the memory of the thousands of unsung registrars and clerks whose work in the nineteenth century has left us the great records we use so much today. In particular I remember my own great great grandfather Whitfield Foster, parish clerk in Wandsworth in the 1840s, whose name appears as the district registrar in August 1846 when the birth of my great grandfather, another Whitfield Foster, was registered. It is a joy to have a personal family link with this great system and to have seen his handwriting on page after page of his registers of births and deaths copied each quarter as part of the quarterly return of registrations to the General Register Office. It was a relief to find that *his* writing, at least, was impeccable, far better than mine.

 * * * * * * * * * * * *

Because of the interplay of structures and procedures in the registration system, and the way these elements are linked with the errors in the system, one can't always separate the parts of the discussion into watertight sections. Topics arise more than once because they relate to another aspect of the system. I hope this will tend to reinforce the effectiveness of the book.

Chapters 2, 3 and 4 are a necessary and logical foundation for the rest of the book. Chapter 5 onwards will, I hope, take most readers into new territory, at the same time putting the earlier chapters in perspective in the total story.

It is inevitable that a book such as this will make suggestions and assertions as well as simply stating facts and findings. Therefore it is also inevitable that some theories or conclusions can be disputed. I believe, if I can be allowed yet another assertion, that the weight of the evidence will speak for itself and that the general conclusions of the book are not in any doubt.

It is an area of research where every finding seems to stimulate two more questions and it is hard to avoid pursuing new lines of enquiry. Even in writing the book I have found myself raising new issues, making new suppositions and even new findings and could very easily and productively spend more weeks or even months at the GRO and at local registries.

"A Comedy of Errors" feels particularly appropriate as a surtitle. It is not only its appeal as a title in itself, but even Shakespeare's plot seems especially apt, a lost son whose marriage is unknown to his searching father and a wife who has been lost without trace, plus the threat of an inflexible legal system (though on that count we can thankfully say that the existence of this book is itself proof that that analogy is rapidly fading).

When I was translating Cicero many years ago, sitting in Latin lessons in a school that was two hundred years old before the system of Civil Registration was set up in England, I had no thought that the old orator would prove useful to me another fifty years on.

In one of his works he tells of visiting Syracuse in Sicily and successfully finding the overgrown and long forgotten grave of Archimedes. The famous city, a centre of learning in the past, would have remained ignorant of the tomb of its most brilliant citizen if a stranger from Arpinum hadn't come to find it. Thus said Cicero. Visiting the General Register Office from New Zealand has seemed to me to have something of that same flavour.

And Cicero is credited with another apposite comment. "Not to know what happened before we are born is to remain a child forever. For what is the value of human life unless it is woven into the life of our ancestors ?" The omissions and errors in the historical record for England and Wales would be seen by Marcus Tullius as a stumbling block on the pathway to a fulfilled life. That throws a very appropriate light on the aims of this book.

Chapter 2 - History & Legislation

If you feel this chapter becoming heavy going, leave it and come back after a few more chapters. When you have been out in the countryside the map may begin to make rather more sense. Do read the first page and a half of the chapter before going on ahead.

The system of registration of births, deaths and marriages in England and Wales was established by legislation passed in 1836. The legislation speaks simply of "England" but this has to be taken as including Wales so far as this chapter is concerned.

The operation of the system began in 1837 and the first published records date from the September quarter of 1837. A slightly earlier start had been intended but was not achieved.

The system is a large one and has grown steadily with population growth over the years. Its existence has been fundamentally important to genealogical research and despite shortcomings it is in continuous use by researchers worldwide, on a scale that can never have been imagined by those setting up the system in the 1830s and indeed in ways and for purposes that would not have been contemplated. See chapter 10 for some population statistics.

The two next chapters will describe the structure of the record system in terms of registration districts and the volume and page reference system used in the index as a means of identifying the material in the records themselves. It will be useful to describe the elements of the 1836 legislation as background . It can be easier to appreciate the workings of a system when you know something of its design.

The discussion in this chapter may well be clearer if we anticipate slightly and note the three levels of registrar that we will meet. Each has a very distinct and vital role and will necessarily appear repeatedly in the discussion.

a)   The Registrar General is responsible for the operation of the General Register Office (the GRO), now a part of the Office for National Statistics (the ONS).

b)   The Superintendent Registrars are the registrars based on the Poor Law Unions, numbering over 600 in England and Wales. The indexes of births, deaths and marriages show the locality of the entries by giving the name of the Superintendent Registrar's district, for example Rochford vol 12, or Eton vol 3a.

c) The district registrars were responsible for registration districts within the overall district of a Superintendent Registrar. Thus Eton included registration sub-districts such as Iver and Burnham.

Two Acts were passed in 1836 :
  1 An Act for Marriages in England
  2 An Act for registering Births, Deaths, and Marriages in England
These Acts are identified as Chapters 85 and 86, 6 & 7 Gulielmi IV. (The calendar year 1836 consisted of parts of the sixth and seventh regnal years of William IV).

The first act amended existing law. It dealt mainly with marriage procedures, licensing of churches and chapels, forms of marriage licences and so on.

Existing Superintendent Registrars of births and deaths "for every Union, Parish or Place" were also made responsible for marriages (section III of the Act). This provision was elaborated in section VII of the second Act.

As well as marriage by licence or special licence or after publication of banns, which remained much the most usual basis for marriage, provision was made for either party to complete a Notice of Marriage in advance of the marriage. This was then copied into a Marriage Notices Book by the registrar and made available to "all persons desirous of inspecting the same". This allowed for the marriage to be forbidden by those legally entitled to do so, as with publication of banns. Time limits were set within which a marriage could or must be solemnised in relation to the date of the Notice. As with banns read in churches, the Marriage Notices were to be read three times at weekly meetings of Boards of Guardians of the Poor Law Unions. Failing any objections to the marriage, the registrar would issue a certificate to that effect. These notices of marriage can be seen at Register Offices today.

In my small collection of twenty three marriage certificates, sixteen marriages were in a parish church after banns, one was by licence, and six were in independent meeting houses or chapels in the presence of a registrar. One in a meeting house referred to a registrar's certificate as allowing the marriage.

Marriages were to take place in the designated "registered building" and were to take place "with open doors, between the hours of eight and twelve in the forenoon in the presence of some registrar of the district in which such

8

registered building is situate and of two or more credible witnesses". Those who objected to marrying in a "registered building" were allowed (Section XXI) to marry in the office of a Registrar, a "registry office wedding".

In 1886 a very brief amending Act, Victoria 49 & 50, c.14, amended the hours within which a marriage could be legally solemnised, extending the time to three in the afternoon. This was further extended to six in the afternoon by an Act of George V in 1934.

Looking at all the provisions relating to banns, Notices of Marriage, the timing of marriage within certain daylight hours, the open doors of the building, the need for two witnesses, all these requirements clearly aimed to ensure that marriages should never be clandestine or hidden or involve any form of deceit or fraud. In a sense this was simply a reflection of the church's own requirement that there should be no "just impediment" to a marriage, but it also reflected the need for a woman's rights and particularly her property rights to be protected. Before the Marriage Act of 1753 was passed, marriages were legally valid without the need for banns or licences and there was no compulsion for the use of a special building or even of a clergyman. The abuses and social costs of the so-called "Fleet marriages" before 1753 were a scandal and a running social sore. "London Life in the 18th Century", that wonderful book by M Dorothy George, contains some graphic accounts of such marriages on pages 314-316.

The Marriage Act of 1836 was to apply throughout England but "shall not extend to the marriage of any of the Royal Family".

The second act was to provide "the Means for a complete Register of the Births, Deaths, and Marriages of His Majesty's Subjects in England" and it repealed previous legislation regulating parish and other registers. It set up the General Register Office and established the office of Registrar General, with a salary not to exceed "One thousand Pounds yearly".

A system of registration districts was to be established, each forming part of one of the parishes and unions for which Boards of Guardians had been set up under the Poor Law legislation, with registrars to be appointed for each of their districts by the guardians and superintendent registrars for "each Union, Parish or Place" (section VII). The Poor Law legislation was recent and the parliamentary debates on the marriage legislation made it clear that there was no wish to set up another national system of officials. Therefore the new Poor Law administrative structure, still in the course of being established, was chosen as the basis for the civil registration system at a local level. Much of the debate in the House of Lords was concerned with the way of appointing the registrars, and with deciding the responsibility for their salaries. Hence the structure arose, that has remained to this day, in which the central organisation does not have direct control over the local organisation.

The clerk to the guardians was specified as first choice for the position of Superintendent Registrar, if he was prepared to serve. An amending Act of 1838, "to explain and amend the two Acts passed in the last session of parliament", allowed the Registrar General to appoint a Superintendent Registrar if a Board of Guardians neglected or refused to make an appointment for 14 days after being required to do so by the Registrar General.

This 1838 Act also gave the Registrar General the power to unite two or more Superintendent Registrars' districts, and to nominate which Board of Guardians would be responsible for the united district. He was also empowered to divide districts, a necessity as cities grew larger.

Each district was to be given a distinct name, for which we can be thankful, even if names like Aston, Ashton, Alton and Alston are all too similar. It was a sensible provision when you think of the large number of identical place names in Britain. Temporary districts were to be set up for all places not yet under the Poor Law Act. The Poor Law legislation had been reformed in 1834 to try to eliminate the abuses and lack of accountability that had been a cause of concern for many years and the organisation of the Poor Law Unions was not fully in order in 1837.

So important was the continuity of the registration system that every registrar was to appoint a deputy to act for him in case of illness, absence or death (section XII). This could otherwise have been a weakness of the new system. The amending Act of 1838 also allowed the Registrar General to appoint an assistant in case of his own absence, though with rather limited powers of decision.

Register Offices were to be set up in each Union for the safe custody of the registers, under the care of the Superintendent Registrars. They would progressively become responsible for the Register Books of births, marriages and deaths for their districts, receiving them from the clergy and the district registrars as they were completed. It is worth noting, in passing, that some of the marriage registers first issued in 1837 have not yet been completed and are still in parish use and custody.

Great care was to be taken of the Register Books. Strong Iron Boxes were to be provided by the Registrar General for each district registrar, "furnished with a Lock and Two keys and no more", one key for the district registrar and one for the superintendent registrar. The books were to be kept in the locked box whenever not in use. Provision was made in the 1838 Act for dealing safely with records when any districts were united by the Registrar General.

The justices of the peace were given sweeping powers to ensure that the registers were duly handed over by any registrar leaving or losing his office, including summary imprisonment "in the Common Gaol or House of Correction" without bail until the registers were delivered up or found. The Act assumed that the registrars would act in their own homes, which had to be within their districts, with their name and function clearly displayed and visible. Register Books for births and deaths were to be supplied to them by the Registrar General.

The procedure for registration of births and deaths would seem a little strange to us now. Each registrar was authorised and required "to inform himself carefully of every Birth and every Death which shall happen within his District" and to "learn and register as soon after the event as conveniently may be done". Then follows one of those provisions intended to regularise the system. Every entry is to be made "in Order from the Beginning to the End of the Book". This is one of the provisions to ensure the completeness of the record system.

The question of compulsion for registration is not entirely clear in the wording of the Act. It provides that a parent (in the case of a birth) or the occupier of any house where a birth or death takes place "may" notify the district registrar within 42 days of a birth or 5 days of a death. On the other hand, if a new-born child or a corpse "is found exposed", then the relevant authority "*shall* give notice and information thereof to the Registrar". This slight uncertainty seems to be at least partly rectified in the following paragraph, by which the parent or occupier *shall* give information to the Registrar on a birth "upon being requested so to do" and a later section in the Act makes a similar requirement for a death. It seems that the intention was for registration of births and deaths to be compulsory. This was very clearly so for any child born at sea or a person dying at sea on a British vessel, and provision was made for a Marine Register Book to be kept by the Registrar General for that purpose.

Special procedures were specified for late registration, after the 42-day period allowed for normal registration. The father, guardian or anyone present at the birth was permitted to make a solemn declaration of the particulars of the birth in the joint presence of the registrar and the Superintendent Registrar who would then jointly sign the entry and would receive additional fees from the informant. The penalty for anyone involved in registering a birth after 42 days and not according to these special procedures was severe, a penalty of "a sum not exceeding fifty pounds".

Beyond six calendar months after a birth, no registration was allowed. Anyone involved in such registration faced the same heavy penalty. Another penalty was that no birth certificate was permitted for such a situation.

The compulsion for registration of deaths was reinforced by a requirement for a certificate of the death to go from the registrar to the undertaker and thence to the minister officiating at the burial. A minister was also to notify the registrar of any burial performed without such a certificate. These were requirements carrying penalties if not met.

Registrars had a financial inducement to register births and deaths completely as they were to be paid a fee based on the number of registrations, duly verified by the superintendent registrar.

It is only in Section XXX of the Act that we first come to a mention of marriages, as these were primarily the responsibility of the churches (and of the Quakers and the Jewish synagogues). The Registrar General was to provide Marriage Register Books *in duplicate* to all the registered and certified places of marriage, the cost being paid by the churchwardens or other responsible persons. Books were of two sizes, some of two hundred spaces while most were of five hundred spaces.

The provision for the registration of marriages was very strict. The duplicate entries were to be made by the clergyman immediately after the marriage ceremony and signed by him, and by the parties married, and by two witnesses. In practice there were sometimes three or more witnesses but the legal requirement was for two. Entries were to be made in order from the beginning to the end of the book, and furthermore the "number of the place of entry" in each duplicate register book was to be the same. There were very minor differences for Quakers and Jews. The registering officer of the Quakers was allowed to make the entries "as soon as conveniently may be". Registration in a synagogue also had to be immediate, and there was the additional requirement that the husband in the marriage should be a member of that synagogue. The Marriages Act required (Section II) that *both* parties to a marriage performed by Quakers and Jews should be "of the said Society, or both persons professing the Jewish Religion respectively".

"Synagogue" marriages were very often not in the synagogue itself, but often at street addresses that were clearly used for meetings. In all marriages there is a tendency for the location of the ceremony to be near the home of the bride rather than the groom. The requirement that a Jewish marriage must be recorded in the register of the synagogue of which the husband was a member meant that a husband might have to take the secretary of his synagogue along with him to some quite distant location where the marriage was to take place. For today's genealogist this can mean that the place of marriage and the registration district holding the record can be far apart if a marriage is a Jewish one. (See chapter 7 and appendix 9 for more comment and examples).

We then come to the requirement for copying the original entries, something that can cause a slight tremor to run down the spine of current researchers, despite the checking that a "true copy'" has been made.

In April, July, October and January, each registrar was to make a true copy of all entries of *births and deaths* in his registers since the previous copy was made, certifying the name and entry number of the first and last entries, and was to pass that copy and covering certificate to his superintendent registrar. Each such quarterly copy was to include all events that were *recorded* in the precise three-month quarter, for example in January, February and March for the April return. For births and deaths the date of the event and the date of the record could often be very different.

The superintendent would verify the registrar's return as a true copy. It is a precisely defined system but has no independent check. There is no requirement, for example, for a Justice or a Justice's clerk to make a few spot checks on some of these copies. Any slackness by a superintendent registrar could quite easily lead to slackness within his whole system.

Marriages were handled in much the same way. In those same months the minister of each church (and the corresponding officers of the Quakers and the Jews) were to make true copies of entries in the register book of marriages and deliver them to the Superintendent Registrar. For marriages the date of the event and the date of the record are normally the same. The minister seems to have been deemed more reliable than local registrars as there was *no* provision for the superintendent registrar to verify the copies as correct. The minister's word was taken as sufficient, whether of the Church of England or an officer of the Jews or Quakers. The dissenting churches, a wide range of chapels and independent meeting houses, Salems, Bethesdas and Sion meetings, had no marriage registers of their own and the local district registrar was present at all marriages that they performed, taking his register office marriage register book with him. Hence the marriage registers completed by the registrars, whether they were district registrars or superintendent registrars, contained a mixture of records of register office marriages and marriages in chapels and meeting houses.

Special forms were printed for making these quarterly copies of the marriages (and of births and deaths). They reflected the procedural differences. Forms used by registrars were printed so as to contain a confirming statement by the Superintendent Registrar that he had compared and verified the copy made by the district registrar. No such statement was included in the forms printed for the other categories, but the forms for the clergy, the Jews and the Quakers all differed to reflect their origin. For the Quakers, who used a different form of wording for their dates, for example "the seventh of the third month, commonly called March", this wording was incorporated in their forms. The forms for the Quarterly Returns were printed on a heavy durable paper, water-marked with the words Register of Marriages, a ream of the forms being some seven centimetres thick.

When each register was filled, one copy of the marriage registers was to remain with the other registers and records of the church (or Quaker/Jewish communities) and one copy was to go to the superintendent registrar, together with completed birth and death registers from the district registrars.

For marriages solemnised not in a registered ecclesiastical building but in a registrar's office, the documentary procedures were not in this Act but in the Marriages Act, sections XXIII and XXIV, one of the several untidy features of these pieces of legislation. The registrar was to record the marriage in his Marriage Register Book and once a quarter he was to make a true copy of the latest marriages and deliver it to the Superintendent Registrar, who was then to verify them as true copies. The two Acts have a consistent standard of trust, or mistrust, in the copying skills of the district registrars.

Only a few of the district registrars of births and deaths were appointed as registrars of marriages. Clergy, after all, were registrars for the overwhelming majority of marriages. The amending Act of 1838 gave the Registrar General the power to fix the number of registrars of marriages to be appointed by any Superintendent Registrar. At the same time it forbade any Superintendent Registrar to appoint more than that number.

The Superintendent Registrar was then required to send the certified copies of entries of births, deaths and marriages to the Registrar General, receiving "the Sum of Two-pence" for each entry submitted. These copies were and are known as "the quarterly returns". For many years these quarterly returns, in bundles according to their districts and volumes, were kept in the less than dry basements of Somerset House in London. Section XXXIV of the Act also informed the Superintendent Registrars that "... if it shall appear, by interruption of the regular progression of numbers or otherwise, that the copy of any part of any book has not been duly delivered to him, he shall procure, as far as possible, consistently with the provisions of this Act, that the same may be remedied and supplied". It will be shown later in this book that there is much evidence that the "progression of numbers" was not faithfully watched and maintained.   Quarterly returns of marriages frequently overlapped or have left apparent gaps in the sequence. Some registrars were no doubt much better than others. The clergy often seemed to have little idea of what a "quarter" actually was.

The original 1836 legislation hadn't defined exactly what a quarter was but this was picked up in 1838, defining the quarters as ending on the last day of March, June, September and December. It obviously continued to mean little to many clergy. They could cheerfully be wrong by at least a month or two.

Section XXXV of the 1836 Act provided that clergy and registrars holding Register Books of Births, Deaths and Marriages should allow searches of the books and provide copies of entries, for prescribed fees. (This would not apply to the Registrar General, who did not hold the Register Books). The wording of this section, with its provision for fees according to the length of search period, could suggest that the registrar would do the searching.

Section XXXVI requires the Superintendent Registrar to index the register books in his office, and "every person shall be entitled at all reasonable hours to search the said indexes" and to have a certified copy made. The fee first set down for searching the indexes was "For every general search the sum of five shillings and for every particular search the sum of one shilling". It seems that the particular search related to a particular register and that the general search involved several registers.

The local indexes seem to have referenced the entry numbers found in the register books rather than the numbers of the pages. It is not said exactly when these indexes would be made but the inference is that the marriage registers could only be indexed when completed and finally lodged with the Superintendent Registrar. The quarterly returns by registrars and clergy to the Superintendent Registrar were in the form of copies but as the Superintendent had to certify the birth and death copies he could have indexed in advance on these occasions, having the registers temporarily in his hands. It is even possible that some Superintendents may have progressively built up parish indexes before sending off the clergy copies to the Registrar General, thus using copies rather than original entries, but this is pure conjecture.

It is clearly stated in section XXXII that after delivering the copies of the birth and death entries to his Superintendent Registrar, the "registrar shall keep safely each of the said Register Books until it shall be filled, and shall then deliver it to the Superintendent Registrar to be kept by him with the Records of his Office".   The clergy, in section XXXIII, had similar instructions relating to the Marriage Register Books.   Thus the Superintendent would have acquired the completed Register Books over a long period of time and doesn't really seem to have been in a position to "index the register books in his office" until the system had been in operation for some while.

In section XXXVII the Registrar General was also required to index the certified copies of the register entries received from the local Superintendent Registrars and to allow those indexes to be searched by "every person". Both this search facility and the one at local level would cost a search fee, a fee that for the Registrar General's indexes was substantially higher for a "general search" than for a "particular search", 20s. against 1s. They were much larger indexes. The Act does not specify that there would be separate indexes for birth, deaths and marriages, and we are fortunate that this was the arrangement that was adopted.

There were severe penalties for false entries, false copies, and any other failures in the registration system, except that clergy or registrars who discover an error may arrange for it to be corrected within a month of the discovery in the presence of family members or reliable witnesses. This requirement emphasises a major feature of the registration system, namely that it has always been "informant driven". Even today's elderly person with no apparent birth registration but needing a birth registration before drawing a pension cannot succeed by simply providing his own evidence. It is necessary to secure some independent informants to verify the birth.

The rest of the Act deals mainly with penalties and their recovery, or with appeals against them, and with providing the Registrar General with free postage for materials relating exclusively to "the execution of this Act". Any officer of the Registrar General who abused this facility in any way would be dismissed and ordered to pay a penalty of one hundred pounds.

The Act of 1838 laid down a penalty of £10 for clergy or registrars who failed to supply their Certified Quarterly Returns or nil returns within one calendar month of being required to do so. This doesn't seem to have prevented late, and very late, returns.

The statistical element in the system of civil registration was largely covered by one brief paragraph (section VI) requiring the Registrar General to submit an annual abstract of the numbers of births, deaths and marriages.

It was also felt necessary that the Act should specify that "nothing herein contained shall affect the Registration of Baptisms or Burials as now by Law established".

Finally the schedules to the legislation set out the format for the entries of births, deaths and marriages, including valuable new detail.

*   *   *   *   *   *   *   *   *   *   *

Such, then, was the founding legislation of the system of civil registration of births, deaths and marriages in England and Wales. It was a huge data system for a time when every process was carried out by hand with simple instruments and without the help of modern lighting and modern workplaces. It has survived in much the same form, though with modification in detail.

Many of the procedures were not defined in the legislation but were left to be set up by the Registrar General, within the structure defined by law. The procedures developed and changed over the years, being formalised at various times in the Registrar General's manual of instructions for the registrars and by a booklet of instructions and guidance for the clergy.

Some fundamentals have been observed from the beginning and reinforced from time to time. They include the need for marriages to be performed with strict legality, be registered and certified by clergy and officiating registrars so that certified records are valid records of legally performed marriages. This is an essential part of the system today, even if we now know that the careful certification is no guarantee that the records are correct.

It has been well argued that the General Register Office indexes are now very inadequate for the sort of research being carried out by genealogists. Without access to original registers, it is often impossible to judge which of many index entries may be the one that is wanted, leading to frustration and to fruitless expenditure on buying certificates. The later indexes are more informative than the earlier ones but much research is necessarily based on the older records. My proposals in chapter 9 would be a big advance.

It has also been pointed out that access to the original registers in Somerset House was permitted up to the late 1800s, mainly to lawyers, and that searches of local registers were possible up to the 1970s, mainly to historians. Indeed the Royal Commission of 1914 gave its view that "it was the evident intention of the [1836] Act that the public should be able to obtain certain information from the registers ... ".   As pointed out above, however, there is a marked difference in the wording of the 1836 Act between the facility for searching the registers and for searching the index that could suggest quite strongly that full public access was only intended for the indexes. The Royal Commission, despite its eminent composition, may perhaps have overstated its case.

The Act specifies the entitlement of "every person" to search the *indexes*, both at the Superintendents' offices and at the GRO. The entitlement to search the Register Books themselves does not have the same reference to "every person" and there may have been a tacit assumption that such searches would only be made by people such as lawyers. When literacy was so low the thought of "all persons" being able to search anything beyond a simple list of names may have been far from the legislators' minds. Certainly a very early copy of the Registrar General's manual of instructions for registrars is quite emphatic that the public have no right of access to the registers deposited with the registrars. The reference in section XXXV mentioned above seems to refer only to registers currently open, as distinct from the deposited registers.

It seems significant as well that access to the Marriage Notice Book was also allowed "to all persons", and this seems to reinforce further the distinction in the wording relating to access to the actual Register books. The Notice Book was also a register that was currently open.

One might have to read the records of the parliamentary debates very thoroughly to throw more light on this apparent difference, but I have read quite a number of the 1836 debates, filed in the GRO library in Southport, without coming across any references to this aspect of the system. There is some untidiness in the way that the two Acts are put together. The parliamentary debates reveal a consciousness of this but at the same time a sense of urgency that it was necessary to pass the legislation into law as quickly as possible despite any minor shortcomings.

But debate on some of these aspects of the legislation may have little purpose today. In later sections of this book, in which the system is described in more detail, I shall be suggesting some remedies along different paths.

Chapter 3 - The Marriage Index

For a clear understanding of this discussion you need this basic picture of the GRO records.

The records of all births, marriages and deaths are held by the Office for National Statistics in Britain. They contain the detail supplied in Birth/Marriage/Death Certificates but are not available for public access.

The records are indexed, quarterly, and these indexes are the access method for the birth/marriage/death records for England and Wales from 1837.

The subject of this book is the marriage records, and no doubt many readers will be familiar with the marriage index. Most will have met the index as the microfiche or microfilm copies of the weighty volumes in the General Register Office in London, now widely available in libraries and family history centres. It is used as a fundamental tool by countless researchers in searching for earlier members of their families. It is an alphabetical index to the marriage records themselves.

Two short segments of the marriage index may help as a basis for discussion. Firstly a short segment from the marriage index for the March Quarter of 1844 (which for simplicity we will now call 1844/Q1) : -

Surname	Name	District	Vol	Page
Crane	Hannah	St Jas Westr	I	76
Crane	Marcus	Samford	XII	543
Crane	Maria Teresa	Liverpool	XX	190
Crane	Mary	Liverpool	XX	153
Crane	Mary	G Boughton	XIX	27
Crane	Mary	Woodbridge	XII	643
Crane	Noah	Plomesgate	XII	499
Cranfield	James	Chesterton	XIV	57
Crankshaw	Ann	Bolton	XXI	63
Crankshaw	Betty	Blackburn	XXI	15
Crankshaw	David	Bolton	XXI	77
Cranmer	Robert	Sunderland	XXIV	213
Cranmer	Willm	Witham	XII	383
Cranmore	Mary	Sheffield	XXII	375

The indexes, and the marriage records themselves, are separate records for each quarter of each year.

This small section of index shows how each name is referenced to a district (i.e. to a particular Superintendent Registrar's district), to a volume and to a page. At that time there were rather over 600 Superintendent Registrars' districts in England and Wales made up by the GRO into 27 volumes, eight of which appear in this small section. In theory the volume number is unnecessary for reference. Each district name is meant to be unique. Hence a personal name could be identified by the General Register Office from the district name and page number alone. On the other hand the volume numbers have been helpful in my work and in practice they are used by the GRO as the easiest way to find a particular piece of information. Each volume number corresponds to a particular microfilm at the GRO and the page refers to a frame on that film. Taken together with the year and quarter of the index, this information identifies the exact location of each marriage record.

Indexes were originally hand-written but many indexes for the early years have now been typed. Five main consequences flow from this. Firstly the typed indexes are often much easier to read (though by no means always). Secondly the old Roman numerals have been replaced by arabic numerals - you no longer need to remember that XXIV means 24. Thirdly, the retyping was made more open and no doubt quicker by only typing each surname the first time it occurred, and also at the top of a new column. Fourthly the old pages of forty names were replaced by pages with far more names (the amount has varied over the years). Fifthly, but this is a major offset to the other advantages, many more errors were introduced into the material (on which I have more to say in later chapters). Here is what our little collection of Cranes really look like in the typed index :

CRANDALL	Amy
CRANE	Hannah
	Marcus
	Maria Teresa
	Mary
	Mary
	Mary
	Noah
CRANFIELD	James
CRANKSHAW	Ann
	Betty
	David

The indexes originally written out by hand were on huge register sheets each holding forty entries in large script. Changes in handwriting can be seen every half dozen pages or so. I have experimented with a quill pen and it seems that each clerk probably wrote for three or four hours at a time.

The arithmetic of the operation is impressive. In 1840 for example 500,000 births, 360,000 deaths and 125,000 marriages meant 1,110,000 names to be indexed, some 27,700 index pages in total. To write such large script with reasonable care, avoiding blots and smudges, reading from hand-written input, must have meant at least 12,000 hours a year. There are only 8760 hours in a year, day and night, so the final index registers must have been a full time job for the few clerks who seem to have been involved.

As explained in Chapter 2, each Superintendent Registrar's district normally held a number of sub-districts, each with its own district registrar of births and deaths, but the indexes only show the district name of the Superintendent Registrar. It is often the name of a town but this can conceal the fact that it extends widely over surrounding country areas, especially for rural districts such as Woodbridge (Mary Crane), Plomesgate (Noah Crane) and Chesterton (James Cranfield).

Quite a number of Superintendents' districts were named after the old administrative hundreds, such as Tendring and Lexden in Essex, or Risbridge in Suffolk. The hundreds were divisions of a county having their own court. The district names can appear in the indexes in a variety of forms. For example St Jas Westr may be simply St James, or St James W, at the whim of the indexing clerk. Several forms may appear on a single page of the index. The GRO record itself normally contains the full form of the name. A glance at the marriage index for 1837, for example, will show districts such as Lexden and Winstree, Loddon and Clavering, and Kingston on Hull but these rapidly became abbreviated to Lexden, Loddon and Hull in the indexes.

Later indexes have gone rather too far. You will often find that Wellington Salop and Wellington Somerset appear simply as Wellington. You can find Newport, for example, in quite an early typed index, not identified as Newport (Mon) or Newport (Salop) but shown simply as Newport. (See Chapter 12 for a discussion on district names).

Sometimes there is no distinction between the three Newcastles (upon Tyne, under Lyne and in Emlyn). Indeed one entry in the typed marriage index of 1837 has the same person on two consecutive lines as Newcastle on Tyne vol 25 p371 and then Newcastle in Emlyn vol 25 p371. In the GRO's records the district name is in the heading of each page rather than in the individual marriage items and the indexing clerk must have known that he was processing the records for Newcastle on Tyne. It is hard to see any reason other than pure ineptitude for errors like this. Even the subsequent typist probably had no discretion to question such an obvious error.

But to return to the main subject. Our concern is just with marriages and for this purpose each Superintendent Registrar's district is mainly a collection of parishes, the clergy of the Church of England being responsible for the registration of most marriages.. Typically the marriages in a Superintendent Registrar's district may come from at least two or three dozen parishes and perhaps one or two register offices. Only a few districts contain Jewish or Quaker congregations. As already mentioned, marriages in dissenting chapels and other meeting houses were recorded in the marriage register of a local district registrar of marriages, a register usually holding an irregular series of register office marriages and those in dissenting congregations.

None of this is apparent from the index. The information in the index is in fact fairly limited. It doesn't tell you the exact date of the marriage, nor the precise locality (and some of the registrars' districts were very large). In particular there is no clue to the other partner in the marriage (until changes after 1900).

Next we come to a segment from the marriage index for 1856/Q1. It will be seen that the numbering system for the volumes has changed. From 1852 the previous 27 volumes changed to a new set of 33 volumes. The structures of the record systems will be discussed in more detail in Chapter 4.

Surname	Name	District	Vol	Page
Jackson	William	Haltwhistle	10b	309
Jackson	William	Islington	1b	293
Jackson	William	Wellingbro	3b	219
Jackson	William	Chesterton	3b	653
Jackson	William	Otley	9a	163
Jackson	William	Macclesfield	8a	153
Jackson	William	Stockport	8a	68
Jackson	William	Dursley	6a	266
Jackson	William	Stokesley	9d	653
Jackson	William	Ashby Z	7a	141
Jackson	William	Oldham	8d	687
Jackson	William	Hemsworth	9c	110
Jackson	William	Kidderminster	6c	245
Jackson	William Henry	Brighton	2b	266

The new volume numbers run from 1 to 11, with the addition of the letters a-e. Unfortunately the letters a/d and c/e can be very hard to distinguish on film and fiche and this led to many errors when some of the indexes were put into typed form. Notice that Chesterton was in volume 14 in the first table and was put in volume 3b in 1852.

It is the marriage records themselves that contain the information you need in order to be sure you are looking at the right person. Nevertheless your only basis for decision is usually the index.

Surnames that are not particularly common can sometimes run into surprisingly large numbers if you are searching over a number of years. William Jackson is an illustration. The name of the district will help to narrow the search but there could be a hundred William Jacksons marrying over a fairly short period. And the district name is not quite so helpful for men as for women. Women were more likely to marry in their own district and men more often married outside their own district.

If you happen to be looking for a marriage for Noah Crane in 1844, in our first table, then you are lucky. It is hardly a common name. You can well use the reference from the index (Plomesgate, volume 12, page 499) to order his marriage certificate and you may very well be delighted to find that Noah is exactly the person you hoped he would be and that his wife, a new discovery for you, is Patience Harling. A case of patience well rewarded ? We shall meet our friend Noah in a later chapter. There is a surprise in store.

If you are looking for Mary Crane the decision is rather harder than with Noah. Even if you know a likely district for the marriage, there may well be other entries for Mary Crane in earlier or later quarters. This index is a wonderful tool but can sometimes present you with agonising choices.

Some names are *less* common than you might expect. Sometimes a name has become a household word because someone in the family was responsible for an invention or an idea, yet the index may show the name as rare. The name of Cranfield in the first of these two tables might seem a name that you could expect to find reasonably often, yet there are only five in my whole collection of names, plus one person with Cranfield as a given name.

I have used the index successfully to find many marriages in my family but equally I have sometimes settled for a guess at the marriage and felt that it was not worth buying several certificates to chase something that might possibly elude me even then. You may well be influenced by how much you need to establish a particular marriage as a step in your research.

The index system has undergone progressive changes over the years but is still very much the same system that began life in 1837. The fact is, however, that the system was designed long before anyone could have imagined the hordes of enthusiastic genealogists whose research brings them to spend hours at fiche and film readers, the hobby rapidly becoming an addiction, and learning more about their past history than their parents or even grandparents ever knew.   It is a level of research and skill far beyond that of previous generations and fuelled by good access to more and more research material.

The GRO birth, death and marriage indexes are an important and heavily used part of this material. They were not designed for this high-volume use, rather for lawyers and historians needing to establish some few particular facts, for whom one or two certificates were their only need as a form of proof, and who often knew all the relevant information that would narrow the search. The later inclusion of age at death and of the mother's maiden name in the births index have improved the value of the more recent indexes by making it a little easier to identify entries more positively.

The indexes are not only used in direct personal research but also in more general research such as one-name studies, name-distribution exercises and the like. They are ideal for such purposes because they are national indexes.

The local indexes

What of the local indexes ? Superintendent Registrars' indexes to the register books held by them were not structured for easy research. Each register was indexed separately and each marriage register related to a particular parish and extended over a different time period. Therefore it was necessary to know which to search. Registers in large parishes in the cities were quickly filled. Registers from small parishes might only have a handful of marriages over several years. Noah Crane and Patience Harling, for example, were the only couple married in Stratford St Andrew in 1844/Q1 and there were only three marriages in the parish in the years 1841-1844. A full-sized marriage register could well last for 500 years at that rate of use.

The "particular" and "general" searches mentioned in Chapter 2 refer to searching a *particular* index or to making a more *general* search over several indexes.

It is only fairly recently that some Superintendent Registrars have begun to build new indexes for their whole districts on an annual basis, giving much better access to information. I shall have much more to say about local indexes later.

Chapter 4 - Looking behind the scenes

A journey of discovery

My interest in the index has gone much further than searching for individuals. After a lifetime of involvement in records of one sort or another, I began to wonder about the organisation of the marriage records themselves.

The indexes refer to volumes and page numbers. What are these volumes like ? Are the marriages arranged in them in some special or interesting way ? Are the records structured in some way ? Can you find a marriage partner by looking for a matching page reference ?

I had one particular marriage in mind at that time, in the East End of London, and I found a quarter with a possible entry for one partner in the marriage. The quarter was the December quarter for 1843 and the reference was Whitechapel, volume 2. I decided to scan the fiche for the whole of that quarter to collect index entries for volume 2. This means starting with the fiche at the beginning of names starting with A and working right through to the names, if any, starting with Z. It requires tireless concentration, looking down the column of volume references for any entries given as volume 2. 1843/Q4 probably has a little over 70,000 names in total.

After several weeks I finished with 3398 entries. As the work developed I began to find a clear pattern. Instead of entries for districts in volume 2 being randomly arranged they began to appear in blocks of pages by district. The page numbering was largely continuous from start to finish, and the districts were arranged in an alphabetical sequence, if a little cryptic in places (you need to decanonise St George and St Luke, a surprisingly irreverent approach). The final outcome was that districts were arranged as follows :

Districts in Volume 2 - 1843/Q4		
Bethnal Green	occupying pages	1 - 33
St George in the East	occupying pages	35 - 63
Holborn	occupying pages	65 - 75
London	occupying pages	77 - 183
London East	occupying pages	185 - 221
London West	occupying pages	223 - 273
St Luke's	occupying pages	275 - 299
Poplar	occupying pages	301 - 322
Shoreditch	occupying pages	323 - 416
Stepney	occupying pages	417 - 491
Whitechapel	occupying pages	493 - 537

This pattern emerged through the simple computer process of re-arranging the extracted names in order of page numbers instead of the alphabetical order of the index itself. What was appearing was something like a picture of the underlying marriage records, minus their detail.

Almost 70% of the total entries were on pages with eight names, four men and four women, i.e. four marriages per page, very much like many of the parish records. There was also quite a strong hint from the localised grouping of Jewish names in the London district that the districts might have an internal arrangement by parish.

The prospect of finding a marriage partner by matching a page reference now seemed much less hopeful. A page of four marriages would give four possible spouses. Only if you knew in advance that you were looking for an Edward or a Matilda could you expect success, and even then you would need to scan the whole fiche for the quarter in order to be certain. If you need to check entries from several quarters the task becomes large.

A curious feature of the sorted results was that the page numbering was not continuous. There were runs of odd-numbered pages, such as 75 77 79 81 83 85 87 89 91, but no such runs of even-numbered pages. The only explanation that seemed to make sense was that I was looking at information supplied on many separate sheets of paper, probably parish by parish, that had been brought together and then numbered, some of the pages having no information on the reverse side. At that time I had not read the 1836 legislation. The procedures specified in the legislation now seem completely consistent with this early supposition. My subsequent work has confirmed it.

This explains why the table for districts in volume 2 consists very largely of odd numbered pages. It is only for Poplar and Shoreditch that the final page of the batch happened to have entries on the reverse (even-numbered) side.

If you turn back to Chapter 3 for the snippets from the 1844 and 1856 indexes you will see that odd pages predominate. This will be true of the marriage index in general but won't apply evenly. In respect of the page references the index is almost a random presentation of information and "lumpiness" is always a characteristic of large random arrangements.

When a book is put together and the pages are numbered, page 1 is always on the right-hand side as the book lies open in front of you. In fact this is how the book will appear if it sits on the table before the various end pages and the covers are added to it. The right-hand page is always an odd-numbered page wherever the book is opened. Therefore the odd numbered pages are known as "recto" pages, meaning that they are on the right. The even-numbered pages, being on the reverse side of the recto pages, are called the "verso" pages. You will learn that the pattern of recto and verso pages is particularly important in the GRO records and these names are a handy and precise way of referring to them. It is a concept that can give you a much clearer picture of the organisation of the marriage records and will give extra meaning to many of the tables in this book.

Here now is a short section from the extracted material collected in this first foray into the marriage index, five pages for the district of Bethnal Green, to illustrate the structure that emerges when the indexed names are arranged by pages : -

---

Bethnal Green - volume 2 - 1843/Q4

page 11 Jane Bean, Henry Collyer, Elizabeth Green, Robert Horright, Mary Littell, Maria Matthews, William Smith, John Whurr

12 Harriet Burgess, Maria Colley, Samuel Cooper, Alice Crockford , John William Hargrave, John William Hargrove,

Shirley Jameson, Mary Ann Johnson, George Palmer

13 Henry Francis Buckley, Eliza Daniels, George James Ellis, Sarah Godson, George Holmes, John Lidyard, Susannah Massey, Mary Ann Oatway

15 Charles Barker, Elizabeth Jane Clemson, Mary Clemson, William Crutchlow, Edwin Johnson, Elizabeth Shambrook, Rebecca Wallis Stanford, John Want

16 William Kennard, Lucy Nunn, Joseph David Royall, Mary Ann Ward

---

The names shown here are simply in alphabetical order within each page. There is nothing in the marriage index to indicate the pairing of brides and grooms. On page 16, for example, you can only say that William Kennard married either Lucy Nunn or Mary Ann Ward. If you happen to know that your William Kennard married a Lucy, then she is identified for you.

Pages 11, 13 and 15 have eight names. Page 16 has four names so it perhaps completes one parish. Visualise this little table in terms of recto and verso pages and you will have a picture of the probable arrangement of the records. You can see that pages 11, 12 and 13 very probably go together as one parish. Pages 11 and 12 will certainly belong to the same parish and 13 is quite likely, though not certain, to belong as well. Pages 15 and 16 are clearly another parish. Page 17 will almost certainly be the start of another parish because page 16 is not a full page.

Page 12 has nine names but Hargrave and Hargrove are duplicates without any doubt.. On the other hand that leaves three men and five women on this page. The five women have all been rechecked and are referenced to page 12 of volume 2 without any doubt whatsoever. This could be an indexing error (or could be a typing error because the 1843 index is typed and not handwritten). Maria and Mary Ann could even be the same person. On almost any assumption there is a need for another man on page 12 and perhaps I missed one man in making up the file. But wait ! No genealogist should be too quick in jumping to conclusions. Shirley is far from being a common name in the 1840s and it was at least as likely at that time to be a man's name as a woman's. It is almost certain that this solves the problem of the five women and the three men.

This little example shows some of the problems that arise in this exercise, and also some that can lie in wait for users of the index. It also shows the difficulty of finding a spouse by matching reference information. No spouses can be positively identified here unless you have a clue such as a given name.

One would expect the indexes prepared by local registrars to be rather different from the national ones. With fewer names their task would be easier and probably done with more care. Local registrars would be more familiar with local names and perhaps with the writing of the local clergy. They would be less likely to make errors in district names. They did not even have the volume number system of the GRO to cope with. Boredom would be a less oppressive enemy. Such may be the expectation. The reality, however, can be rather different, as I shall show in a later chapter.

I had finished my exercise on volume 2 in 1843/Q4. All this was a fascinating picture but every discovery in any genealogical endeavour seems to raise even more questions. For example, would the picture found in the East End of London be similar in a rural district ?

One thing leads to another, and another ....

I chose volume 12 for the same quarter of 1843 as an example of a rural area and went to work to scan the same fiche again from A to Z. Volume 12 covers Essex and the southern part of Suffolk. Essex is my home county so the whole area was of personal interest and was fairly familiar.

This was another revelation. As I expected, the pages were again numbered right through from the start to the end of the volume. The districts were again alphabetically arranged but there was a county structure as well. The Essex districts all came first and were followed by those for Suffolk.

The pattern was as follows :

ESSEX	Billericay	pages . . .	1 - 31
	Braintree		33 - 55
	Chelmsford		57 - 120
	Colchester		121 - 149
	Dunmow		151 - 192
	Epping		193 - 221
	Halstead		223 - 251
	Lexden		253 - 305
	Maldon		307 - 356
	Ongar		357 - 385
	Orsett		387 - 413
	Rochford		415 - 443
	Romford		445 - 467
	Saffron Walden		469 - 503
	Tendring		505 - 557
	West Ham		559 - 575
	Witham		577- 605
SUFFOLK	Bosmere		607 - 655
	Cosford		657 - 697
	Ipswich		699 - 735
	Plomesgate		737 - 789
	Risbridge		791 - 828
	Samford		829 - 867
	Stow		869 - 923
	Sudbury		925 - 987
	Woodbridge		989 - 1049

The pages in this volume were numbered without any breaks between districts or even between Essex and Suffolk. Notice again that few even pages occur. The pattern that emerged from the data suggested strikingly that rural parishes were far smaller, as of course one would expect. Far more pages contain only one marriage. Far more sheets have no entries on the reverse side - there were only 91 verso pages referenced in the index but 523 recto pages.

I now became curious to know if there was any seasonality in the marriage pattern. I proceeded to extract volume 12 entries for the rest of 1843 and then eventually for the whole of 1844. A strong seasonal pattern emerged.

In both years the marriages in the December quarter were over 40% of the total for the year. The figures in the next table are the numbers of names collected, not the number of marriages.

A possible inference from these figures is that Q2 and Q3 were extremely busy times in the rural community, covering the main activities of the farming year from seedtime to harvest. Q1 would have been a hard time in the countryside and probably a lean one. The last quarter of the year was probably the one time when life was a little easier and marriage was therefore more possible. Marriages on Christmas Day were common.

Number of index entries in volume 12 (Essex/Suffok)

1843	Q1	1162
	Q2	1306
	Q3	1465
	Q4	2836
1844	Q1	1284
	Q2	1495
	Q3	1490
	Q4	2875

From the marriage records as a whole it is clear that this extreme pattern was especially a feature of rural areas. National records for this part of the century show a little over 30% of all marriages in the December quarter. Arable agriculture probably gave the most extreme pattern. Chapter 10 has more details, some surprising, on the numbers and seasonality of marriages.

As a rural marriage example, look at Samford in Suffolk in 1843/Q2 :

Samford marriage entries 1843/Q2

Page	533	Mary Brown, Thomas Tabor
	535	Hannah Cuthbert, Thomas Heckford
	537	Thomas Borrett, Thos (sic) Borrett, Susan Coe, Frederick Mills, Frances Read, John Richer, Martha Wollard
	539	Laura Barthorp, George Pyke
	541	George Keeble, Susannah Steward
	543	William Mann, Hannah Ratliff
	545	George Stannard, Mary Wiseman
	547	Lucy Abbot, Francis Jennings
	549	Caroline Daking, Stephen Marshall
	551	Mary Anne Cole, Joseph Wright Smith
	553	William Baldwin, Harriet Parker

The sparse pattern of the rural marriage data is quite strikingly different from the ranks of full sheets typical of inner London districts such as Bethnal Green, Stepney and Shoreditch. There are still some full pages in the larger centres such as Chelmsford, Colchester, West Ham and Ipswich.

In the Samford example each page is balanced, no page is full, no entries on the verso pages. The only oddity is that the indexer has thought it necessary to include Thomas Borrett twice exactly as he was recorded in the entry. (Also the indexer wrote Mary Ann Cole instead of Mary Anne Cole as she appears in the actual marriage record and as I show her here).

The general pattern of the records was now quite clear. The records for the large cities consist mainly of pages that are full, front and back, and the small rural parishes have many more pages with only one or two marriages. Even the large cities, however, are far from uniform. The registration district that carries the name of a large city will often include smaller outlying parishes and there will usually be a few light pages.

I extended the East Anglian analysis by extracting Essex/Suffolk entries for 1839/Q4. It was a fortunate choice in terms of learning more about the system because it proved to be a quarter with a very high level of detectable errors. Many of them very clearly arose in the typing of the original hand-written index. The inference must be that the index for this quarter is badly flawed throughout and probably that indexes for neighbouring quarters also have high levels of errors. (It is all too obvious that the scope for this research is virtually unlimited).

Spreading the net . . .

One lesson from collecting over 13,900 entries for East Anglia in this way was that one inevitably misses a few. Scanning microfiche to look for references to a particular volume reference or for particular district names is all too likely to be an imperfect process.

Even if a large proportion of the extracted material fits neatly into balanced male/female pages, showing that the search has been generally successful, nevertheless there are some that escape the net. Some pages have too many names or too few and it is not always possible to be sure whether the error is in the index or in the process of extraction. I subsequently found that I had missed 79 names in the 1843 collection and 50 names in 1844, an average of 0.92%. This is perhaps some indication of the likely "miss rate" for anyone combing the index to find a marriage partner.

The solution ? Well, perhaps not the solution but the next venture into the unknown. I opted to record all entries for a single quarter. Might this overcome some of those problems of index errors where entries have wrong district names or wrong page references ? Might it also overcome the problem of missing some of the names ? Collect them *all* and in theory you don't miss odd ones if your concentration slips. It should also give a detailed picture of the whole system, not just of East Anglia. Embarking on the computer entry of nearly 60,000 more index entries was a huge addition to the work but by this time I was firmly hooked.

(Jumping the gun for a moment, one segment of the Essex/Suffolk names for 1843/1844 that we have just discussed came from a much later collection of all index entries for England and Wales for 1844/Q1 and I only missed *two* names from volume 12 in making that collection (as I subsequently discovered at the General Register Office). This confirms that collecting in bulk is much more efficient and helps to explain my better "miss rate" for 1844 than for 1843, simply because my 1844/Q1 material was so much more complete than the other seven quarters.)

To resume, I decided to collect the whole of 1849/Q1, thus extending the time period covered by the exercise. The microfiche for this quarter is in manuscript, a mixed blessing, much harder to read but not subject to errors from the typing process.

A year or more later saw this large task completed. Some parts of the fiche were quite impossible to read and I was fortunate in having a friend visiting London who was able to read several hundred of the "impossibles" from the original index registers. I later discovered an alternative source of the 1849/Q1 index on microfilm and was able to correct a large number of dubious readings (I discuss film and fiche sources in a later chapter).

As I have already said, the marriage records for the early years up to 1851 are in 27 volumes. The original manuscript used Roman numerals for the volume numbers, changed to arabic numerals when parts of the index were typed. Hence many of the errors in volume numbers in the indexes.

Sorting of the country-wide entries for 1849/Q1 based on page numbers confirmed the marriage records as being held four to a page as was the case for 1843 and 1844. There was again a clear pattern of pages being brought together singly or in groups from separate parishes, the same preponderance of odd-numbered page references as previously (especially in rural areas), and the same sprinkling of duplicated entries and various kinds of indexing errors. Some district names were clearly wrong in the index, as were some volume numbers. Wrong page numbers showed up when entries fell into wrong districts when sorted. One can find entries such as Leicester that should have been Lancaster, a Norwich entry shown as volume 12 instead of 13, and entries with page numbers that are clearly wrong.

The coverage of the volumes, illustrated by the 1849/Q1 material, is :

Volume I	Central London, including Marylebone, Strand ...
Volume II	East London, as outlined earlier in this chapter
Volume III	North West London, including Uxbridge and Staines
Volume IV	South West London and Surrey, from Newington to Guildford
Volume V	Kent
Volume VI	Bedfordshire, Berkshire, Buckinghamshire, Hertfordshire
Volume VII	Hampshire and Sussex
Volume VIII	Dorset, Isle of Wight, Wiltshire
Volume IX	Cornwall and Devon
Volume X	Devon and Somerset
Volume XI	Gloucester, plus Bath etc
Volume XII	Essex and part of Suffolk
Volume XIII	Norfolk and part of Suffolk
Volume XIV	Cambridge, Huntingdonshire, Lincolnshire
Volume XV	Leicester, Northants, Nottinghamshire
Volume XVI	Oxfordshire, Warwickshire
Volume XVII	Staffordshire
Volume XVIII	Shropshire and Worcestershire
Volume XIX	Cheshire and Derbyshire
Volume XX	Lancashire
Volume XXI	Lancashire
Volume XXII	Yorkshire
Volume XXIII	Yorkshire
Volume XXIV	Durham and N Yorkshire
Volume XXV	Westmoreland and Northumberland
Volume XXVI	Herefordshire and S Wales
Volume XXVII	Central and N Wales

There is the same alphabetical arrangement of district names within counties that was found in the work on volume 12 in the 1843/44 period. Volume 6, for example, contains the Bedfordshire districts from Ampthill to Woburn, then Berkshire from Abingdon to Wokingham, Buckinghamshire from Amersham to Wycombe, finally Hertfordshire from St Albans (remember to decanonise the name) to Watford.

All the detail of the 1849/Q1 registration districts is shown in Appendix 2. This is one of four "Page Range Tables" in appendices 1 to 4. They describe the structure of the system in four particular quarters but also give a good general indication for other periods. They are a valuable by-product of this research. See Chapter 12, page 149, for a further discussion of these tables.

The exploration goes on

After the exercise on 1849/Q1 I then took two other complete quarters, 1856/Q1 and 1844/Q1. As partial exercises I processed some 30,000 entries from 1881 and 1891, as well as a number of smaller extractions for particular volumes or parts of volumes for a number of other quarters of the 1800s. The total number of entries extracted rose to 250,000 and every piece of new work continued to uncover new items of interest and new information about the underlying marriage records. Total marriages in the period 1837 to 1899 are published as a little over eleven million (see Chapter 10) so my sample is a little over one per cent of the index entries.

1856 March Quarter (1856/Q1)

The fiche for this quarter is again in hand-written form with all the attendant problems of legibility. It was much the most protracted part of these exercises, some two years' work overall, some of the index being very illegible.

The record system was significantly changed in 1852 and these changes are reflected in the results of the 1856/Q1 study, already partly foreshadowed in Chapter 3. The main points of difference are :

a) There was a change in volume structure from 27 volumes to 33 volumes.
b) The volume numbering system was changed from 1, 2, 3 ..... 27 into a system from 1a, 1b, 1c, 1d, 2a ...... 11b.
c) The registration districts were totally rearranged within and between volumes, no longer in alphabetical sequence but arranged generally on a "neighbouring" basis.
d) Some new districts were created, e.g. St Olave, Farnborough and Hampstead. Bloomsbury disappeared. Swindon changed its name to Highworth.
e) The page structure was changed from pages of four marriages (eight names) to pages of two marriages (four names).

Because of the 2-marriage pages, the prospect of finding a marriage partner by matching page references is a great deal better from 1852. On the other hand there was a little old stationery that seemed to be still in use up to 1856 and probably beyond so there is still a small chance of coming across a page with eight names.

The new arrangement of volumes from 1852 is shown below. County boundaries were again able to be broken. Parts of Hampshire are in both 2b and 2c, while volume 5c leaps across the gap from Cornwall to Somerset.

Volume 1a	Central London
Volume 1b	North East London
Volume 1c	East London
Volume 1d	South London
Volume 2a	Surrey and Kent
Volume 2b	Sussex and Hampshire
Volume 2c	Hampshire and Berkshire
Volume 3a	Middlesex, Hertford, Bucks, Oxfordshire
Volume 3b	Northants, Huntingdon, Bedford, Cambridge
Volume 4a	Essex and Suffolk
Volume 4b	Norfolk
Volume 5a	Wiltshire and Dorset
Volume 5b	Devonshire
Volume 5c	Cornwall and Somerset
Volume 6a	Gloucester, Hereford and Shropshire
Volume 6b	Staffordshire
Volume 6c	Worcestershire
Volume 6d	Warwickshire
Volume 7a	Leicester, Rutland and Lincolnshire
Volume 7b	Nottinghamshire and Derbyshire
Volume 8a	Cheshire
Volume 8b	Lancashire (and volumes 8c, 8d and 8e)
Volume 9a	Yorkshire, W Riding (and volumes 9b & 9c)
Volume 9d	Yorkshire, East and North Ridings
Volume 10a	Durham
Volume 10b	Northumberland, Cumberland, Westmorland
Volume 11a	Monmouth, Glamorgan, Carmarthen, Pembroke
Volume 11b	The rest of Wales

The arrangement of Superintendent Registrars' districts into volumes is an arbitrary part of the GRO system. It is simply an expression of the GRO filing system, defining the way that the GRO files the records received from each district. Some districts are so very small that there can be one or two marriages in one quarter and none in the next. Therefore a tabulation of districts over several quarters would be needed in order to be completely definitive and could differ in minor respects from the Page Range Table for 1856/Q1 given as Appendix. 3.

This GRO system is quite unrelated to the way that the Superintendent Registrars control and index the registers that they hold in the local registry offices. The legislation simply said that the records were to be held and were to be indexed, both at the national and the local level, but said nothing about how it was to be done.

Here is a snippet from the 1856/Q1 material, including one page of eight names :

Islington 1856/Q1
261 Frederick Gale Chard, Edward Dawes, Sarah Ann Petchey, Eliza Phillips
262 Elizabeth Jane Atkinson, Charles Hill, George Lance, Sarah Jane Waters
263 George Bryant, Sarah Mead, Ann Philpott, Thomas Henry Wintle
264 William Davidson, Thomas Kirby, Emma Leffler, Maria Slade
265 Peter Coleman, John Driver, William Peirson, Louisa Rogers, Frederick John Sleap, Ann Elizabeth Thomson, Therisa Willson, Mary Ann Wyatt
266 Georgina Lucy Innes, William Morris, George Petrie, Amy Wilson

The spellings of Peirson and Therisa on the 8-name page are exactly as given, right or wrong. These 8-name pages have popped up from various parts of the country. When the Registrar General wrote to clergy in 1852 to tell them about the new 2-marriage sheets he stressed that they were to destroy the old sheets as they would not fit his filing system. Several years later the frugal clergy were still producing some 8-name pages.

The rural areas once again have a much thinner density of records and are a good place to seek matching page references. Here as an example are the complete entries from Billericay in Essex :

Billericay 1856/Q1
123 Eliza Page, William Such
125 George William Hatfield, Eliza Low, Susannah Rush, Henry Speller
127 Chilton Mewburn, Emily Stone
129 William Fell, Isabella Pudney
131 Elizabeth Ann Stone, James Wright
133 William Reeve, Mary Thompson
135 Alfred Jewell Alexander, Caroline Stratford
137 Mary Ann Ayley, William Whitby
139 Catherine Gibson, Henry James Peacock
141 William Barnes, John Eady, Elizabeth Hughes, Mary Jane Osband
143 Ellen Collis, William Charles Moore

The absence of any even-numbered pages in Billericay indicates that all these entries came from different churches, though there were occasional exceptions by the clergy that broke that rule.

In the 1856 material there are still large numbers of duplicate entries. This practice is discussed in more detail in chapter 6. In volume 4b, for example, covering Norfolk and the northern part of Suffolk, there are 1433 entries in the marriage index and 76 of these entries are duplicates of another entry, just over five percent. In the district of Flegg the indexer had a major problem with one name. Two marriages are involved, the four names being James William Diboll, Sarah Elizabeth Diboll, William Page and Mary Plane. Each of the Diboll entries has been made three times, using alternate surnames of Dyball and Dybull.

The same volume has two identical marriages appearing twice with different page references, and there are three names entered twice in the index in exactly the same form, Sophia Stibbons in Aylsham, Thomas Barwick in Aylsham, Mary Ann Howard in Norwich. Sophia was probably a slip-up by the clerk as the other bride on that page was a Sophia Stibbings. Unless, of course, Stibbons and Stibbings are really one person and he has omitted the actual second bride altogether. Another problem person for him was Samuel Burroughs Ranel in the district of Guiltcross. He appears four times in the index :

> Samuel Burroughs Ranel   Samuel Burroughs Rauel
> Samual Burroughs Reanel   Samuel Burroughs Reauel

It is just as well that the clerk had no doubts about Burroughs.

Volume 4b has no less than two recto pages apparently unused, or very probably used but not indexed, page 431 in Guiltcross and page 455 in Wayland. I need another day at Southport !

Thus 1856/Q1 can be seen to continue many of the quirks and slips already found, that are described extensively in Chapter 6. This is just a foretaste.

As expected from the outset, 1856/Q1 was a difficult quarter in fiche quality. I was fortunate to have help from friends in Australia, the USA and elsewhere in New Zealand who sometimes had access to better material. A friend in Britain provided invaluable help by looking up some hundreds of unreadable page references in the original index registers in Myddelton House. Even so, and despite returning again and again to the fiche to try to resolve pages appearing to have wrong numbers of men or women, some imbalances obstinately remained. In this respect volume 4b has several pages where the switch of a name between two likely pages would resolve both. Some such problems are problems of legibility, some are indexing errors.

1844 March Quarter (1844/Q1)

This is another typed quarter of the index, in a format that is not too hard to read. It was an exercise that I completed in a small fraction of the time taken by the two previous exercises and, not unexpectedly, it didn't have the uncertainties in reading the page references that characterise the handwritten fiche. It hasn't been possible to discover just when the various indexes of the 1800s were typed from their original handwritten form.

The general structure of the record system in the pre-1852 period has already been well enough described in the findings from the 1849/Q1 exercise. The structure in 1844/Q1 is essentially the same. It is a quarter that was chosen partly as a contrast to 1849/Q1 in being typewritten, and partly as a means of adding 1844/Q1 to the earlier set of data for Essex and Suffolk and completing the two-year seasonal pattern that was begun several years before and was described earlier in this chapter.

I expected at first that 1844/Q1 might share some of the typing problems found in the 1839/Q4 material but I then came to feel that it was probably typed much later and has probably been better handled in many ways. Ultimately, however, 1844 proved to have plenty of problems of its own, as will be seen in Chapters 6 and 8. It proved to have been a very good choice.

1891 March Quarter and other oddments

In addition to the large-scale extracts, my journeyings in the marriage index have picked out many small segments, often for particular districts and for particular reasons, and have ended with one final major exercise, the March quarter of 1891.

With the growth of population, this is a quarter with nearly a hundred thousand entries.   When the exercise is completed it will bring the total entries in these studies to more than 300,000. On the other hand this is no longer a priority exercise and it is a sobering thought that devoting just one hour a day to the data entry of about a hundred index lines would create a two-year horizon for completing the quarter.

1891/Q1 was selected for five main reasons. Firstly there was a need, I felt, to see whether the characteristics of the earlier period had changed significantly. Secondly, it seemed likely that the district structure might have changed. Thirdly, one interest in these studies has been the changing patterns of personal names and it seemed very probable that name patterns had changed a good deal by that time. Fourthly, the indexes of the late years of the 1800s are laid out in a different, tightly typed format, and it seemed worth seeing how well this material could be read. Fifthly it is a quarter that lies just before the taking of a census and virtually all those who were married in 1891/Q1 will appear in the 1891 census as man and wife.

From an initial sample of over 18,000 entries a picture has emerged :

a) The quality of the indexing has not apparently improved to any real extent. There are still errors in terms of wrong page numbers, volume numbers and the like, and these are still at much the same frequency as found in the earlier years, around one in every 700 index entries. Many Superintendent Registrars' districts are now so large that faulty indexing is harder to detect. Duplicate entries in the index still occur, with a frequency of around one per hundred entries. The sample is still too small to regard these ratios as reliable, but they are still an indication that the quality of the quarterly copies and the standards of indexing have apparently not changed in forty years or so.

b)   The pattern of 33 volumes remains unchanged. The 35 years since 1856 have even left the pattern of Superintendent Registrars' districts remaining surprisingly similar. All the same there are plenty of differences in detail to notice between appendix 3 and appendix 4, including changes in district sizes. Appendix 4 still shows some quite large gaps in page structure even with 18200 names but these entries are still quite thinly spread over about 630 districts and are less than 20% of the index entries for the quarter.

c)   The pattern of given names has changed quite dramatically by 1891 and these changes are discussed in detail in Chapter 14.

d)   The legibility of much of the later index material, when viewed in the form of microfiche, can vary from reasonably clear to very difficult, with some entries subject to damage in the typeface to the extent of making them almost or wholly impossible to read (discussed in Chapter 11). The Page Range Table (of appendix 4) has been a sine qua non for reading a good many references.

e)   The characteristics of duplicated index entries are much as in earlier years. This is an indication, as chapter 6 will show, that the handwriting of the clergy had not greatly improved, also evidenced by some of the outlandishly improbable names in the index.

*   *   *   *   *   *   *   *   *   *   *

So much for the journey of exploration. Now to look briefly at the journey taken by the marriage records. How did the record get from the bride and groom to the fiche drawer in your favourite library ?

Chapter 5 - The bridal path

Before we venture into the wilderness of the errors, oddities and other stumbling blocks in the marriage records and the marriage index, it is worthwhile to take a bird's-eye view of the landscape. Let's look down at the path followed by the marriage information, from the entry of the marriage in the marriage register to the final appearance of the names of bride and groom (they hope) in the marriage index for the benefit of their descendants.

The marriage registers

As we saw in Chapter 2, each parish (and other registered chapel) was provided with two copies of a marriage register book. Similar pairs of books were provided to Jewish congregations and Quaker meetings, and a single register to each registrar of marriages.

In all cases there was a requirement for each entry in a marriage register to be numbered in a consecutive sequence from the beginning of that book to the end. The duplicate copies were to be kept as exact duplicates with precisely the same numbering. This number is the one you see in the extreme left-hand column in any marriage (or other) certificate that you obtain, though there is nothing on the certificate to tell you what that number is. No doubt many peoples' wedding photographs have a picture of the "signing of the register" and will show, as ours does, the two registers open together on the table.

The register kept by a registrar of marriages, used as necessary both for marriages in the register office before the registrar and for marriages in the dissenting congregations in the district, was also consecutively numbered from beginning to end, whatever the source of the marriage.

The information recorded in the marriage entry depended primarily on what your ancestor said and/or on what the writer thought was said. One of my wife's ancestors had the misfortune to lose three wives. When first married he said his father was a pensioner (deceased), next time his father was a gentleman, and at the third and final marriage his father was a labourer. The system relied on the information provided. It is very unlikely that this father's position agreed with all these descriptions at different times, and certainly not in the order given. We have no doubts as to the identity of this thrice-wed person. We have a record of his wives and family in his own hand.

Some clergy had, and perhaps still have, a tendency to try to save time by entering the marriage details in the registers in advance of the marriage, thus creating a problem if something delayed or prevented the marriage. The GRO has tried hard to discourage the practice. It is very possible that this practice may have had something to do with the many fairly extreme homophone variations in the marriage records and index, entries such as Mary Ann Shew and Mary Ann Shoe, Maria Walters Beauditch and Maria Walters Bowditch.

The format of the marriage entry is basically the same in the marriage registers and in the quarterly returns, and is shown in Appendix 6.

The quarterly returns

A short while after the end of each quarter, the clergy, the Jewish congregations, Quaker meetings and district registrars were required to make copies of all marriages recorded in that prior quarter and to send them to the Superintendent Registrar for the district. There seems to have been no specific requirement at first that these copies were to be based on one or the other of the duplicate registers so the return is likely to have sometimes been a copy of a copy. It was only much later that the Registrar General recommended that clergy should base all their returns on one register.

All were provided with loose forms for these copies, four marriages to a side up to 1851 and two to a side from 1852. These forms were slightly different for each of the four providers of marriage information. Appendix 7 shows the details of the declarations to be made, preprinted as part of the forms.

The declaration at the foot of each of the forms, on both sides, said how many entries were being supplied on that side of the form and gave their entry numbers in the register.

The clergy's form had a declaration to be signed by the Rector or Vicar to attest that the copies were true. The declarations for the Jewish and Quaker marriages were similar but they were preprinted to refer to "Secretary of a Synagogue of persons professing the Jewish religion" and "Registering officer of the Society of Friends commonly called Quakers, for the monthly meeting of [place]". The Quaker form also provided for the date to be in their special format, for example, the "7th day of the eleventh month commonly called November". The Monthly Meetings are those at which business is transacted, hence their status in the structure of the Quaker congregations. Regular weekly meetings are for worship. The declarations that the quarterly returns are "true copies" form the basis for the description on all certificates of births, deaths and marriages that what you hold in your hand is a "Certified copy of an entry of marriage".

The forms used by a district registrar for his quarterly return were significantly different. They contained an additional statement to be signed by the Superintendent Registrar to the effect that he had compared the copy with the original and had found the copy to be a true one.

It is of the greatest significance for the integrity of the whole record system that the legislators didn't find it possible to provide for such a check on the information supplied by the various congregations. The clergy in the nineteenth century were extremely prone to error in many different ways and their handwriting in many of the returns was little short of atrocious. I have even had to read the name of a parish many times in different records before finally being able to deduce the name properly.

It was not simply the poor writing of the clergy that led to errors and uncertainties in the indexing. When some 120,000 to 260,000 marriage entries were copied each year by hand, involving some 250,000 to 500,000 personal names (excluding the parents and witnesses), then it was inevitable that there would be many, many errors. Yet the system provided no check at all on the accuracy of most of this copying. In fact any such system with two completely different methods of keeping the records and indexing them might have been designed to make any checks as hard as possible to achieve.

There is now ample evidence, as I will show, that it was the quality of the copying that led to many of the errors and uncertainties in the indexing. There is evidence of errors in the copying and of gaps in the returns. Even today some clergy are said to treat the record system as a rather tedious chore that is undeserving of high priority in their work. It was not unusual for clergy to be many months late with their returns, even years late, and they often seemed to have little idea which months actually fell in a particular quarter.

In a letter of 25th July 1837, just after the civil registration system came into operation, the Registrar General pointed out to all clergy that they were "…. required by law, in the months of October, January, April and July respectively, to make …. a true copy, certified by you under your hand, of all the entries of marriages in the register books of the church or chapel of which you are the Rector, Vicar or Curate, during the three calendar months last preceding …". In view of what has actually happened, this wording was perhaps not the very best that might have been chosen. Clergy were often late in making their returns. How might they then interpret the "three calendar months last preceding" ? Certainly they all too often included marriages almost up to the date of their return. It is also rather a pity, as we can see now, that the Registrar General was not courageous enough to urge the need for accuracy and legibility.

Even if the clergy were known as "Clerks in Holy Orders", aptitude for clerical work was often not their strong suit. It has always been required that the quarterly copies must be made by a fully ordained minister of the church. It was not a task that the minister was able to delegate to his parish clerk.

The Registrar General certainly did his best to gain the goodwill of the clergy. In the same 1837 letter referred to above he concluded "I trust I may confidently rely on your co-operation for the furtherance of the important public object for which these certified copies are designed. They are to be deposited in the General Register Office in London, to be there preserved, and to be so arranged that a copy of the entry of any marriage solemnized in England and Wales after June 1837 may be obtained without difficulty on application at that office, which copy, duly stamped, `shall be received as evidence of the marriage to which the same relates without any further or other proof of such entry;' and thus the proof of marriage, which hitherto has been frequently coupled with much delay, difficulty and expense, may from this time forward be obtained promptly, easily and with very trifling cost. But such benefits cannot be secured to the community without the due and regular transmission of certified copies. I cannot doubt that this consideration will, to a Minister of Religion, be a sufficient inducement for the exact fulfilment of the civil duties thus assigned to him by law, especially when he feels that by neglecting to perform them he may inflict an injury, he knows not how serious, on the descendants of those who have received at his hands the holy ordinance of marriage."

What are we to think of the serious injuries inflicted by the errors and omissions that we are now looking at ?

With this letter the Registrar General enclosed ten blank forms for the quarterly returns and four blank forms for nil returns. These last would have been quickly used up by small parishes. It would not have helped in the orderly control of the system. In referring to the forms for the nil returns, he described them as forms "wherein, if there shall have been no marriage registered, you may certify the fact under your hand, and deliver in like manner". It would surely have been better to express this as a requirement and not, as it almost appeared, as an option.

The General Register Office

The Superintendent Registrar was responsible for forwarding to the General Register Office the quarterly returns accumulated for his whole district. He kept no copies of them. Only when a register was filled was it sent to the Superintendent Registrar to form part of his record and to be indexed by him.

It is important to appreciate that the General Register Office only has *copies* of the original marriage entries. It will be seen that this is a major deficiency in the accuracy and completeness of the national record system. The registration system was set up in the belief that the central record would be a faithful and valid copy of the recorded events. This study is the first review of what actually happened in the 1800s (or what so often failed to happen).

As we have seen, the General Register Office grouped the returns from the Superintendent Registrars into volumes. This was arbitrary, based mainly on counties, parts of counties, or groups of counties, and has been subject to gradual change over the years in addition to the major change introduced in 1852. The sequence of Superintendents' districts remained the same in each volume (apart from the 1852 changes). Thus the district of Billericay will be found as the first district in the Essex/Suffolk volume XII from 1837 to 1851.

Each "volume" was put together as a large bundle of papers, tied up and held (originally) in the basements of Somerset House. Each volume now consists of a microfilm copy, in most cases one film per volume, from which certificates are produced on film reader/printers. Master copies of these films, known as "silvers", are used from time to time to print a new film if a working film gets too worn and has to be replaced.

Before indexing could take place, each volume had to be given page numbers throughout, beginning with page one and numbering the pages consecutively to the end of the volume.

As small parishes often had no more than one marriage to a return, that sheet would be numbered both front and back but seven of the eight spaces on the form (or three of the four spaces from 1852) might be blank. The front of the form, forming the recto page of the "volume" or bundle, always gets an odd page number and the verso page gets the following even number. Thus even numbers arise when a parish has at least five marriages (or three from 1852).

But no, even that is not quite true. Occasionally a vicar would write his first or only marriage of a return in the bottom space, perhaps because he was copying from a bottom entry in his register, or perhaps he just found that more comfortable. I have even seen examples where a return of two marriages has been written as the bottom items on two separate forms. The pattern of the marriage records is that there is no fixed pattern.

The indexing

There is evidence to suggest that the indexing process was often carried out some considerable time later. It seems very likely that the large workload was a factor in this but I suspect that the tardiness of many of the returns from the parishes was a main reason. I have seen some returns that were nearly a year late in being submitted but were nevertheless correctly placed in their normal position and were part of the normal consecutive page numbering. I suspect that the indexing clerks would have dealt with the births and deaths first. These came from the register offices and were not subject to the vagaries and delays of the clergy.

No one in the Office for National Statistics now seems to have any knowledge of the indexing and sorting procedures used in the nineteenth century. Even the GRO library, despite many very old volumes and records, seems to have no procedural records covering this aspect of the work. Nor is it generally known when various parts of handwritten indexes were typed.

The first step in indexing must have been for a clerk to work through each volume to copy out the names of bride and groom from each marriage together with the district name, volume number and page number. As we will see later, in Chapter 6, all imaginable errors and omissions occurred in this process. A strange feature of many of these errors, as I shall demonstrate, was that clerks tended to make an error with one party in a marriage and not the other, or made errors with part of a page of marriages and then completed the page correctly without going back to correct the previous errors.

The next step in indexing would have been to sort all the names, some fifty to a hundred thousand married persons for a single quarter, into an alphabetical sequence based on their names. The most logical process for such a step, in the absence of effective sorting methods of a mechanical nature, would be to sort each volume separately and then to merge the volumes into a total index as the final step. This is similar to computer sorting procedures in which sort strings are built up and merged. It has been suggested that some mechanical aids based on Jacquard needles were available in the nineteenth century, and indeed there may have been, but there is no current knowledge of this within ONS and no mention of it in the literature covering the work of Jacquard, Babbage and Hollerith. Hollerith's work with punched cards doesn't seem to have achieved mechanical sorting until the early 1900s.

Sorting individual volumes wouldn't have been a long process and labour was abundant and inexpensive. It is not hard to visualise a large room with tables for the sorted cards for each volume and a central table at which the top cards from each volume would be progressively merged and presented to the clerk who was writing out the final national index. The work would have been done under gas lighting. We are before the days of electric lighting.

There would be no room in such a process for checking on an apparent error. Interrupting the process would be virtually impossible. This would account for the way that exactly identical entries are sometimes repeated in the index.

It will be clear that there were at least two copying processes involved in the indexing procedure, in addition to the copying already involved in making the quarterly returns.

Generally the sequencing of the indexing was very good but some glaring exceptions can be found when an addition has been made by inter-lining it in the handwritten index. In 1856 a Rachel Williams is right out of place in the March quarter index, added among the entries for Ann Williams, eleven full pages away from the other three occurrences of Rachel Williams. There is a Sarah Palmer who is a page away from her proper place. It would only be a very careful or a very lucky researcher who would find such entries. I have found sequence errors in the typed indexes as well.

It may be as well to repeat that the legislation said nothing on *how* the marriages were to be indexed. For example the GRO adopted the practice of indexing under both names if an alias situation appeared in the marriage entry. A widow who remarried is recorded in the marriage entry under her last married name and is indexed as such. Some local indexes record both the married name and the maiden name in such cases, i.e. the surname of the father. Researchers have occasionally reported finding widows in the GRO marriage index under the maiden name. It was not uncommon for a new wife to sign the register with her newly acquired surname and for this name to be used by the indexing clerk, another trap for later researchers.

Typing the indexes

All the original indexes were hand-written. We now find many of these indexes in typed form. Typing, however, is only another form of copying and errors and omissions happened at this stage too. A typed index has usually passed through at least four copying processes altogether. Omissions at the typing stage could easily be much larger than those at the earlier stages. My one- per-cent sample uncovered one instance of eighty names clearly missed in typing one index, a simple omission of two of the 40-name manuscript index pages. I've also met examples of whole blocks of names with a wrongly typed surname. Later chapters describe examples of typing errors.

I strongly suspect that many of the "non-indexed" marriage partners are simply typing omissions but it would now be impossible to prove that the loss was in the indexing or the typing. It could certainly explain why one partner in a marriage may be missed but the other is present. It must be very possible that such omissions could have occurred right through the 1800s.

The major omission of eighty names is from the index for 1844/Q2, where inspection of fiche or film will readily show an obvious gap in the entries for Jenkin and Jenkins. At Southport I was able to trawl through the films for volumes 26 and 27 (Wales) to recover some fifty of the missing entries, plus two that I found in Somerset (see chapter 8 and Appendix 8).

This Jenkins example tells us something of special significance. Not only is it a gap in the fiche and film in libraries around the world. It is also missing from the massive typed registers in the GRO basement at Southport. Furthermore it has been checked against the fiche and microfilm made by the LDS and held in Salt lake City and, as one would expect, it is missing from those as well. I was told at Southport that the original handwritten versions of the typed indexes no longer exist. We therefore have to say that any names missed from the indexes in the typing process are lost for ever (our few lucky Jenkins names excepted). I suggest in Chapter 8 that most individual names missing from the indexes are probably typing slips. There is no realistic way that these losses from the indexes can ever be repaired within the system as it stands. My proposals in Chapter 9 are the only solution.

Although our concern here is with marriage records, it is obvious that birth and death indexes would have been subject to the same typing errors. On one very limited check on a small group of births I found surprisingly many spelling differences between the index entries and the record on the GRO film. It is all the more surprising because the quarterly returns for births and deaths are theoretically checked and verified as correct by the Superintendent Registrar. Such checks may have helped to some extent, but how thoroughly could any Superintendent Registrar check hundreds of birth and death entries, not just personal names but all the other associated detail ?

I have also come across other clear examples of errors in the birth and death indexes, simply in passing. Births and deaths involved as many copying processes as marriages.

It is extremely hard to track down omissions that may have happened in the typing process. On many occasions I have been very suspicious of apparent gaps in name sequences in the indexes but proof is almost impossible, even with access to the GRO films. The Jenkins example was an outstanding exception, simply because it is such a localised name, but there is no way of saying whether an individual name has been lost by the indexer or by the typist once the handwritten indexes have been disposed of.

Correcting the indexes

One sometimes notices that a worn entry in the manuscript index has been helpfully inked over, or an entry in the typed index has been carefully amended. I have found that some of these well-meant amendments were in fact incorrect and were clearly not checked against the actual marriage record. Some of the errors created in this way are startlingly wrong. After six years of work on the indexes I find that such errors will often jump out of the page at me even if I am looking for something quite different.

Filming the indexes

Making the indexes available on microfiche and film is simply a further copying stage and has proved at least as subject to error by way of omissions. Gaps of several or indeed many pages have been found in film and fiche, as described in chapter 11.

Obtaining certificates

Marriage certificates (and likewise those for births and deaths) are produced in the General Register Office by means of microfilm reader/printers (Regma machines). These print the required entry onto the preprinted and sealed certificate forms, green for marriages, red for births and black for deaths.

The display on the microfilm reader can be masked so that the print will show nothing beyond the detail of the one marriage. It is perhaps worth mentioning that the full pages of which the films consist contain all sorts of jottings, messages, cross references, numberings and so forth. They are very far from being the neat and tidy records that most people no doubt imagine them to be.

David Hey, in the "Oxford Guide to Family History", 1993, was actually wrong when he wrote "The copy of the certificate that is provided upon payment of the fee is usually freshly made, and as with all copying runs the risk of transcription error". He was perhaps misled by seeing what may appear to be handwritten entries on a preprinted form.

He may also have been thinking of certificates from years before direct printing was possible. Before the days of printing, certificates both from the General Register Office and from other sources were handwritten or typed on the blank certificate forms. Many different pre-printed forms can be seen. Some certificates issued by a local registrar soon after an event clearly state that that registrar still has the "Register Book lawfully in my custody". A certificate issued somewhat later by a Superintendent Registrar may indicate that it is a copy from a register now in his custody (having been passed to him by the district registrar or clergyman when filled). A certificate issued by a clergyman at the time of a marriage is described as "a true copy of the Marriage Register of the church of ...".

A few certificates *are* still handwritten at the GRO but only where the handwriting of the quarterly returns is so atrocious, wholly or in part, that a good print is impossible. A small section at the GRO, with staff rostered for a week or so from other sections, carries out this small-scale operation.

The bulk of the certificate production is carried out with great care on the film printers, with plain-paper prints made and carefully checked before committing to a print on the official form. The microfilm printers have good control for focus and brightness. Newer equipment is under trial, digitising the microfilm images and printing by computer.

The actual wording on a certificate from the General Register Office is significant. On a marriage certificate, for example, the words are "Certified to be a true copy of an entry in the certified copy of a register of Marriages in the Registration District of . . .". It differs from the wording on a certificate from a Superintendent Registrar, which is certified to be a "true copy of the entry no. --- in the Marriage Register no. --- of . . .". The GRO certificate says that it is a true copy of a copy of a register. The local certificate is a true copy of an original entry in a register. The GRO wording is not simply long-winded, as people may imagine, but is a careful and exact reflection of the mechanism underlying the GRO records.

The words "true copy" have been in use since the days when certificates were filled out by hand or by typewriter. Thus they purported, rightly or wrongly, to guarantee total accuracy in copying or typing. Yet even in the early days of civil registration it would have been known that the certified copies themselves were unreliable. Clerks were making many thousands of duplicate index entries because the quarterly copies were impossible to be sure of. The only recourse open to the system was to stand formally on the "certified copies" made by the clergy, as provided for in the legislation, and to take the optimistic view that true copies could be contrived from quarterly returns that were being variably indexed, at the same time turning a blind eye to the fact that no checks existed for the accuracy of the clergy copies.

The certificate from the GRO is undoubtedly a "true copy of a certified copy" in these days of photo-printing.

The 1837 letter from the Registrar General to the clergy is a reminder, if it is needed, that the whole system was designed to yield these certified copies of entries of births, deaths and marriages that would be deemed legally acceptable by way of proof. It was also aimed at avoiding fraudulent use of information. Most genealogical researchers today would be fully satisfied with a lesser standard of certification. The paradox in the situation is that the standard of certification has been nominally maintained at the highest possible standard whereas this research has proved such widespread error in the record system that the notion of universally true copies must now be an invalid one. Even the Registrar General's booklet of 1900 for the guidance of the clergy (see chapter 7) admitted that errors were inevitable.

*   *   *   *   *   *   *   *   *   *   *   *   *   *   *

It is probably true that most people have found themselves unable to track some of their past family in the BDM indexes. I hope that the findings from this study will not only help to explain how some of this information may have gone astray or may have been hidden in the process of getting from the marriage register to the marriage index, but may in some cases provide some encouragement or some new leads that will help to track them down. I also hope that my vision of a revamped marriage index put forward in Chapter 9 may find favour and may lead to a very much better research environment for the future.

*   *   *   *   *   *   *   *   *   *   *   *   *   *   *

The Parishes

This description of the paths and arrangements of the marriage records would be incomplete without taking a look at the basic level of the marriage records, namely the parishes. Although this aspect of the system is not immediately obvious from the index, the sorted computer files did detect the appearance of such an internal arrangement within the district records.

The hierarchy of the GRO marriage record system in the 1800s is :

1.   The volume structure, firstly 27 volumes and then 33, ranging in size from less than a thousand marriages per volume up to several thousands.

2.   The Superintendent Registrars' districts, grouped into the GRO volumes as shown in the Page Range Tables in appendices 1 - 4.

3.   The parishes and register offices, their individual sheets and groups of sheets forming the quarterly returns of marriages within the district of each Superintendent Registrar.

The parishes in major cities such as London, Bristol, Liverpool and Manchester were few in number but some of these parishes sent in more marriages than whole districts in the rural areas. We will look at both.

Here is the marriage pattern for one district of a rural Superintendent Registrar in volume 12 for 1843 and 1844 :

Numbers of marriages in Samford, Suffolk, 1843 and 1844								
Parishes	Q1	Q2	Q3	Q4	Q1	Q2	Q3	Q4
Belstead		1		2	1	1		
Bentley	2			1	2			1
East Bergholt	4	1	2	4	2	1	2	3
Brantham	1	3	2	2		1		2
Burstall							1	3
Capel St Mary	3	1	1	1		3	2	
Chattisham		None				None		
Chelmondiston		1	2	4	1		2	2
Copdock				1		1		
Edwardston						1		
Freston						1		1
Hawkstead				3	2		1	
Higham		1						1
Hintlesham			1			2		1
Holbrook	1			2		2	1	2
Holton St Mary	1			2				1
Playdon				2	1		2	2
Shelley		1		1	2		1	1
Shotley	1		1				1	3
Sproughton	1	1	1	3	1		1	1
Stratford St Mary	2			2	2		1	1
Stutton			3	3		2		1
Tattingstone	1		1	1		1		1
Washbrook		1						
Wenham Magna		1		2		1		1
Wenham Parva	1		1	1		1		
Whenstead		None				None		
Woolverstone	1			1	2			1
Register Office			1	1	1	2		

Within the bundles of Quarterly Returns at the General Register Office, and hence within the GRO films, the parish sheets are arranged more or less in a stable alphabetical order of parish names within each Superintendent Registrar's district, followed by the sheets for any Jewish or Quaker marriages in that bundle and by the sheets for any register offices in the district. Here in Samford there was only one marriage registrar.

The table of Samford marriages for 1843/Q2 shown in Chapter 4 can be aligned with this table of parishes. The two parishes of Chattisham and Whenstead each had three marriages over the two years 1841/42 yet had no marriages in 1843/44. The only parish with marriages in every quarter of 1843/44 is East Bergholt. The majority of the quarterly returns had only a single marriage.

Most of the large parishes tended to solemnise marriages in every quarter but small parishes in rural areas could appear very sporadically. It is typical of a Superintendent Registrar's district in a rural area that it may contain thirty or forty parishes but only receive marriages from a dozen or so in a particular quarter. The smallish district of Orsett in Essex, down by the Thames, registered 254 marriages in the four years 1841 to 1844, an average of sixteen marriages a quarter, but this includes the remarkable March quarter of 1842 when only three marriages were registered, one in Fobbing and two in Stanford le Hope, right down by the marshlands of the river.

Here by contrast we have marriages for West Ham, becoming part of London in Essex :

Numbers of marriages in West Ham, Essex, 1843 and 1844							
Parishes							
	Q1	Q2	Q3	Q4	Q1	Q2	Q3	Q4
East Ham	2	3		4		1	3	2
Leyton	1	6	10	6	4	4	9	8
Little Ilford					1			2
Walthamstow	2	2	2	1	4	3	3	1
Wanstead	1		2	1		1	1	1
West Ham	11	5	17	17	11	16	18	14
Woodford		1	2	4	1	3	1	4
Friends' Mtg Ho						1		
Register Office				1		5	4	4
St James' Chapel, Walthamstow								1
St James' Chapel, Stratford								3
St Peter's Chapel, Walthamstow								1

By the end of 1844 the marriage register for Leyton reached 227 entries and the register for the parish of West Ham reached 385 entries, both since 1837. West Ham parish would probably have filled its first register by some time in 1846. Notice too that more chapels were springing up in developing areas such as West Ham. These three chapels celebrated their first marriages in the December quarter of 1844.

By contrast the most active parish in the Samford district was East Bergholt with 67 entries and the next was Chelmondiston with 34. The whole district of Samford had had 564 entries from 1837 to 1844 (assuming that no entries were spoiled) and West Ham district had reached 912. This is a reflection of the difference in patterns between town and country.

It is possible that there are one or two parishes in the Samford district that saw no marriages at all in the four years 1841 to 1844 and have therefore escaped my table completely. After all, Edwardston and Washbrook only had one marriage each in the two years 1843 and 1844.

Do you recall Marcus Crane in that first extract from the marriage indexes on page 19 ? He was indexed (in 1844/Q1) as Samford, volume XII, page 543. Marcus's marriage is one of those in our table of Samford marriages on page 51. His is the one and only event in the parish of Chelmondiston in that quarter, marrying Mary Ann Bailey. They occupy position 30 in the marriage register of the parish (as you could have deduced from the comment about 34 marriages up to 1844).

Chelmondiston is a village by the River Orwell, a little down river from Ipswich. Even an old 1/4-inch map of the area shows nearly all the parishes listed in the table on p51, the exception being Wenham Parva (or Little Wenham), but shows no additional places. Perhaps our table is complete after all. Not surprisingly a few spellings differ from the best that could be read from the GRO film. We find Erwarton for Edwardston, Wherstead for Whenstead and Raydon for Playdon. Samford itself does not exist as a settlement.

Chapter 6 - Chapter of accidents ?

The scene has been set and ample hints dropped. Now is the time to look at some of the errors and oddities that have come to light in these studies.

Errors have come out of the research in large numbers. Some emerged directly from my processing and examination of the sorted index files. Others were only found when the files were checked in detail against the GRO films in Southport. You will find examples of both in this chapter.

Working with errors seems to increase sensitivity to them. Now they jump out of the fiche. A few popped out in an odd half hour when I was looking for something quite different in the 1844 marriage index :

Name	District	Volume	Page
Olive Boulton	Walsall	10	297
Robert Brindle	Stroud	10	589
Agnes Ann Burnett	Uxbridge	10	490
Emma Carter	Abridge	10	577
Thomas Heaven	Dursley	10	357
Abraham Hurle	Dursley	10	363
Frances Maria Pollard	St Martin	10	128

Only Emma Carter has the right volume number but her Essex village of Abridge is an error for Axbridge. The others have wrong volume numbers. Unless, of course, Uxbridge is another error for Axbridge, in which case Agnes has the right volume number but the wrong district. I find after six years with these records that a mis-match of a district and a volume number is generally obvious. It makes it the harder to see how clerks working with this material each and every day were able to make so many errors. Walsall is volume 17, Uxbridge is 3, Stroud and Dursley are 11 and St Martin is 1.

So much for the introduction. Now for some of the findings from the research.

Organising the story

We could perhaps look at errors by type, or we could look at the errors in a particular piece of the index. It seems best to take the second course first so as to give a sketch of the density and variety of errors, and then to range far and wide to look at examples of the many different errors to be found. Apart from indexing errors in the sense that references or names are wrong, there is ample evidence of marriages and individuals who were not put into the index and evidence of marriages that never found their way from the marriage registers to the Registrar General's records. There are people in the indexes who shouldn't be there, and marriages repeated in two quarters. An endless variety of errors.

Keep in mind that the evidence comes from a one per cent sample of marriages from the 1800s and that only about ten per cent of that sample has been checked in detail against the marriage records. We have to suppose that the untouched 99% of the record, not to mention the 99.9% not checked in detail, will have errors or omissions that could well be of the same magnitude (or greater).

This chapter ranges widely and needs a list of contents :

Some Essex/Suffolk quarters in detail

At the GRO I checked my files of Essex/Suffolk index entries for nine quarters of the 1830s and 1840s and this report on three of those quarters is only a small part of the results. In other quarters there was a wide range of similar errors. The number of errors detected ran to around one per 20 marriages on average.

1843 June Quarter - volume 12 (Essex & Suffolk)

This film contains 563 marriages and I have noted 24 probable errors. Here are some of them.

Page 3 of the film (parish of Brentwood in the Billericay district) includes the marriage of George King and Sarah Jiggers. George is mis-indexed as p33, and Sarah's entry in the film looks much more like Jiggens than Jiggers.

Page 55 of the film includes Ann Susannah Aldridge, very clearly written, who is in the index as Aldriige.

Page 97. Two marriages are indexed as Lexden, p97. The page heading in the film was once Lexden and Winstree but this was at some time crossed out as an error and changed to Colchester. The page is in the Colchester section and both marriages should have been indexed as Colchester. Quite often an alteration in the record is not carried through to the index.

Page 259 Louisa Leith Saward on this page is mis-indexed as page 359.

Page261 The one marriage on this page is James Benjamin Kearsey and Eliza Cook. The indexer wrote down the bride as Edward Cook.

Page 362 Mary Jane Morley on this page (East Ham) is mis-indexed as p562. Her bridegroom John Loxley is correct as p362.

Page 375 Of the two marriages here, that of William Algar and Mary Partner took place in the September quarter but was wrongly in the return for the June quarter. Though later crossed through in the film, it was already indexed. This is common. Many marriages are in two successive indexes.

Page 432 Patrick Timmins is in the index as Sheffield vol 12 page 432. There is no page 432 in the volume 12 film and this is one of the many mis-typed Roman numerals, XII in place of XXII.

Page 441 In the Ipswich parish of St Clement we have John Simpson Clark marrying Emma Noy. His signature is given as John Simpson and this is very likely to have been an error in the quarterly copying, creating a fictitious John Simpson in the index.

Page 446 In the Ipswich parish of St Margaret, one of the ten marriages is of Henry Pepper and Mary Ann Pepper. Mary is indexed as Mary Ann Turner, probably because her marriage is immediately after Samuel Turner and Hannah Brown.

Page 644c This page is a late insertion for the parish of Haskerton in Woodbridge district. It has on it the one marriage of Robert Tyler and Ann Girt. Robert is indexed as p644c and Ann as p544c.

1843 September quarter

This index has eight entries with references to volume 12 that have proved to be either a wrong volume reference or a wrong page reference.

Here are a few other errors that are worth pointing out :

Page 29 This page in Braintree district has a marriage entry for Charles Field and Elizabeth Raven but the index entry is for Thomas Field. Thomas was the father of Charles Field and it seems that the quarterly copy put Thomas Field as the signature in error, not an uncommon error. Charles Field is not indexed.

Page 69 The one marriage on this page is William Turp and Mary Wright, submitted by the vicar of Margaretting in Q2 *and* Q3 - indexed in both quarters.

Page 129 Another example of the Thomas/Charles Field error. In Gt Dunmow were married James Tyler and Ann Collins. James' signature is shown as Thomas Tyler who happened to be his father. Thomas is indexed, James is not.

1843 December quarter - volume 12 (Essex/Suffolk)

This film has suffered quite badly from the indexers. Here are some examples :

Page 7 Elizabeth Sarah Spearman is mis-indexed as Sarah Spearman

Page 35 Three Braintree marriages were included by the Vicar of Bocking for this quarter and again three months later for 1844/Q1 and all have been indexed in both quarters. One belongs in 1843/Q4 and two in 1844/Q1.

Page 40 That same common error was repeated by the Vicar of Finchingfield for the marriage of Thomas Stock and Charlotte Turner, married on 3 February, only days before the vicar mistakenly included them in his return for 1843/Q4. He submitted them in the following quarterly return as well.

Page 137 Thomas Bibby married Mary Anne Wilson in Colchester, Nayland parish. The index entry is for George Bibby, one of the witnesses. Thomas is not indexed.

Page 153 Elizabeth Byford in Bardfield Saling in Dunmow district is indexed twice, once in error as Colchester p153 and once correctly as Dunmow p153. This is a good example of an indexer appearing to realise and correct a mistake but nevertheless leaving the error to stand. It has happened time and again.

Page 181 My index extraction had found six men and four women referenced to this page. The explanation has turned out to be that the signatures for the parties and the witnesses for the three marriages were transposed and the indexer put four of the witnesses in the index. The spurious entries are for Thomas Dawkins, Samuel Lane, Benjamin Newell and Martha Tadgell.

Page 481 Another father/son mix-up in Hempstead parish in Saffron Walden district. Here John Ward married Jane Waylett but his signature was mis-copied as Henry Ward, Henry being his father. The indexer entered both John and Henry. The marriage record was later altered by crossing out Henry and replacing with John. Henry remains in the index as a trap for any researcher.

P553 The Tendring parish of Wix saw the marriages of Hannah Pickers and Susannah but the indexer saw Susannah Pickers twice and omitted Hannah.

P582a This film page is for the parish of Ulting in the district of Witham. The indexer missed it and missed the marriage of Charles Lucking and Eliza Bowles.

P583 The vicar of Hatfield Peverel reported the marriage of John Green and Ann Elms twice in his return. Both passed the check (if any) of the Super-intendent Registrar and went on to the Registrar General. There their pages were numbered 583 and 585 and they were indexed in respect of both, though the writing was worse on 585 and the indexer felt the need to index Ann as Ann Elems as well.

p707 Many Ipswich quarterly returns were very badly written and here we have, I believe, George East who married Ann Green. The indexer was less sure and also indexed him as Eort, Gest and Gort.

p758a This page holds two marriages. William Nunn and Harriet Pitts married on 9/11/1843 and were entered as no.17 in the marriage register. John Smith and Harriet Packard were entered as no.18 in the register but with the marriage recorded as 29/9/43. John and Harriet seem to have fallen victim to some misguided vigilance in the system as they are crossed out and not indexed. Those responsible for discarding them perhaps thought they were already in the Q3 return and in the Q3 index. If so, then they were wrong and clearly failed to check.   They are nowhere else in the record, so far as I can see, and I believe the date was a simple copying error by the vicar, an error for November or even December. Therefore John Smith and Harriet are lost from the index system.

P871 Elizabeth Gladwell married Thomas Hanton in the Stowmarket parish of Buxhall and the marriage record reads as though Elizabeth then signed as Elizabeth Hanton. The indexer then indexed her under both names. I have found several examples of a bride signing her married name and being doubly indexed as a result but here I suspect the mistake may be the vicar's and not Elizabeth's, as he also described her as a single man and Thomas as a single woman. One needs to see the register to be sure but these errors could all be in the copying.

Page 941   In the parish of Bulmer in Sudbury district William Howard married Jane Spalding, not, as the indexer would have us believe, Jane Spaine. (Page 80 points the finger at the typist rather than the indexer).

Page 973   This is one of the many recto pages that failed to appear in my lists, a good indication that a page was missed in indexing. Sure enough, the marriage of Isaac Josling, butcher, and Elizabeth Sillitoe, widow (maiden name Frost) was not indexed. They are in the district of Sudbury.

    *   *   *   *   *   *   *   *   *   *   *   *   *   *   *

It can be readily imagined that one could write at very great length about the errors found in these studies but it would become an interminable catalogue, legitimate in my report to ONS but not appropriate here.

I will now give examples of errors taken from various of my computer files. They show the very many ways in which mistakes were made and may perhaps throw some light on the way the indexers worked and the reasons for some of the errors. In Chapter 7 I take up another theme, evidence suggesting and indeed proving that there are gaps in the marriages in the quarterly returns.

Then in Chapter 8 I take the investigation one step further back into the system. All I have dealt with up to this point is *the comparison between the records in the General Register Office and the GRO marriage indexes* made from them. It is important to keep in mind that the GRO records are *copies of the original records* and often poor copies. The work I have done on the GRO indexes is also an ideal launch pad for comparing them with the primary records, the marriage registers held by the Superintendent Registrars. At this stage I have been able to come very close to such a comparison by comparing the GRO index for one district with the local Superintendent Registrar's index for that district. The Superintendent Registrar's index is based on the original marriage entries and *not on those terrible quarterly copies.* The results in terms of differences and omissions have been startling to say the least. This work is the basis for Chapter 8. I have made proposals to the GRO for an exercise that would extend this smallish comparison from about 800 names to around 14000. Then Chapter 9 outlines suggestions for redeveloping the 19th century marriage records and indexes, a proposal that seems to be a logical conclusion from the situation that has been uncovered.

Many ways to be wrong

Now let us look at a range of examples of various types of errors that have been found in the index system. This is necessarily only a portion of the very large number of errors recorded in my six weeks in the General Register Office.

Recto (or other) pages missed by the indexers

My sorted index files have sometimes signalled a possible problem not so much because something looked wrong but because something failed to appear at all.

In chapter 4 (page 26) we looked at the quarterly returns of marriages in terms of bundles of individual sheets brought together and then numbered in a continuous series, the result being that each recto side has an odd number (and always contains marriages) while the verso sheets may be used or unused according to the number of marriages in the return. My sorted files had no references to occasional recto sheets . Could these sheets have been missed by the indexers ?

It turns out that there are at least three explanations for these absent recto pages:

1. Pages were indeed missed by the indexers.
2. Pages were sometimes given a wrong reference by the indexer.
3. Page numbers sometimes badly written in the handwritten
      index were mistyped when the indexes were typed.

I have not checked all the missing recto pages in my files but the following examples will illustrate each type of error.

Volume 12, 1839/Q4, p453 ff

In my file of index entries for the 1839/Q4 for Essex/Suffolk (a file that revealed an extremely large number of typing errors) I was surprised to find no references to the two recto pages 453 and 455 in the district of Saffron Walden. I wrote to what was then OPCS (Office for Population Censuses and Surveys) to ask whether these pages held marriage entries. I was assured that they didn't.

At Southport I checked these pages myself and found more than I expected.

a)   Page 451 contains two marriages.   Joseph Wilson and Elizabeth Wombwell have been indexed but Peter Wombwell and Susan Dyer have *not*.

b)   Page 453 also contains two marriages.   William Seach and Ann Smith have *not* been indexed.   David Moore and Sarah Woodley, an entry that is fully recorded, signed and witnessed, has been crossed through and not indexed, no reason being given.

c)   Page 455 has one marriage, John Debnam and Susan Harvey, *not* indexed.

d)   Page 457 has four marriages.   John Stalley and Sarah Woodly and also Charles Cornel and Eliza Harriet Saville are indexed.   The other two marriages are *not* indexed, John Taylor and Elizabeth Chapman, Emmanuel Baynes and Elizabeth Haydon.

Volume 11, 1849/Q1, p195   This unindexed page from the Bristol Register Office contains :

> Thomas Tincknell and Elizabeth Sparrow
> Thomas Mathling and Elizabeth Mathling
> Daniel Nutt and Susanah (sic) Hill
> Matthew Gaynor and Mary Ann Voisey

It turns out that these names are not missing. All are mis-indexed as page 194.

Volume 12, 1849/Q1, p174a   This page was possibly added to the marriage records a little late but its two marriages never reached the index.   The marriages are for the parish of Pebmarsh in the Halstead district of Essex. They are :

> John Wass and Elizabeth Mays, married 6/1/1849
> John Franklin and Susannah Sycamore, married 18/3/1849

Volume 14, 1849/Q1, p163.   My file showed p161 as the highest page in Newmarket district and p165 as the first page in North Witchford.   P163 was unreferenced by the index and could be in either district.   The GRO film shows it to be Newmarket and it has the following unindexed marriages :

> Thomas Sherwin and Elizabeth Bocock
> Samuel Fuller and Mary Gooch
> John William Johnson and Rachel Saunders
> Henry Braham Rumbelow and Eliza Elizabeth Hammond

Volume 25, 1849/Q1, p261   This unindexed page adds fifty per cent to the marriages in the tiny Haltwhistle district in Q1, namely :

> William Phillipson and Margarett Nicholson
> John Laing and Mary Dickerson

They are from the parish of Whitfield, with which I can feel a personal affinity.

Volume 19, 1844/Q1, p479   This unindexed page proved on inspection to contain the marriage of John Eaton and Selina Barton which had been crossed through. It carries a date of 6/2/1844 but there seems to have been a thought that it may have been an error for 1843. My notes are not complete enough to comment further.

Volume 13, 1844/Q1, p79   This is an unindexed page in the district of Depwade. It is one I have not checked but probably has one or two marriages.

Volume 12, 1844/Q1, p417   This unindexed page is from the parish of Willisham in the district of Bosmere and contains :

> George Stearn Mumford and Anne Boby

As with another example above, they are mis-indexed to page 407 (parish of Debenham), probably through a typing slip induced by bad writing. Consider, however, that these names lie in two very different parts of the index so the misreading must have happened twice. Possibly the indexer wrote a heavy "blobby" "1" and it was thick enough in both instances to be misread as a zero. The opposite error has also occurred with a tall thin "0" misread as a "1".

Volume 12, 1844/Q4, page 42a.   Not quite an unindexed page but a half-indexed page, from the Essex picture-postcard village of Finchingfield with its well known green, duck pond, windmill and church on the hill. Here half our picture seems to be missing. Three marriages are on page 42a :

> James Hitchcock and Ann Chapman
> William Turner and Mary Townsend
> John Wendy and Mary Harvey

There are no index entries for Turner, Townsend or Wendy, as if the indexer was somehow distracted, turned back to work and picked up with Mary Harvey.

What about the IGI ?

The International Genealogical Index (IGI) produced by the Church of Jesus Christ and Latter-day Saints (the LDS) is an index to births, baptisms and marriages, based very largely on the filming of parish registers.

Would any of the unindexed marriages be found in the IGI ? People have sometimes claimed finding entries in the IGI that are absent from the GRO indexes. The great strength of the IGI record lies in entries from before 1837 and it also holds far more information on births and baptisms than on marriages. The coverage varies because filming of registers has depended on permission from incumbent ministers.

Essex and Suffolk entries in the IGI are generally thin beyond the early 1800s and none of these unindexed items from the GRO's volume 12 can be found.

Northumberland proved a different matter. Here the two missing marriages from volume 25 in 1849/Q1 are listed by the IGI, as :

> William Phillipson and Margaret Nicholson
> John Laing and Mary Dickinson

Both couples are shown as marrying in the parish of Whitfield, on 11/1/1849 and 17/3/1849 respectively. They are the only missing entries in this study that I have been able to track down. Notice that the IGI shows Margaret and Dickinson where the GRO film has Margarett and Dickenson. The IGI entries are from film of an original marriage register whereas the GRO film is based on the quarterly copies. This feels like yet another straw in the wind pointing towards bad copying as the source of the GRO's problems.

For the simple reason that many marriage entries haven't reached the General Register Office (as you will see in chapters 7 and 8) or haven't been indexed (as you have seen in this chapter) or have been lost in the typing process, then it must follow that some of these missing marriages will be found in the IGI to the extent that the LDS happen to have filmed those particular marriage registers.

It could be a worthwhile exercise to take a sample of several thousand marriage entries from the IGI record, perhaps for the period 1837 to about 1860, and to check these against the GRO indexes for the same period. This could be a good indication of indexing omissions and indexing variations. It is a study that I have initiated and is briefly described in chapter 15.

Errors in index references

When data from the marriage index are sorted into a sequence based on volume and page references, the pattern of volumes and districts appears. What also appear in sharp relief are errors in district names, volume numbers or page numbers.

To take an example from 1844/Q1, there is an entry in the index for John Russell, in the district of Bethnal Green, volume 1, page 7. This volume/page reference would put John in the middle of the entries for St George Hanover Square which occupy the first 42 pages of volume 1. Bethnal Green is in volume 2 and when the data entry for 1844/Q1 was complete it became obvious that John Russell would fit perfectly on page 7 of volume 2, with two other men and three women. The indexing error in this case was in the volume number.

Sometimes the district name and volume number are right but the page number is wrong. Then that entry may show up in a different district. It may or may not be easy to pick the page where it actually belongs. In 1844/Q1 John Farley is indexed as Mere in volume 8 and with page no. 419. This places him in Cricklade rather than Mere, a distinct embarrassment to Emma Cuss and Charles Millard who are the rightful occupants. Districts in volume 8 are quite small and it is immediately obvious that John Farley should be on page 519, where he is awaited by either Elizabeth Cook or Eliza Viney, a relief to James Howell.

Cricklade	
419	Emma Cuss, John Farley [Mere], Charles Millard
421	Jonas Little, Ann Stapleford
Mere	
517	John Brooke, Ann Lampard, Elizabeth Miles, George Scamell, George Scammell
519	Elizabeth Cook, James Howell, Eliza Viney

If a page number in the index is wrong it may still lie in the right page range if the district is large. This means that wrong page numbers can be very hard to sort out when they occur in large districts in London or in places like Liverpool or Manchester. A few wrong page numbers in those locations will certainly create unbalanced pages in my files but with little chance of correcting them.

Sometimes a district name may be wrong and I am able to say that the volume and page reference are both right. An example from 1844/Q1 comes from volume 5. A Mary Clark in the index is given as Tendring vol 5, page 419. Tendring is in Essex and Essex entries are in volume 12. The Tendring pages in volume 12 cover the range 331 to 361. In volume 5 the Tenterden pages are 417 to 423 and it is clear that Mary Clark does belong in Tenterden but has been mis-indexed as Tendring, an error or poor writing by a GRO clerk.

Tenterden
417 Elizabeth Austen, John Brooks, Rachel Ellen Freman, Stephen Redman,
     Josiah Smith, Josias Smith, Margaret Wellstead, Margaret Welstead
419 Mary Bayley, James Beech, Frederic Britcher, Mary Clark [Tendring],
     Thomas Hutchinson, Sarah Sharp, Thomas Underdown, Mary Ann
     Wicken

In Tenterden Mary Clark is happily at home with three other women and four men, one undoubtedly her husband. It was the district name that was wrong in the index. It is tempting to imagine that Elizabeth Austen may be one of Jane Austen's two nieces of that name. Note the variant entries on page 417.

In the Superintendent Registrar's district of St James Westminster in the same quarter the indexer processing volume 1a correctly lists four of the eight names from page 73 as St James but lists the other four from the same page as Westminster. This is a different district, higher in the same volume.

These examples illustrate the sort of indexing errors that show up in this processing of the data. In general such errors seem to occur with a frequency of one for every 500 to 1000 entries. Very often they are errors that no user of the index could reasonably suspect.

But much worse can be found. The last of the early exercises carried out on volume 12 (Essex and Suffolk) was for 1839/Q4. Index errors were numerous. Instead of the usual two or three per volume there were twenty four. These included entries for Gloucester, Ticehurst, Brighton, Depwade, Malton, Cheltenham, Stoke, Stamford, Liverpool and so on, all indexed as volume 12. There were references to Sudbury as Ludbury. With so many entries from other districts indexed as volume 12, some volume 12 entries could well have been indexed to other districts. I scanned the fiche a second time and found fifteen errors of Essex/Suffolk entries indexed as other volumes, adding ten names to the file of volume 12 entries and supplying spouses for ten lonely individuals. The balance of five entries were referenced as Stow, volume 17 and turned out to be the district of Stone. From later study of handwritten parts of the index it became very obvious that Stone could all too easily be misread as Stow.

A total of thirty nine indexing errors in an extraction of 2585 entries is overwhelmingly the highest density of errors that I have found at long range. Was there perhaps an inexperienced clerk at work on the indexing ? I would say not. The answer almost certainly lies with the typing from the original manuscript, and especially the reading of Roman numerals. Detailed checking of the GRO film would undoubtedly multiply this error rate just as it has done with all my other files that have been checked.

The inference must be that many of the other indexes for 1839 and perhaps for neighbouring years are just as badly served by these typed indexes. It is quite impossible that entries just for Essex and Suffolk could be so badly flawed and that other entries in the same index could be largely correct.

Another typing error that can be mentioned here was in 1844/Q1, where the index contains the two following entries :

Ingram	John Thomas	St Saviour	2	353
Ingram	John William	St Luke's	4	238

The problem with this example is that St Saviour's is in volume 4 and St Luke's is in volume 2. Change the volume numbers and the entries both fall into their rightful places. This could be a typing slip, from the badly written Roman numerals II and IV, or it could have been a moment of confusion in the indexing process. Are John Thomas and John William possibly interchanged as well ?

It was in the births index that I first noticed what you might call a "bulk" error. I was checking a Sayel reference in 1849. It is a name that only occurs very occasionally, just before the fairly numerous entries for Sayer and Sayers. In one of the 1849 quarters I came across a big block of Sayel, followed by Sayers, but no Sayer. Clearly most or all of the Sayel entries should have been Sayer.

This is a typed section of the index, where the surname is only typed once even if there are several entries for that name. This makes it very easy to propagate an error over a series of entries. The typist probably started with a Sayel and must have forgotten to switch to Sayer. I have found other similar examples. Few users of the indexes would notice errors of this sort. A clue may lie in the sequencing of the given names but this is not very likely to be noticed.

A bargain bag of errors from Essex/Suffolk

My set of Essex/Suffolk files contain dozens of indexing errors, far too many to describe in detail. Here are a few thumbnail sketches :

William Woollard indexed as Woolland (Bosmere 1838/Q4)
William Elijah Chaplin indexed as Eyah (Colchester 1843/Q1)
Simon James Mazey indexed as Senior (ibid)
Elizabeth Noakes on p243 indexed as 343 (Rochford 1843/Q1)
Thamar Hicks indexed as Thomas (Risbridge 1843/Q1)

William Johnson (groom's father) indexed, later amended but still in index
    (Samford 1843/Q1)
James Eady mis-indexed as Earley (Sudbury 1843/Q1)
Mary Ann Hockley mis-indexed as Stockley (Sudbury 1843/Q1)
Mary Jane Morley on p362 mis-indexed as 562 (West Ham 1843/Q2)
Henry Beard on p44 indexed as p114 (Colchester 1843/Q3)
James Tyler not indexed (his father Thomas is) (Dunmow 1843/Q2)
Ann Elizabeth Troubridge is mis-indexed as Elizabeth (Orsett 1843/Q3)
Catharine Hewit mis-indexed as Hervitt (Ipswich 1843/Q3)
Mira Farrance on p567 is indexed as p367 (Risbridge 1843/Q3)
John Gentle is imis-indexed as John Gent (Woodbridge 1843/Q3)
Elias Suckling mis-indexed as Eliza (Chelmsford 1843/Q4)
William Bush is indexed as Bust (Rochford 1843/Q4)
John Totham indexed as Torham (Samford 1843/Q4)
William Cunnolds indexed as Cunnolls (Stow 1843/Q4)
Caroline Hickford indexed as Huckford (Halstead 1844/Q1)
Emma Cresswell indexed as Crupwell (Lexden 1844/Q1)
John Doe indexed as Joe Doe (Lexden 1844/Q1)
Emma Whipp indexed as Phipp (Tendring 1844/Q1)
George Jubillee Botham indexed as George Botham (Witham 1844/Q1)
Joshua Smy indexed as Spry (Bosmere 1844/Q1)
Frederick Ling on p504 mis-indexed as p564 (Plomesgate 1844/Q1)
William Goodram on p539 mis-indexed as p509 (Samford 1844/Q1)
Lucy Attridge mis-indexed as Attredoe and Attridoe (Billericay 1844/Q2)
John Day indexed in error (father of George Day) (Dunmow 1844/Q2)
Susanna Westwood indexed as Susann (Dunmow 1844/Q2)
James Knight indexed as Orsett p151 (which is an Epping page) and no place
    in Orsett found for him (Orsett 1844/Q2)
Joseph Binks on p181 in Halstead district, doubly mis-indexed as Henstead
volume 13 (Halstead 1844/Q2)
Thamar Warren indexed as Thamor (Lexden 1844/Q2)
Eliza Marrells indexed as Merrells (Rochford 1844/Q2)
Sarah Halls on p317 doubly mis-indexed as Rochdale vol 11 p317 (Rochford
    1844/Q2)
Abraham Weston not indexed (West Ham 1844/Q2)
George Nankivell mis-indexed as Nankwell (West Ham 1844/Q2)
George Wightman not indexed (Risbridge p595, 1844/Q2)
Elizabeth Hasler indexed as Haster (Dunmow 1844/Q3)
Sarah Jane Bawtree and Charles Henry Hawkins indexed as Halstead p177 but
    are actually Lexden (Lexden 1844/Q3)
Hannah White indexed as Henry (Maldon 1844/Q3)
Thomas Sparman indexed as Spearman (Ongar 1844/Q3)
Eliza Hayden on p303 mis-indexed as Rochdale vol 21 p303 (Rochford
    1844/Q3)
David Ling on p585 mis-indexed as p385 (Risbridge 1844/Q3)
Charles Oetzman indexed as Octzman (Samford 1844/Q3)
Willliam Osborne p633, probable mistype as 638 (Stow 1844/Q3)
William Simpson indexed as Simsin and Simson (Woodbridge 1844/Q3)
Sarah Ann Orwin indexed as Onwin (Chelmsford 1844/Q4)
Eliza Tunnap indexed as Tunnah (Chelmsford 1844/Q4)

> John Garrard and Mary Ramsey are indexed as p138 but this page is blank in
>   the film and I didn't spot them elsewhere (Colchester? 1844/Q4)
> Marianne Argent is indexed as Rebecca (Halstead 1844/Q4)
> John Culver in Maldon mis-indexed as Malton (Maldon 1844/Q4)
> John Parsons mis-indexed as Jane (Maldon 1844/Q4)
> Elizabeth Webb is indexed as Eliza (Saffron Walden 1844/Q4)
> Harriet Cornell is indexed as Comell (Saffron Walden 1844/Q4)
> Daniel Suckling is not indexed (Witham p564a 1844/Q4)
> Leonard Pead is indexed as Halstead p595. This is a Bosmere page and
>   Leonard belongs neither here nor in Halstead. Probably an error from
>   elsewhere.
> Louisa Junnis and Sunnis as indexed are probably Lunnis (Samford 1844/Q4)

This list excludes the many minor slips such as Ann/Anne, Harriet/Harriett, Ellin/Ellen and the like, and all the many errors of entries in wrong quarters.

Duplicate entries

A feature of the index that caught my imagination from the start was the fact of names being entered twice. When a clerk is creating the index entries for a particular marriage he feels the need to enter one (or both) of the names twice with some variation. These names may be adjacent in the index, or fairly close, or far apart, depending on the variation in the name. Variants like Jelf and Self will be a long way apart, but having the same page reference they are re-united again when sorted by page. I have been most surprised at some discoveries.

My first extraction of the East End of London found 71 entries that were duplicates of another entry, such as Robert Horner Sealey and Rober Horner Sealey, Mary Ann Shew and Mary Ann Shoe, Ann Honora Macdonald and Ann Honey Mackdont, Elizabeth Irawin Tracy Clapp and Elizabeth Prawin Tracy Clapp. The variety of duplicates is infinite. Often they result from two versions of a name on the certificate, often a difference from the name in the marriage entry and the name as signed. Sometimes they come from difficulty in hearing a name. Very frequently they result from the sheer difficulty of identifying a name from the bad writing of the returns. Sometimes it is not so much bad writing as a style so florid that more than one reading is possible. Sometimes the duplicate entries will be helpful to a user of the index, sometimes they will mislead, sometimes they will do no harm and no good.

Duplicates are brought together in my files when the collected entries are sorted by page. They are not always immediately obvious, for example Eliza Buffer and Huffer, Rebecca Hatcher and Slatcher, James Linfield and Tinfield, Emily Onion and Unwin, James Barker and Parker.

Duplicate entries are generally between about 1% and 2% of the entries for one volume. I have found several volumes where the duplicate entries amount to just over 5% of the entries. Most can be put into a number of general categories :

a) Clark and Clarke. There are large numbers of duplicates of this general type.

b) Butler and Butter, Barnett and Burnett. These are duplicates where a distinctly different name is given by a small variation.

c) Mary Susanna Maltman and Mary Susannah Maltman. These small variations in given name are extremely common with names like Ann and Anne, Susanna and Susannah, Catherine and Catharine, Elisabeth and Elizabeth, Harriet and Harriett, Mary Ann and Marianne. I have even found An and Ann, Ada and Adah.

d) Will Dunlop and William Dunlop. There are quite a lot of duplicates of this sort involving Tom and Thomas, Chas and Charles, Wm and William, Fred and Frederick, all dutifully entered twice.

e) The homophones, such as Maria Beauditch and Maria Bowditch, Mary Ann Shoe and Mary Ann Shew, John Joseph King and John Joesseth King.

f) n and u, as in Kate Branfoot and Kate Braufoot, Rebecca Blont and Rebecca Blout, John Bonck and John Bouck, Emma Ando and Emma Audo. This is another common source of duplicate entries.

g) The additional given name, e.g. George Smith and George Dixon Smith

h) The truly ridiculous variant, a long and utterly distinctive name varying by only one or two letters, such as the remarkable pair of Zaphnath-paaneah Challis and Zaphnath-paaniah Challis. He was the son of an agricultural labourer. These are by no means uncommon.

i) The improbable variants, such as Avis Ducklow and Evis Ducklow, Evis being improbable. In a similar class is the variant entry of Stephanie in Dover in 1844 as Hephanie. Yes, "St" can look like "H" but surely Hephanie is wholly unjustified. Yet similar examples are many.

j) The "rebuilt" variants, such as William Collishaw and William Collis Law, Emma Woodbridge and Emma Wood Cridge.

I have come across names entered not just twice but up to four times, such as Maud Mary Bartrell, Bartsell, Burtrell and Burtsell in Winchester in 1891.

Conversely there are quite a large number of names entered twice where the name is given exactly and completely the same in both cases. Occasionally such identical pairs turn out to be two separate people, especially in the Welsh districts. It pays to be aware of this when ordering a certificate for a Welsh marriage (see page 91).

Duplicate entries were part of the system throughout the 1800s. The duplication tends to be a patchy phenomenon and this makes it harder to be precise about its extent. In 1849/Q1 there were 710 duplicate entries in a total of 57834 entries, one duplicate in 81 entries. By 1891/Q1, based on a partial file of 18200 entries (out of some 99000 in that quarter), there still seem to be over 200 duplicates, or one duplicate in less than 100 entries. I would have expected a change for the better but this is much the same as the earlier years.

There tends to be a regional difference. It is much less likely that duplications would arise in very strongly established regional names like Richardson, Atkinson, Harrison, Butterworth. There are many such names that are very strongly localised in the north. In Wales the names of Evans, Jones, Williams, Griffiths, Roberts, Thomas and so on are even more dominant.

One extreme variant comes from the very small district of Pateley Bridge in 1849/Q1. There is one duplication in this district, that of Christopher Holliday who is also recorded as Chittrister Holliday. The marriage record contains a clear version of the name as Christopher but it also contains a version that is far from clear. The indexer must presumably have been working to instructions that required him to look at all occurrences of the name and to make a "best assessment" of any apparent variations. I believe that Chittrister is a poor rendering of what is on the film.

Finally we come back to our old friend Noah Crane. My sorted Essex file, bringing entries together from the ends of the alphabet showed that he was also entered as Noah Ware. I fully expected that the GRO film would show that he was an "aka" person, Crane also known as Ware. It was a real surprise to find his surname so written that it was possible to read it as either of those names, different as they are. I believe on very close scrutiny that Crane is correct. There can be no doubt that the original marriage register will be clearly Crane or clearly Ware. No copyist could copy an uncertainty of that sort so that it remained identically uncertain in the copy.

I was taken to task by one eminent genealogist and columnist some years ago for saying that these duplicate entries could be errors. These studies have now shown that most are indeed errors in one way or another. The majority of them arise from the struggle of the indexers to read the terrible script in the quarterly returns or from variant errors that have obviously arisen in the quarterly copying. I have already commented on the many cases of a father's name being wrongly entered as a groom's signature. It is very significant that the comparison of the local Taunton index with the corresponding GRO index has shown that the GRO index has many duplicates where the Taunton index has a single name.

I shall have more to say on this topic in chapter 7 when considering some of the practices of the clergy.

A small window into the problem has been provided inadvertently by clergy who managed (all too often) to submit the same marriage for two consecutive quarters. I have several examples where the writing was worse on one of two submissions and led to duplicate or different indexing. Thus Koosher in one index became Roosher and Koosher in another, Nankivell in one index became Nankwell in another, Benjamin Hills in one index was completely miscopied with a signature of Hicks in the next quarter, becoming both Hills and Hicks in the second index, and Secker in one became Sicker in the next.

Another common cause of duplication is where a party signs a shortened name. For example Sarah Ann Ford in the parish of Clopton is given with her full name in the marriage entry but signed as Sarah Ford. She is indexed as both. The example of George Smith and George Dixon Smith is the same. To my mind this is taking the principle of uncertainty too far and it has happened very often. The Registrar General's advice to clergy was that signatures in marriage entries need not express the full name but should simply be the normal signature. This makes it even less appropriate that both forms should be given in the index, where it will simply make it harder for users to decide the most likely entry.

The most amusing indexing of a signature comes from Dover in 1849. Here Ann Maurice Gabriel de la Fare (bridegroom) married Margaret Isabella Petch. The groom, in French fashion, signed himself simply as "La Fare". The indexer, carefully following the procedure for unnamed infants, indexed his full name from the marriage entry and also indexed him from his shortened signature as "Male la Fare".

Overall I now have no doubt at all that most of the variant indexing arose from bad copying and from some inappropriate indexing instructions and it has certainly inflated the size of the marriage index in the 1800s by at least two percent, over 500,000 entries. I am equally sure that the badly written quarterly returns are also responsible for the thousands of names in the index that are extremely improbable.

The double submissions

Some clergy had trouble in knowing where a quarter began and ended. In the eight quarters of Essex/Suffolk marriages in 1843/44 there are well over twenty marriages submitted in one quarter and re-submitted in the next.

A common error in making a quarterly return was the inclusion of a marriage that had happened since the end of the quarter. Sometimes these were noticed at some point in the system, crossed through and not indexed. Much more often they reached the index. Sometimes they were subsequently crossed through (but remained in the index) but often there is no sign that the error was seen at all. A few marriages were picked up from a prior quarter and resubmitted.

By way of an example, the parish of Coggeshall in the Witham district submitted two marriages wrongly in the quarterly return for 1844/Q3.

Coggeshall 1844/Q3 index	
Marr Reg item 90	Charles Dennis and Emma Sach
item 91	James Rootkin and Rose Wiseman
item 92	David Goodson and Mary Ann Alden
Coggeshall in 1844/Q4 index	
item 91	James Rootkin and Rose Wiseman
item 92	David Goodson and Mary Ann Alden

Items 91 and 92 took place in October. All were indexed. The two intruders were crossed through in the film. Both were sent in again for Q4.

Sometimes one wonders about the clerical short-term memory. The Rector of Birch married George Bond and Ann Pryor on Sunday 29 September 1844 and on the following Wednesday he wrote his return for 1844/Q2 that should have been submitted in July. He included the Bond/Pryor marriage from just four days earlier. Perhaps it was a peace offering for being late. It went through the system without any comment. It was then resubmitted and re-indexed in Q3.

Down in Romford a vicar made his 1844/Q2 return somewhat earlier, on Saturday 10 August, perhaps a day when he had already written his sermon. 1844 had sultry showery weather from the end of June to the middle of

August so perhaps the garden was too wet to tempt him out of doors. He copied the marriages of James Lester and Susannah Trapp, John Norman and Jane Eve, and must have trotted straight round to the Register Office between showers.

The following Wednesday he made a second copy of the Norman/Eve marriage on a new sheet and the Superintendent Registrar clearly accepted it. Both copies were sent off to the Registrar General, both were included in the bundle, both pages were numbered (pages 341 and 343) and Norman and Eve were duly indexed twice. There is no perceptible difference between the two records. Perhaps for some reason the vicar thought that he had forgotten to send in the Norman/Eve marriage on the Saturday.

The reverse situation happened in Suffolk in 1843. The Reverend William Bathurst of the parish of Hollesley in Woodbridge District wrote four marriages in his quarterly return for 1843/Q1. He was fairly late with this return and two of the marriages were Q2 events, taking place on April 4th and June 11th. Both of these were crossed out and not indexed.

So far so good. For Q2 he resubmitted the June 11th marriage but forgot the one from April 4th. Thus William Wilmshurst and Harritte Taylor are not in the Q2 film where they should belong, nor have they been indexed. The irony is, of course, that they are sitting, crossed through, in the GRO film for 1843/Q1. Clearly there was no clerical system for checking that marriages crossed out for such a reason were later resubmitted for the correct quarter.

Good writing was not one of William Bathurst's accomplishments. The indexer made both Richard Lewis and Richard Leuis out of his Q1 return, and made Mary Ann Koosher and Mary Ann Roosher out of the Q2 return. Mary Ann was very clearly Koosher when submitted early in error.

In the Rochford District in 1842 the local registrar of Rochford district included the Q2 marriage of Samuel Giggins and Elizabeth Target in his quarterly return for Q1. This reached the GRO index for 1842/Q1. He resubmitted the same marriage in 1842/Q2, so this marriage is in the index for both quarters. Quite by chance, as so often seems to happen, the indexing of this couple for Q1 has yet another error. Samuel was indexed to p261 and Elizabeth to p269. Their location, illegal though it may be, was on page 269. A case of a moving target ?

William Sutton and Sophia Cook are a Writtle marriage in 1841/Q2 but were included again in the quarterly return for Q3. They were also indexed for Q3. Likewise the Dovercourt couple of William Willow and Mary Carter who married in 1841/Q3 were resubmitted and re-indexed in 1841/Q4.

For 1844/Q2 the Reverend Mr Dicken (if that is a correct reading of his signature) sent in five marriages from the parish of All Saints with St Peter in Maldon. as follows :

Maldon 1844/Q2
241   James Algernon Piggott and Sarah Ann Pledger, George Howard and Sarah Bourne, Levi Bright and Ann Collins, James Baxter and Charlotte Baxter
242 William Smith and Caroline Bapham

He duly certified these as true copies and they were accepted by the Superintendent Registrar and forwarded to the GRO and indexed in the 1844/Q2 index.   What no one in the system noticed is that while the Piggott/Pledger marriage took place on 27 June, the other four marriages took place in Q3, on 2 July, 10 July, 25 August and 22 September.   It was 22 October when they were sent in to the registrar (by which time Mr Dicken should have been working on his Q3 return).

When we come to 1844/Q3, the energetic Mr Dicken picked these last four marriages once again and submitted them. (Perhaps energetic is a little amiss because he again sent them rather late on 13 January 1845). They once again passed right through the system without any query and were indexed in the 1844/Q3 index.

It is all too obvious from the timings of many of these quarterly returns that the returns for two or three quarters were often at various stages of passing through the system at any one time.   This is all very different from the neat system of quarterly returns envisaged in the legislation, all flowing through the system in the month immediately following each quarter.   It is hardly surprising that the Superintendent Registrars seem to have passed on all the returns without apparently checking them.   Their chances of effectively checking the "due succession of numbers", as required by the legislation, must have been rather poor.

The parish of Bocking in the district of Braintree submitted three marriages in the Quarterly Return for 1843/Q4, namely :

> Joseph Moore and Emily Oxbrow
> George Rayner and Eliza Gentry
> Thomas Mott and Maria Parker

In the following quarter exactly the same names were re-submitted.   The Moore/Oxbrow marriage was in December 1843, the other two were in the March quarter of 1844.   All three marriages are indexed in both quarters.

I suspect that a vicar was occasionally persuaded into error. The return for Woodham Ferrers for 1844/Q3 was creditably prompt, dated 23 October, and contained the four September marriages that were items 42 to 45 in the marriage register book. The next return, for 1844/Q4, contained items 46 to 51.

Much later, in mid-1845, someone seems to have noticed that marriage no.47 (Samuel Jobson and Susannah Sarah Perkins) was dated 29 September 1844, and on 14 July 1845 the vicar resubmitted no.47 on a new sheet. It was included in the bundle of records for 1844/Q3 and inserted in the index as a supplementary page 86a.

It is all too likely that the date on item 47, falling as it does between the Q4 marriages 46 and 48 in the marriage register, is wrong and should have been October or November. In the preface to C R Cheney's "Handbook of Dates" (page ix) he says that when dates show inconsistencies it is generally the month that is wrong rather than the day. It would have been a more valuable piece of surveillance if someone had noticed that item 49 from the same parish of Woodham Ferrers shows the bridegroom both as James Keeling and as Samuel Keeling, very probably an error in copying or perhaps recording.

There was a major overlap in Finchingfield in 1841/Q1. The quarterly return was decidedly late (on 9/8/1841) and the vicar submitted four marriages, items 67 to 70 from his marriage register :

> Robert Wakelin and Sarah Warter, married 28/1/41
> John Whitehead and Elizabeth Moore, married 10/4/41
> William Chapman and Mary Suckling, married 10/4/41
> Samuel Pryer Field and Harriette Sophia Westerman, married 8/6/41

All were indexed in Q1 and were not crossed out in the film. He resubmitted items 68 to 70 for Q2 and they have been indexed again.

The usages of the Society of Friends added another element of obscurity to the process. Take as an example the marriage of Matthew Alsop and Martha Brock at the Friends' Meeting House in Maldon, Essex, in 1844. It was dated the "10th day of the 7th month" yet it was submitted as a Q2 marriage. It was later re-submitted as a Q3 item and it has been included in both GRO films and indexed in both quarters. The submissions were by the same Meeting Secretary and both submissions are referenced to item 12 in the marriage register book.

The submission as a Q3 item was made on "the 6th day of the 11th month commonly called November". It was hardly a dating practice lending itself to a data processing system. Those who work with children today are only too well aware that many find it hard to cope with the sequence of the months.

This same Quaker Meeting started its erratic returns even earlier with its return for 1844/Q1, namely two marriages for April 1844, William Batt and Eliza Marriage, William Impey and Elizabeth Marriage. In the Q2 return these two April marriages were ignored. The only return was the erroneous one for Alsop and Brock. All entries seem to have gone through the entire system unremarked. All were indexed for the quarters for which they were (erroneously) submitted.

With so much that was erratic in the quarterly returns the Superintendent Registrars would have had to maintain very good records of the marriages that they had handled if they were to exert any real control. It seems hardly surprising that they failed to live up to the requirements laid on them by the legislation, at least so far as marriages were concerned.

There are also quite a number of marriages entered twice in the index in the *same* quarter with very different page references. Four examples from 1844/Q1 are shown below. My time at Southport was too short to check every possible item of interest and these were among the casualties.

Brighton (vol 7)

340   *Harriett Bowley*, Frances Collings, John George, *William Hagon Goble*, Henry Hollamby, Mary King, George Pollard, Harriett Williams

357   Robert Attree, *Harriet Bowley*, Elizabeth Clarke, John Cooke, *William Hagon Goble*, Harriett Hills, Mary Potter, George Richardson

Yarmouth (vol 13)

612   Martha Easter, Harriot Norfor High, *Agnes Holland*, George Bately King, *Richard Morley*, Mary Ann Rolfe, Denny Wade, Robert Wright

614   Susan Benns, Lydia Ellis, *Agnes Holland,* Eliezor Johnson, George Jubby, *Richard Morley*, William Read, Mary Ann Wright

Derby (vol 19)

417   *Mary Bridges Barber, John Clark*, Thomas Clews, Esther Redshaw

430   Isaac Allen, *Mary Bridges Barber*, John Carter, *John Clark*, John Evans, Ann Gibson, Ann Ison, Martha Price

Carlisle (vol 25)

55   James Burgess, *Whitfield Eddy*, Jane Graham, *Jane Kellett*, Robert Quin, Elizabeth Wilson

56   *Whitfield Eddy, Jane Kellett*

The structure of the data in my files suggests that in the first three of these examples the second instance of the marriage in italics is in the quarterly return from a district registrar and that the first instance is in a return from a parish. You will see in chapter 7 that the Registrar General recognised that those married in a register office might want to repeat the ceremony in a church but warned very specifically that the second ceremony wasn't to be recorded in the marriage register or included in the quarterly return. Obviously this had been happening and had been going through the whole system without detection.

In the fourth example, the Eddy/Kellett marriage, the two marriage entries were in the same return and it looks very much like a return from a district registrar. Either the registrar copied it twice in error, once on the recto side and then again on the verso side, or he possibly made a slip in the first case and repeated it as a correction. Either way it seems that both entries were accepted and indexed.

The Buttsbury/Ingatestone saga

Some six miles along the road from Chelmsford to London are the neighbouring parishes of Ingatestone and Buttsbury. Ingatestone sits on the main road and Buttsbury is about a mile away in the direction of Stock, just beyond a little headwater of the River Chelmer.

Something appears to have happened to the Ingatestone Marriage Register, apparently some while before 1843, and the vicars of Buttsbury and Ingatestone took to the practice of sharing a register. This seems to have been the Buttsbury register. It went to and fro as needed and both vicars made their separate quarterly returns from it, each duly attesting that the marriages were true copies from their own register ! In the two years 1843 and 1844 we have the following picture in terms of the entry references in this peripatetic register :

Buttsbury register 1843/44			
Parish	*Ref*	*Parish*	*Ref*
Ingatestone	39	Ingatestone	51
Ingatestone	40	Ingatestone	52
Ingatestone	41	Buttsbury	53
Buttsbury	42	Ingatestone	54
Ingatestone	43	Ingatestone	55
Buttsbury	44	Ingatestone	56
Ingatestone	45	Buttsbury	57
Ingatestone	46	Buttsbury	58
Buttsbury	47	Ingatestone	59
Ingatestone	48	Ingatestone	60
Buttsbury	49	Ingatestone	61
Buttsbury	50		

To judge from the GRO films, it looks as if this situation already prevailed in 1839 and was still happening in 1856. It must have been against all intentions of having control of the system based on the orderly progression of numbers. If the Ingatestone register was damaged, destroyed or lost, what happened to the earliest Ingatestone records ? Are they a gap in the Superintendent Registrar's record ? Ingatestone would have had two duplicate registers. Were both lost or destroyed ? How often did this sort of situation happen in the other 99 percent (or more) of the system ? Some of the answers to these questions probably lie in the office of the Superintendent Registrar in Chelmsford.

"St Leonard" in 1849

This is not so much an error as a very strange piece of indexing, capable of causing confusion. In the index for 1849/Q1 there is a curious situation in the Shoreditch entries in volume II. These run from page 285 to 362. Of the 8 names on page 313, one single name is referenced as St Leonard's instead of Shoreditch. Thereafter St Leonard appears without rhyme or reason.

Shoreditch 1849/Q1 examples (SL indicates district entered as St Leonard)
313   Martha Ackland, John King Barclay, Robert Ford, Ann Goffee, Mary Ann Plummer, John Smithers [SL], John Charles Solkhon, Ann Matilda Talby
315   Joseph Charles, Lydia Fanny Cole, Sarah Coote, Mary Crawley [SL], Elizabeth Crofts [SL], George Forman, John Hatchett, John Thomas Hobbs
332   Sarah Winifred Cross [SL], John Dexter [SL], Elizabeth Gale, Elizabeth Groves, William Harris [SL], Matilda Hughes, William Wallace [SL], John William Wallbank [SL]

St Leonard's is a major parish in Shoreditch but why would an indexer write St Leonard's for John Smithers but Shoreditch for the other seven entries on that page ? Why choose two women on page 315, and all the men and one woman on page 332 ? Look more carefully at that page exactly as the names appear in the GRO film of marriages :

Shoreditch 1849/Q1 page 332
John William Wallbank (St Leonards) m Elizabeth Gale (Sditch)
William Harris (St Leonards) m Elizabeth Groves (Sditch)
William Wallace (St Leonards) m Sarah Winifred Cross (St Leonards)
John Dexter (St Leonards) m Matilda Hughes (Sditch)

It is hard to see the reasoning in an indexer's mind in indexing in this way. There are also some actual indexing errors in this Shoreditch section.

St Leonard references occur sporadically as far as page 361 and on 29 pages. Only on three of those pages can the St Leonard reference possibly apply both to a bride and a bridegroom. On most occasions it is quite unsystematic and is certainly applied to one party in a marriage but not to the other.

The Southport records yield no explanation, no hint of pattern or reason. They make it all more puzzling. Within the records for the Superintendent Registrar's district of Shoreditch, St Leonard's parish occupies pages 327 to 360, preceded by St John the Baptist in Hoxton and St Mark's Old Street. Pages 361 and 362 are the marriages at the Register Office and at chapels and meeting houses.

The puzzle is why the St Leonard references extend back into the Hoxton entries and even pop into the Register Office section at the end of Shoreditch district, where Edward Jopson (St Leonard) married Mary Ann Barber (Shoreditch). The explanation must surely be that the indexing clerk saw St Leonard and Shoreditch as completely synonymous and used them at whim with no conscious thought. The case of Cornelius Parr on page 360 indexed as "*St Shoreditch*" then looks rather like his ultimate comment.

This St Leonard phenomenon seems to occur in several quarters around 1849 and 1850.

Typing, retyping and over-inking

Often it can be a relief to come to a typed section of the index or a figure over-inked to make it clearer, especially in one of those dog-eared corners where the index has become badly worn.

Don't be too sure of these bold page numbers. No doubt most revitalised figures are right but this isn't always so. I have found at least a few instances when the new clear figure is unmistakably wrong, evidence that the helpful clerk didn't go back to the original record to check the correct reference.

In 1850/Q1 there is an entry referenced as Liverpool Vol 1 page 174 where the volume number has been heavily over-inked. Liverpool is in volume XX and there was a correctly referenced Liverpool entry only a little way away in the index. To show Liverpool as volume I proves unfamiliarity with the data.

The 1849/Q1 index has an entry for Catherine Hyland in Wolverhampton, volume 17. The page reference is heavily re-inked as 300 but page 300 in that volume is in Wolstanton. Something amiss ? That Wolstanton page has two happy couples and an extra woman would surely be unwelcome as a permanent resident. I was lucky to find a clear reading on an LDS film with a fragment of an "8" poking out behind one of the heavily inked zeroes. The real page number was 380, a valid Wolverhampton page with four men and three women waiting to have their position regularised. If the "8" is visible in the LDS filming it is hard to see how a clerk could overwrite it as a zero.

As for typing, there is no doubt that the typing in the earlier parts of the marriage index is full of errors. I have already said that my file of Essex/Suffolk data from the typed index of 1839/Q4 showed far more errors than found elsewhere and most were created by the typing. In checking of 1843/44 data at Southport one unindexed name uncovered a gap of eighty names in 1844/Q2 in the area of Jenkin and Jenkins, a very obvious omission of two of the handwritten pages of 40 names. I was able to find fifty lost names by winding through the GRO marriage films for all the Welsh districts. I have included them here as an appendix. The other lost Jenkins entries will be scattered one or two at a time in the rest of the 24 films for that quarter.

Do you recall Jane Spalding on page 59 ? The indexes for 1844 and three quarters of 1843 show Spain (18) and Spalding (28) and no Spaine. 1843/Q4 has Spain (2), Spaine (6) but no Spalding. We know that Jane Spaine was Spalding and the same must go for the other five. Several nearby years show no sign of a Spaine. Several handwritten years show no name that might have sent the typist off the rails. The typing looks worse and worse.

Even a carefully typed amendment in the typed index can prove wrong. Robert Parsons was married in that troublesome year 1844 in Wellington, Somerset in the parish of St John the Baptist. He appears in the index as Wellingborough, volume 15, page 698a ! It can be seen that the figure "15" is a careful alteration of whatever was there before, almost certainly the figure "10". The error was in the district name and not in the volume number. No doubt the clerk had the best of intentions but in fact he made the situation irretrievably worse.

It goes almost without saying that there must be hundreds if not thousands of such mistaken amendments. I have come across others from time to time but have not noted them.

A plethora of problems

Whatever the collective term for a multitude of problems may be, I now present some indexing errors that have been interesting exercises to resolve.

Volume 3 in 1844/Q1 has an entry for William Augustus Brown, indexed as *Islington volume 3 p 199*. Page 199 happens to lie among the Kensington entries and William is surplus to the other eight names on that page.

Kensington 1844/Q1
197   John Powell, Frances Smith
199   Eleanor Bee, William Augustus Brown [Islington], Elizabeth Maria
      Camp, Thomas Young Chapman, Henry Davis, James Davis, Ann Ladd,
      Ann Pearce, George Frederick Wright
200   George Godfrey, Amy Hall, Susan Wells, John White

Step one was to scan the Islington pages (141 to 175) for a possible home for William. Page 152 was the first option but is a problem in its own right as I have two men and five women. Page 153 is another bad page, this time four men and two women. If the errant William is made part of this mishmash of entries, he would at least bring the totals to seven men and seven women.

Page 159 is another page with a vacancy, three men and four women, and seems more likely because 159 and 199 could be more easily confused.

Therefore William Brown probably belongs in page 159 and at least some of the names on pages 152 and 153 are wrong, in the indexing or the typing. All have been rechecked in the fiche and all are exactly as entered.

But we can't leave this Islington/Kensington trouble-spot without considering page 145, an Islington page with a reference to a Hackney bridegroom :

Islington 1844/Q1
145   Robert John Artis, William James Bartholomew, Sophia Crouch, James
      Frederick France [Hackney], Elizabeth Isaac, George Sexton, Jane
      Starling, Elizabeth Tompkins, Henry George Wiggins

James France is indexed as Hackney p145. He is an embarrassment to the other four men and four women, so where does he belong ?

Hackney pages run from 97 to 141 and the first places to look are 105, 115 and 125. Pages 115 and 125 are happy as they are but page 105 has three men and four women. It is the obvious choice.

These examples show it isn't always easy to unravel an index error, even with information laid out clearly as in my files. Without them, how would you find these answers ? Indeed nothing in the normal alphabetic index would lead you to suspect them in the first place. Once alerted, you could check all the Hackney and Islington marriage records at Southport to find them and you might well do so, but this would still fail completely to uncover the mix-up of references in pages 152 and 153. Only the sorted index discloses such a problem. This volume is not one that I managed to check at the GRO.

The only other obvious error in volume 3 is Mary Groves, indexed as Staines, page 268a. That is an Uxbridge page. She is undoubtedly the bride of Frederick Wooderson on page 262a, a genuine Staines page, who is languishing alone.

It is necessary to inspect the sorted index files in detail to find all the possible problems. I can use a small computer program to find the unbalanced pages and check just those pages visually for the reasons. Even this will miss the many imbalances on pages that appear balanced. If a page has a duplicate entry and is also unbalanced in terms of gender it can still have an even number of names.

Some of these detailed checks do have their lighter side, revealing some interesting juxtapositions like Amelia Parish and Henry Record on the same page. Though the chances that they were bride and groom are not favourable, it would be nice to think this may be the only true Parish Record marriage in the system. In similar vein, my files show Mary Muddle and Thomas Tidy in close proximity in Uckfield in 1849.

Those St Leonards entries in 1849 have a little echo on page 248 of volume 22, one of the pages in the Hull district. Of the 8 people with this page reference, one person is in the index as "*Grebby Caudace   Kingston XXII 248*". This is obviously a reference to Kingston upon Hull but would a normal user of the index always realise that ? Was it just a little joke on the part of the indexing clerk or is there some other explanation ? By a process of elimination, Caudace Grebby must be a woman and this extraordinary name may be an error for Candice. The GRO film shows that Caudace married Thomas Collinson and the parish was Holy Trinity, Laidlaw. We shall never know why the indexer used Kingston for this one name in Hull. Perhaps his patience was wearing thin after several dubious names. He mis-indexed one name on the following page.

Another 1849 example, this from volume 19.

Runcorn (volume 19)
196   John Frodsham, Mary Jones, Edward Prescott, Alice Sandbach, Abraham Spade, Peter Steward, Hannah Tickle, Martha Young [volume 14]
197   Alfred Ackerley, Mary Anne Ackerley, Joseph Burkett, Joseph Hewitt, Robert Prescott, Sarah Prescott [Thomas district], Jane Spruce, Catherine Taylor

Of the eight people on page 197, which is a page in the Runcorn district, Sarah Prescott is indexed to the district name of "Thomas". I suspected that this was a parish but in fact the entry is in the parish of Runcorn itself. The other seven names are Runcorn pure and simple. The Ackerleys and the Prescotts were each brother and sister. The marriages were on 27 March. There is no visible reason for the Thomas reference. On the preceding page the clerk had also slipped up by listing Martha Young as volume 14 instead of volume 19. Was it the end of a tiring day or was the clerk temporarily unnerved by having just had to index a Hannah Tickle ?

Some little blocks of strange index entries are found. In 1844/Q1 the records for St George Southwark occupy pages 325 to 351 in volume 4, except, that is, for ten entries indexed with page references 426 and 427. Without these two extra pages volume 4 would end with the Wandsworth entries (which cover pages 377 to 393). How could there be a big gap in the page numbering and then these two isolated pages of entries for St George Southwark ? I took the entries on pages 426 and 427 at first to be later insertions but then had second thoughts.

1844 is a year when entries were four marriages to a page, but in the entries for St George Southwark I found one marriage on page 326 and two marriages on page 327. Page 426 has three marriages and page 427 has two marriages. I decided the references to pages 426 and 427 must be indexing errors and it seemed more and more obvious that they should refer to pages 326 and 327, restoring them as two full pages. The error must have happened somehow at the indexing stage. It couldn't have happened at the typing stage as no typist could have made consistent errors with names scattered through the alphabet. All the same, it is still hard to understand that an indexer could make this sort of mistake on two consecutive pages and only for *some* entries on those pages.

St George Southwark 1844/Q1
326 Nicholas Joseph Fisher, Sarah Simmons
327 William Beldham, Elizabeth Boorer, William John Burridge, Lydia Barham
        Heath
Wandsworth
392 William Bruce, Sarah Fleming
393 Mary Ann Guy, Eliza Meyer, Henry Parfitt, Hannah Street, Joseph
        Trueman, William Young
St George Southwark
426 Sarah Ann Bone, Rebecca Sharman Forder, Edward Harold, Mary Holman,
        William Potter, David Twyford
427 Julia Holt, Mary Hopgood, Thomas Robert Locke, James William
        Westbrook

The GRO film confirms that all these entries belong on pages 326 and 326 and that the film does end with the two Wandsworth pages.

The indexing of Volume 4 in that quarter has several other oddities. St George Southwark is quite often indexed as Southwark St George but generally only for one of the eight names on a page. One isolated name was simply indexed as Southwark. The next district in the Volume 4 records is St Olave, and the indexer embellished one single entry as Southwark St Olave. The district after St Olave is St Saviour's and here the wayward indexer has one entry as St George Southwark. A few pages later he has one St Olave entry as Southwark.

The indexing clerks also seem to have had trouble with Martley in Worcestershire in 1844/Q1. For a start the district of Worcester, covering pages 485 - 511 of volume 18, has two strangers according to the index, Sarah Bishop and John Brookes, with their district given as Martley.

Worcester 1844/Q1(volume 18)

495   Robert Lee, Ann Merick, John Monkland, Mary Price, Mary Summers, William Ward

496   Sarah Bishop [Martley], John Brookes [Martley], Robert Lee

497   Caroline Milley, Henry Smith

The Martley district occupies pages 407 to 427 in the records and it is very possible that Sarah and John are actually on page 416 or 426 in the marriage records and have been mis-indexed as page 496. And, yes, Robert Lee does appear in the index twice, as shown above, but one would think that he is actually on page 495 and that page 496 is a blank and unused page.

But Martley has a second problem. Martley itself has four strangers, index entries with Martley page references but Kings Norton as the district name.

Martley (volume 18)

413   Philip Euey, Maria Johnson

415   Ann Bark, George Gould [K Norton], Joseph Harwood [K Norton], James Paine, Ann Shaw [K Norton], Emma Tallis [K Norton]

417   Sarah Igenritt, Sarah Iquahitt, James Roberts

Kings Norton records are just before Martley, on pages 379 - 404. The observant reader may have picked up that page 405 is in neither Kings Norton nor Martley. The almost certain answer is that the indexer wrote 405 for these Kings Norton wanderers in that very difficult hand where a tall thin "0" and a "1" are almost indistinguishable and that the typist later misread the 405 and typed 415. This resolves my problem, but for any user the problem persists. The GRO film confirms these marriages as being on p405.

As for the names of Euey, Igenritt and Iquahitt, these come from the index, improbable though they are. Pages 413/417 are from different parishes.

Another example of these groups of mis-indexed names comes from 1856/Q1, volume 3b, covering the Fenland areas of Cambridgeshire, Huntingdonshire and Bedfordshire. I found seven names appearing in the index with the district name of Huntingdon but with page references putting them in the district of Chesterton.

```
Chesterton   ([H] indicates index entries shown as Huntingdon district)
658  John Pettet, Sarah Tibbett, James Waters, Rebekah Wolf
659  John French, Elizabeth Saunders
660  James Corney [H], Jane Harris [H], Jane Payne [H], Jesse Peacock [H]
661  James Jackson [H], John Levitt, William Palmer [H], Emma Rollings [H],
     Mary Ann Wallis
663  Elizabeth Mary Raymond, William Stonebridge
```

The solution seemed to be in finding a place among the Huntingdon pages, and it seemed that 660 and 661 were most likely to be errors for 360 and 361.

```
Huntingdon
359  William Bridgment, Cornelius Dixon, Caroline Leaten, Elizabeth Rolt
361  Martha Palmer
362  Paulin Phillips, Rhoda Rose, Emily Shelton, Charles Veasey
```

The solution leaves the unanswered question "How did the clerk make seven errors but still managed to put Martha Palmer in her right place ?" Is this example trying to tell us something significant about the indexing process ?

A similar example is the case of five entries for Risbridge district in Suffolk in 1844/Q1 (volume 12). They were indexed as page 425 which happens to be in the Cosford district. It is possible to see that they must actually be on page 525 of the marriage record, among the Risbridge marriages. Once again the vexing question is "Why did the clerk indexing that page get five of the spouses wrong and yet index three of them correctly as page 525 ?" Volume 12 wouldn't have scored high marks for accuracy in that quarter as there were four other errors, making a very high error rate of nine indexing errors in 1284 entries (plus, of course, all my other discoveries at Southport).

Kensington in 1849/Q1 gives us another example of an erratic indexer. He ran off the rails when he reached page 245 in volume 3. The following list shows the marriages that are on pages 245 to 247 and the numbers in square brackets show the pages quoted by the indexer in the index.

Kensington 1849/Q1 volume 3

p245   Willliam Langton and Ann Sophia Ringer   [245]
        James Woods and Charlotte Giles   [246]
        Henry Woolmer Gilbert and Susan Cocks   [246]
        Charles William Cooper and Esther Matilda Leary   [246]
p246   Frederick Bury and Henrietta Pryce   [247]
        Joseph King and Jane Snook   [247]
        Evan Evans and Constantia Vertue   [246]
        Robert Whibley and Sarah Ellis   [246]
p247   Frederick Gibbons and Mary Ann Herring   [247]
        William Edward Sowter and Ellen Pickman   [247]
        William Pocock and Maria Butt   [247]
        John Vinden and Jane Prior   [247]

This accounts for my file showing far too many people on pages 246 and 247 and also my difficulty in allocating Evan Evans (whose page number was virtually illegible) because his rightful page 246 was already overfull. The indexer obviously slipped one cog while on page 245, moved up to 247 with the new page, realised that he was wrong half way through the page and reverted to 246, then got 247 right, forgetting that he had already referenced two of the other marriages to that page. Total errors in the index are ten.

I believe the reason for many of the errors where a clerk got part of a page right and part of it wrong may lie with the disciplines employed in the system. In the Risbridge example he correctly indexed the marriage on page 523 (Stansfield parish). Turning to page 525 (Stradishall parish) he wrongly wrote 425 for the first two marriages and for the groom in the third marriage. Then he must have realised his error. He wrote 525 for the bride and for the fourth marriage. There must surely have been some reason in the system that acted against going back and correcting the five errors he must surely have realised he had made. The same sort of situation has arisen in many of these examples. It is a characteristic of many of the indexing errors and other quirks that have come to light in this exercise that the improper reference is applied to one person in a marriage and not to the other or to some persons on a page but not to others.

In 1844/Q1 there are two entries for the Clutton district that are indexed as page 643 and page 645. The Clutton entries (volume 11) are all in the range 73 to 95. These two rogue entries, for Septema Hall and Richard Hutchins, have no obvious slots in the Clutton area as all the Clutton pages are balanced by gender. Therefore Hall and Hutchins are likely to belong on the same page and could thus be on any of several pages.

In 1849 there is a block of four entries labelled Bromyard whose page references put them in the middle of the Hereford pages. They are in fact already included in Bromyard as well. Their raid into Hereford is in the form of "late insertions", with an "a" appended to the page reference. It is hard to imagine a reason for this situation.

There is a fishy story in the East End of London in 1844/Q1. There are two entries in the 1844/Q1 index that came together when my file was sorted into page order, namely John Frederick Pike and John Frederick P Scrivener, both indexed as St Luke's, page 46a. Now it happens that pages 31 to 49 in volume 2 for that quarter hold the marriages for St George in the East. The St Luke marriages occupy pages 233 to 252. John Frederick is certainly surplus to requirements on page 46 itself, and no spouse for him has been indexed to page 46a. My guess would be that he is actually on page 246a and that the clerk became confused when indexing him. It may even be that it was his spouse who had the surname of Scrivener. This is a volume I didn't manage to check when in Southport.

Father and son

In the notes on 1843/Q4 (page 58) I mentioned the marriage of John Ward and June Waylett in the Hempstead parish in the Saffron Walden district. Here the quarterly return gave John's signature as Henry Ward, Henry happening to be his father. The error was realised later and the signature was crossed out and replaced by John Ward, both John and Henry appearing in the marriage index.

There are many such errors but this is the only corrected one I have noticed. If a vicar has just copied out the details for the man and the woman, then it is the father's name rather than the son's that could easily be uppermost in the mind of the copyist. I would expect some thousands of examples in the 1800s.

Ahead of their time

You sometimes find entries in a pre-1852 index that have a page reference in a post-1851 format.

When combing the 1844 indexes for the Taunton study (see chapter 8) I found index entries in the June quarter for John Bowring and Agnes Clark, both as Ilminster volume 10 page 644a. In 1844/Q1 I had already found an index entry for James Hallett as Ilminster volume 5c page 596a. There is no spouse in the 1844/Q1 index for James.

Ilminster is not a Superintendent Registrar's district. All these entries should be referenced as Chard. I suspect that two marriages were inserted at the same time, perhaps as the result of a chance discovery, and hence no earlier than 1852, perhaps much later though before the manuscript indexes were typed. They are probably omissions from the quarterly returns, not noticed at the time but picked up many years later.

I have found several such post-1851 references in early indexes.

Index entries without a home

Among the many index errors it is possible to find some index entries that simply cannot be linked back to the correct marriage record. ONS frequently receives requests for certificates that cannot be correctly identified.

When I was checking my sorted index file for 1844/Q4 against the GRO film I came to page 429, the page for Dagenham parish in the district of Romford, where my search of the index had come up with seven names, three men and four names. My missing man, revealed by the GRO film, was the bridegroom in the second marriage on the page, marrying Jane Rush Grimwood. His name - William Burrel. Had I missed him in the index ?

I returned to the index to look him up. There he was. His reference was not Romford vol 12 but Bromyard vol 26 p429. He was obviously the right person, the name was right and the page number was right. We went down to the basement to check the actual index register. There he was, exactly as in the fiche but with a little pencilled question mark against his name. Someone must have asked for a certificate for him and he couldn't be found. There is in fact no way in which a totally misindexed name can readily be tracked back to the right place in the marriage records. It is just pure chance that a search such as mine could come at him and surprise him, so to speak. It is the same in most filing systems, something misfiled is to all intents and purposes lost for ever unless someone happens to stumble upon it.

In theory it could be possible to track down a person like William Burrel. If his page number was right, then it would be possible to look at p429 in each of the 27 films for 1844/Q4. If his volume number was right, one could work right through the film for the quoted volume, anything between about 1500 and 5000 names. If the district name was right, this would give the shortest search. In practice searches on this scale are not usually feasible in terms of cost.

In the large register in the Southport basement it looked rather as if the volume number for William Burrel had been altered to 26. It seems very possible that he was put into the index as Bromyard vol 12 p429, the error being Bromyard for Romford. A careful clerk then changed the volume instead of correcting the district name. This is far from being the only such example I have found where the district name looks very like a homophone error, suggesting that some of the indexing may have been done by pairs of clerks, one reading and one writing. Likewise this isn't the only example where a clerk has wrongly taken the district name to be right and the volume number to be wrong.

Those "a" and "b" references

It may be happier to close this chapter with illustrations of problems that are not exactly errors.

Users of the marriage index will be familiar with the index references that have an "a" or some other letter added to the page reference.

In handwritten parts of the index these items are usually inter-lined, written in between the existing lines. In general they are what they seem to be, late insertions for marriage records received after the index was written out. Be aware that they are not always in strict alphabetic sequence. Sometimes they can be well out of position. Because they are smaller and squeezed between the existing entries they can be hard to read in film and fiche, especially where the page references are squeezed between the existing references.

In the typewritten indexes they may be fully integrated into the typing or may be handwritten at the foot of the page, usually with a marker to show where they fit in the name sequence. Those integrated into the typing are generally those in the earlier years because the typing was a much later upgrade of the index. In later years there was no prior published handwritten index.

Here is a little segment of a file from 1849/Q1 :

Worthing 1849/Q1	
Page	*Marriage*
639	George Budd, William Murton, Harriet Adelaide Porter, Ann Twine
641	Sophia Benn, Thomas Mitchell
642a	Frances Morris, George Morver
643	Jane Blackman, Noah Leach
645	Jane Goldring, Elizabeth Jenkins, Michael Murphy, William Tupper
647	Sarah Ayling, Sarah Ayting, John Ruff

In chapter 7 we will see some huge examples of late material where there was an omission by a large city congregation. Much more often the insertions seem to be a single omitted marriage, as in the Worthing example.

More often than not the inserted page seems to have been given an even page number. I believe there is a better than even chance that an inserted page has only a single marriage on it. The chance of finding a marriage partner may be somewhat improved if you are starting with a reference containing an "a". If you meet a page reference with a "b" or higher, then perhaps you are dealing with a batch of omitted pages, all full.

You might ask why the Morver/Morris marriage couldn't be added to the part-full page 643 which in 1849 had three unused spaces plus four more on the verso side. Firstly they are almost certainly from different parishes. Secondly the GRO couldn't simply add the entry into a vacant space. The essence of the whole system is the signature of the originating clergyman at the foot of the page, certifying that the entry is a true copy from his register. Nothing else would do.

I have been told of one supplementary entry where the groom is added in one quarter and the bride in another. That is not at all impossible with the handwritten indexes where the index for a single quarter was broken into different physical volumes. It would not be at all difficult to pick up the wrong volume for the second party of the marriage.

These supplementary pages are much more numerous than the marriage index reveals. The marriage record has very large numbers not directly referenced by the index but cross-referenced from the primary entry. When working on the Southport films I often found a sheet with a single marriage that was one of a set of marriages on the following one. Many times there was no visible difference between any of the names, dates or any other information, even in legibility.

Who's who

In Chapter 3 we noted that if you were looking for Sarah Crane or for William Jackson it could perhaps be difficult to choose among several possible entries in the index. One can illustrate this to an extreme degree with a small section of the sorted index from that area where half the people in the street sometimes seem to have the same name ! That area is Wales. We will now look at the Lampeter section of volume 27 in 1844/Q1, a district that had 34 entries in the index, all coming together in the sorted index on pages 67 to 85.

Lampeter 1844/Q1
67 David Davies, Elizabeth Jones
69 David Jones, Elizabeth Jones
71 John Davies, Margaret Evans
73 Henry Daniel, John Richard, Sarah Thomas
75 John Davies, Sarah Davies, Elizabeth Evans, John James, Mary James
77 Rachel Jones, Thos Jones
79 Anne Davies, Sarah Davies, Thomas Fox, Evan Jones
81 Jane Evans, James Morgan
83 Mary Davies, David Lloyd, John Richard, Mary Richard, John Richards
85 David Davies, David Dudley, Margaret Evans, Martha Evans, Elizabeth Jones, Martha Jones, David Thomas

It is all too probable that one of the three women on page 75 should be on page 73. The index is clear but there is probably a typing error or an indexing error. We also seem to have a spare woman on page 85, unless Martha Evans was "also known as" Martha Jones.

But the point of the example is to show the problem of researching some of these popular names. Elizabeth Jones is here three times, and there are two occurrences of David Davies, John Davies, Sarah Davies, Margaret Evans and John Richard (plus a duplicate variant as John Richards), all in a few pages in one locality in one quarter. This may perhaps be an extreme but it serves to show how hard it is to research these names via an index offering no other clues. The GRO film contains the name of the parish for each marriage. Not so the index.

In fact if we take a quick aerial view of volume 27 for this quarter we can spot no fewer than twenty with the name Elizabeth Jones. In a file of 1183 names, of which some 590 would be women, this means that one woman in every 30 was Elizabeth Jones. This name was narrowly beaten by Mary Jones with a count of 21, and the prize goes to John Jones with 23 occurrences. As the other quarters of 1844 would have broadly similar patterns, the difficulty of researching some of these Welsh names is extreme.

There are even three occurrences in this particular volume of pages containing two women of the same name. Unlike most such occurrences elsewhere in the records, these are two *different* people with the same name and with the same page reference, two each of Mary Griffiths, Anne Hughes and Ellen Hughes. If you order a marriage certificate with those references you seem to have a 50% chance of one marriage or the other and there wouldn't really be anything to indicate that you should perhaps have ordered the other certificate. There is nothing in the index to indicate that two identical entries are two different people on the same page. Sometimes they are. Sometimes not. You may very well accept and file away your certificate without even suspecting that there is another marriage on that page with exactly the same name. Once or perhaps twice, in checking the East Anglian files, I have found two identical names on the same page to be father and son, the widowed father marrying within a short time of the marriage of his own son.

Summary

Summarising a heterogeneous array of errors is almost impossible. I feel very privileged and fortunate to have been able to carry out this research into the marriage records, both through having the time to pursue the studies on the marriage index on a scale large enough to reveal so much about the system and also through subsequently being permitted to carry out further work in the General Register Office for the benefit of genealogy in general and also for the benefit of the Office for National Statistics.

I can almost visualise some readers working their way through this book with their heads in their hands and emitting occasional groans of despair. This was my own feeling at times, though in my case it was at least a rueful satisfaction that the work was proving itself worthwhile. I hope that I may carry such readers through into a belief in the proposals that finally emerge.

Even though the "large sample" of sorted indexes is tiny in relation to the whole body of 19th century marriage records and is heavily concentrated in the earlier years, the research has produced a unique insight into the quality of the system. The errors uncovered are on a scale far beyond my initial expectations and probably ONS would now say the same. The variety and numbers of the errors found and illustrated in this chapter give a vivid impression of a system that was often quite chaotic. More time at Southport would have revealed more. Many errors are systematic. They reflect shortcomings in the structure, a structure largely unchanged. There are some more black clouds to come in chapters 7 and 8, but the forecast for chapter 9 is "possible sunshine".

There are indications, as I have mentioned in Chapter 4, that the indexes for the later part of the century are not so very different from the early indexes.

Chapter 7 - Twixt the registers and the General Register Office

or "How complete were the Quarterly Returns ?"

The legislation, as Chapter 2 shows, required Superintendent Registrars to ensure that returns from the parishes were complete in terms of the "progression of numbers". No doubt many did so, but some clearly didn't. Chapter 6 has already given examples of erratic returns made by some clergy. There is also evidence suggesting, and in some cases proving, that there are marriage register entries that were omitted from the quarterly returns.

It was fortuitous that my early work on the indexes produced a set of eight consecutive quarterly files for Essex and Suffolk and also that I decided to take those files first in the comparison with the GRO films at Southport.

It quickly became obvious that I would learn more about the parochial structure of the records by noting the names of the parishes as well as simply checking the index entries. In any tedious job it pays dividends to create an additional focus of interest. It maintains concentration in a situation where errors are inevitably well scattered.

A chance early discovery at Southport then made me retrace my steps and jot down the reference number from the marriage registers (see page 40) against each entry. My print-outs rapidly became a tangle of jottings and squiggles.

The outcome of this extension of the work at Southport was a complete tabulation of the marriage register references submitted for volume 12 in the two years 1843 and 1844. In other words I now knew not only which marriages had taken place and in which parish, but I also knew the position of each marriage entry in the marriage register of that parish. There were enough discontinuities in the reference numbers to make me decide to devote some time to a quick foray through the films for 1841 and 1842, simply to record the reference numbers submitted in those years. Many times I found myself caught out, thinking I had found a discontinuity when the fault was my own in missing a reference that was found on a second check.

The final result of this tabulation was that over 60 marriages appeared to be missing in terms of the "progression of numbers". What is more, every one of those missing numbers constituted a gap *between* returns and not *within* returns, in other words they look like items not picked up by clergy when starting or finishing a return, or missed because a return was not sent in for a particular quarter. They have been reported in detail to ONS. If verified as missing, they represent one omission in about 210 marriages. If this pattern is common to all the 1800s, then we would have 50,000 marriages missing from the GRO record and 100,000 entries missing from the marriage index, quite apart from the other evidence of many marriages simply not indexed.

Here are a few examples of apparent omissions :

Pleshey parish in Chelmsford district returned item 23 from the register for 1844/Q1 and then item 25 in Q4. There is no sign of item 24.

Alberton parish in Lexden district sent in item 13 for 1844/Q2 and item 15 for Q4. There is no sign of item 14.

Tiny Bovinger parish in Maldon district sent in item 8 for 1841/Q1 and then items 10 & 11 a year and a half later for 1842/Q3. I did not spot item 9 in the quarters between.

The Sampford parishes in Saffron Walden are a situation where one would want to look a lot deeper. From 1841 I found items 17 & 18 for New Sampford in Q2 and then item 21 in 1842/Q1, then nothing in 1843/44. From Little Sampford I found items 19/20 in 1841/Q4, looking rather like omissions from New Sampford, but items 21 to 23 from Little Sampford then appeared in 1844/Q1. The returns thus look like two separate series from two reasonably active parishes, though the complete silence of New Sampford for over two years is another worry.

The tiny Saffron Walden parish of Struthall entered the first marriage in its register in 1842/Q4. No further activity is evident in 1843 or 1844. There are several situations like this. It is not a proven gap but a long open-ended period without marriage entries does create an uncertainty.

Great Clacton in the Tendring district was an active parish and seems to have seen 50 marriages up to the end of 1842. Then item 56 came in for 1843/Q1, nothing for Q2, and then a resumption of frequent marriages for the rest of 1843 and 1844. What happened to items 51 to 55 ?

Another busy marriage register was the one in the Register Office in Witham, an area with many dissenting congregations. There are no items in the film for 1844/Q1. Items 75 to 86 were 12 marriages celebrated in 1843/Q4 and items 91 to 98 were submissions for 1844/Q2. It seems likely that items 87 to 90 were marriages in 1844/Q1 that were never submitted.

Such, then, is just a little of the evidence of omitted entries.

On another omission we can shift blame from the parish to the GRO. Childerditch parish in Billericay district sent in item 8 from its marriage register for 1841/Q4. Then item 12 appeared three years later for 1844/Q4. A change of vicar in the meantime seems likely. A request for items 9, 10 and 11 must have then have been made, probably after a delay, and they were submitted on 11/7/1845. Item 9 is for a marriage on 1/5/1842, item 10 is for one on 10/10/1842 and item 11 is for one on 3/7/1843. All three were unfortunately written on one sheet. This was filed in the bundle for 1842/Q2 and appears in the GRO film for that quarter. The other two marriages were thus lost to the record and not indexed. They were Benjamin Barker and Sarah Stokes, followed by George Wright and Eliza Ann Richardson. The vicar had acted reasonably in sending in the three marriages as required.

This is yet another example of the multiplicity of ways in which errors occurred. It is also an example of the way that the legislative safeguards largely failed. The inference from all the examples is that the checking of the "progression of numbers" was far from complete. Each parish was also supposed to send in a "nil return" on a prescribed form for a quarter without a marriage, ensuring that the Superintendent Registrar would always know the positions of all his parishes. No doubt some registrars were excellent but my evidence of gaps for Essex and Suffolk is scattered widely over the districts.

A local register offers proof

Chapter 8 describes in some detail my findings in comparing a local index, the index for the whole of 1844 prepared by the Superintendent Registrar for Taunton, against the index entries for 1844 from the GRO index. The discovery that is relevant here is that the Taunton index contains the marriages for all four quarters of 1844 for the parish of St John the Baptist in Wellington (Somerset). The GRO index has the marriages for the June, September and December quarters but has none of the names for the first quarter. It would appear that the following eight marriages were not included in the quarterly return or were in some way lost :

> John Hammet and Jane B Sercombe
> James Marks and Elizabeth Manley
> John Hayes and Sarah Lane
> John Mayner and Mary A Dockings
> James Westcott and Maria Forward
> George Cavell and Mary Ann Baker
> James Keates and Susanna Wright
> John Burston and Mary A Stevens

The inference is that the loss of these marriages was not noticed, or if noticed was not acted upon. These are not the only apparent omissions of Taunton marriages from the GRO indexes for 1844, as chapter 8 will show. Altogether there seem to have been about twelve missed in this year of 400 Taunton marriages, as well as numerous other examples of indexing errors or omissions. This is a very high rate of default.

These Taunton examples are clear evidence of marriages recorded in one index but missing from the other. Many genealogists have reported finding marriages in local records but failing to find them in the GRO index. The evidence of this study tends to support them. It could be a major problem.

Some of the erratic clergy

Some of the clergy and their brethren were far from pursuing the straight and narrow path and two extreme examples can be brought in here as illustrations (I hesitate in calling them extreme because the untouched 99% of the records will no doubt surpass them many times).

For the City of London District in volume 1c of the March quarter of 1856 the extractions of index entries uncovered a huge collection of entries referenced to page 258. They were clearly late additions to the record and late insertions in the index, squeezed between the existing lines, often hardly legible, and referring to pages 258a through page 258i. Much of the material in this City of London section contains Jewish names and the inference seemed to be that the records were from the Jewish community.

This assumption has proved completely correct. Pages 243 to 258 are all returns coming from a Mr Oppenheim for the months of January and February 1856. The explanation for the supplementary pages is that Mr Oppenheim must have completely forgotten that March was part of the first quarter of the year. Pages 258a to 258i contain all the March marriages, still under Mr Oppenheim's signature. He copied the January and February marriages on 9th May 1856. On 9th September he sent in the Q2 return, apparently forgetting the omission of March. Either he or someone else must have noticed the gap. He sent in the missing March entries on 30th October.

This material also shows that marriage registers for the Jewish community were thinner than others. Mr Oppenheim's return for January and February took him to item 200 in his marriage register and then into items 1 to 3 in a new register. A normal marriage register will contain up to 500 marriages.

It makes one doubt the wakefulness of the Superintendent Registrar. As Mr Oppenheim filled one register with his January/February entries he should have deposited the full register with the Registrar at the time of his Q1 return. After all, he made the Q1 return in May and would have had the register in his possession at that time, by which time he was well into the following register. One would have thought that the Registrar would at least have looked at Mr Oppenheim's offering.

These Jewish marriages are also particularly interesting, as I have mentioned before, because they are not all in a single building as with marriages in a parish church. Although roughly half took place at the Great Synagogue, many were at street addresses where meetings no doubt took place, such as 10 Hester Villas or 9 St George's Crescent. A list of these Oppenheim entries is given as appendix 9. They show that these "City of London" marriages took place in many different districts, St Luke's, Clerkenwell, Lambeth, Walworth, Stepney, Paddington. A look through the entries for other quarters may well find some marriages from much further afield.

Mr Oppenheim's subsequent marriage data arrived without any problems.

The same cannot be said for the parish of St James in Bristol. Here there was an even greater explosion of supplementary entries in the record for 1838/Q4, consisting of pages 158a to 158k. When you recall that pages in 1838 contained four marriages and those in 1856 contained only two you can see that this was a very great explosion indeed, 40 marriages. These marriages were sent in by the Reverend Jonathan Woodward on 17 June 1840, covering all the marriages for St James's for 1838/Q4.

The story behind this is that there was an officiating minister earlier in 1838 who had duly submitted a quarterly return for 1838/Q3, of 39 marriages. Thereafter there seem to have been a number of curates holding the fort until the name of Jonathan Woodward appears in the marriage record on 8th April 1840. Clearly no marriage returns came from this major church of St James to the Superintendent for the Bristol district from 1838/Q4 until 1840. One might have thought the Superintendent Registrar was aware that St James was still responsible for large numbers of marriages (it was a fashionable church in Bristol in those days), or perhaps he leaned unsuccessfully on the curates responsible for all this wedlock. For wedlock perhaps read deadlock. (To be fair to the clergy, they were not entitled to make and attest the quarterly returns unless they were fully ordained ministers).

Be that as it may, Jonathan Woodward took pen in hand and submitted the marriages for 1838/Q4 and for 1839/Q1 on 17 June 1840. At the same time he also submitted the returns for 1840/Q1 and these were consequently on time. For some reason the return for 1838/Q4 was given supplementary page numbers at the GRO and the papers for St James's were placed between the two other parishes where they had always belonged, St George's Brandon Hill and St John the Baptist, while the other two quarters were tacked on at the tail end of all the entries in volume 11. It probably felt like too much clerical trouble to repeat this exercise for two more quarters.

Perhaps Jonathan thought he had done enough at this stage, even though 1839/Q2, 1839/Q3 and 1839/Q4 were still outstanding, a total of 130 marriages. He allowed more time to pass, nearly eight months up to 3rd February 1841, when he again set to and sent in returns for the three out-standing quarters and also the last three quarters of 1840. Up to date at last !

Time, he thought, to relax once more. No further marriages came from his pen until 2 December 1841 when he came up to the mark again with the first three quarters of 1841. Another long break until 12 September 1842. He then published three more quarters up to 1842/Q2.. Nine more months passed and he then produced returns for 1842/Q3 to 1843/Q1, all on 12 June 1843. At the end of November 1843 he came up to date again with two more quarters and was actually on time with 1843/Q4, dated 28 February 1844. There I have left him, in the hope that his performance was stable thereafter.

The GRO clerks battled manfully with this erratic flow of material, sometimes putting it in its rightful place among the other Bristol parishes but rather more often tacking it at the end of the record.

One wonders whether Jonathan Woodward was just being awkward or perhaps taking a frivolous approach to something he objected to. The fact is that his handwritten copies are among the best produced by any of the clergy. They are eminently readable and certainly not dashed off in haste as so many seem to have been. If he kept a diary it would be fascinating to read it.

These are just a couple of isolated examples of the irregular flow of material. They make one realise just how impossible it was in reality to keep the system in some sort of order. Vicars very often fell behind with their returns.

Sometimes a vicar's quarterly return was incomplete but in a different sense. The vicar of Saxmundham in Suffolk reported three marriages in 1843/Q1 but the last of the three has no signatures for Robert Yellop and Margaret Cattermole or for their witnesses, whoever they may have been. The likeliest explanation is that the vicar was interrupted at the point of nearly completing his return, or perhaps his candle went out. Of much more significance for the integrity of the system is that this deficient submission went through the hands of the Superintendent Registrar and through the General Register Office without anything being done to correct it. Even the clerk who indexed the item must have ignored the defect. One presumes that the marriage did take place and was valid but there must be a small element of doubt.

A sermon to the clergy

We have seen that the design of the record system relied heavily on the performance of the clergy, on accurate and legible copying, on complete returns, and indeed on correctly completing the original marriage entries. We have also seen evidence that these expectations were not met and that the system was not designed to enforce them.

A booklet of instructions for clergy was produced by the General Register Office in 1900 and issued in 1901. The General Register Office itself had no legislative right to direct the clergy, though the legislation did place certain duties on the clergy. This is reflected clearly in the title of the little booklet, where the iron hand was carefully enclosed in a velvet glove :

SUGGESTIONS

FOR THE GUIDANCE OF

THE CLERGY

RELATIVE TO THE

DUTIES IMPOSED UPON THEM

BY THE

MARRIAGE AND

REGISTRATION

ACTS.

The title encapsulates the essence of the problems with the marriage records. It carefully notes the legal responsibilities lying on the clergy but can only express the advisory role of the Registrar General.   So careful is the presentation that there is nothing on the title page to show that it was produced by the General Register Office, simply that it was published by Her Majesty's Stationery Office. Even in the text the references to the Registrar General are few and far between.

No doubt the booklet would have been sent out to clergy under cover of another of the Registrar General's letters expressing "his earnest desire that the clergy would find the booklet helpful".

Within the book you will find phrases such as :

> "It is most desirable that . . . . ."
> "It is recommended that . . . . ."
> "It may be useful to direct attention to . . . . ."
> "The Registrar General will be glad if . . . . ."
> "The Registrar General thinks it well to point out . . . . ."
> "Clergymen will do well to see that . . . . ."

Imperatives have slipped into the text where the detail of completing the marriage entry is described.

It is not known whether this booklet of 1900 is the first such to be issued but there is no indication that it is a revision. It may perhaps have been first issued at the time of the marriage Act of 1886. This particular version (of 17,000 copies) was written for the clergy but there would have been parallel versions for the Jewish and Quaker congregations and officiating registrars.

The Registrar General's "advice"

Parts of the Registrar General's suggestions consist of some of the text of the Marriage and Registration Acts but our interest here is more with the procedural notes aimed at correcting some of the problems with the records.

"No entry in the Register Books should under any circumstances be commenced until after the marriage is legally complete". This was (and I am told still is) a not infrequent problem. A marriage can so easily be postponed or even cancelled.

"Every entry (in both books)" must be signed by all the parties, the clergyman, those married, and the witnesses, this "affecting the legal value of the entry".

"All the particulars for the several columns of the entry should, before being copied from the Banns Book, Certificate or Licence, be carefully read over to the parties by way of verification, and then if correct should be inserted in their proper places in full, abbreviations being undesirable".

It is completely clear that the intention was that all the checking of details for accuracy and then the writing in of all the register entries, in both copies of the register, were to be done *after the marriage had been completed.*

How many marriages were but one in a rapid succession of several ? How many married couples will recall simply "signing the registers", all the preliminary entries having been made before the ceremony ? How many couples would have been thinking consciously of the strict accuracy of the marriage entry at that time ? How many genealogists will have copies of certificates with entries such as Chas, Jas, Thos, Richd and Wm ?

How many people who have worked in a typical office environment will recall doing all their work by verbal instruction or "learning as they went", booklets of instructions long since buried or lost ? How many of the Registrar General's booklets of suggestions would have become lost on the ecclesiastical bookshelves ?

"The parties must, if they can write, sign their names *in their usual manner* in both registers; they should not be required to sign their names in full if they are not in the habit of doing so."

"If either of the parties or witnesses is unable to write .... then (**X** the mark of -------) should be written, followed by the Christian name or names and the surname of the party or witness whose mark it is, written at full length".

Variations between full names and signatures have routinely led to two entries in the marriage indexes, creating decisions and uncertainties for present-day researchers. If indexing had used only the full name, thousands of index entries and a great deal of doubt and despair would have been avoided. It seems illogical that John Jacob Jones who signed as John Jones should be indexed under both names, yet this happened thousands of times. It was even more improper that the "full length" of name after an **X** mark was not always observed and has then also led to a variant index entry.

The booklet has several things to say about some of those "aka" names (also known as) :

"If either of the parties has adopted or is commonly known by a Christian name or Surname other than his or her true name or Surname", both are to be recorded, separated by the word "otherwise".

In cases of illegitimacy of one of the marriage partners and where he or she "has been known through life by his or her putative father's surname", the vicar was to allow the *option* of entering the maternal surname and then the paternal surname, separated by the word "otherwise".

A little later the booklet says that "Persons of Illegitimate Birth are sometimes unwilling or unable to state the name and the rank or profession of their fathers". If a party is reluctant, the vicar might leave those spaces blank in the entry and draw lines through them.

Taken in conjunction with the requirement that none of the entry was to be made until the marriage was complete, a vicar might have to think quite quickly if he was to follow these rules. If we see an entry with the father's name and occupation blank, then we may fairly assume that that party to the marriage was illegitimate. If only one surname is given for that party, then it seems that strictly it should be the maternal name, being the true name under which he or she would have been registered at birth as an illegitimate child. However it seems at least possible that a putative father's surname might be used on occasion instead. It is also possible for an illegitimate party to be in the marriage record under his or her "true" maternal surname and for the putative father's name to be entered as well. In a system that was driven by the information provided by the parties to the event, it would often be hard for a clergyman to know the true facts of the case.

It seems a great pity to us now, at the end of the twentieth century, that the Registrar General could not find it possible to allow a mother's name to be given in place of a father's name when the father was unknown. We would see that as a valuable and considerate option.

One recourse by the parties was deliberate mis-information. I have learned of an example on a marriage certificate where a known illegitimate daughter, normally using her mother's surname, has listed her father but given him her own surname. This was at her mother's bidding with the express motive of creating respectability. Marriage certificates for her siblings leave "Father's name" blank.

"It may be useful to say that in keeping duplicate register books it would be practically impossible to guard against accidental variations occasionally arising at the time entries are being made, and it would be most undesirable that because an error had been inadvertently committed in one book it should be deliberately repeated in the other for the mere purpose of securing uniformity."

If an inadvertent error could be made in one book, then it is equally possible that an error could inadvertently be made in the second book. Likewise there is no guarantee that the clergyman will follow the instruction to "satisfy himself of the correctness of the entries", so it is entirely possible for an error to occur in one entry or the other and to go unnoticed.

> "When the marriage register books of a church or chapel are filled, one ... must be delivered to the Superintendent Registrar of the district in which such church or chapel is situate, at the same time as the certified copies containing the last entry in such register book are delivered to him ".

This is useful confirmation of the timing of the hand-over and indicates that James Oppenheim (page 97 in this chapter) should have deposited his full register at the same time that he delivered his (deficient) returns for 1856/Q1. Yet the Registrar evidently failed to notice that the return only had three entries from the new register and none for March.

> "In the event of register books having, as the result of long usage, or damp, or other cause, become damaged either as to the condition of the paper or of the binding, the Registrar-General will be glad if the clergyman in whose possession they are will communicate with him with a view either of the books being repaired, or of their being closed and fresh ones substituted if the damage has gone too far for repair".

So what really happened to the Ingatestone registers (chapter 6) ? We know the Buttsbury registers were shared with Ingatestone parish for some fifteen years. Was this situation common among the 35000 or so registers in use at any one time ? What is the condition of the registers that started life in 1837 and are still in use ? How are the early entries standing up to the passage of time ?

> "When persons who have been married in a district register office desire to add the religious ceremony of the church, they may ... present themselves .... to the clergyman, who upon production of their marriage certificate before the Superintendent Registrar, may, if he shall see fit, perform the marriage service according to the rites of the church".

The booklet goes on to say that the first marriage is the legal one and the second is not to be entered in the parish register books. Some of the doubly entered marriages noted on page 76 look like such wrongly entered second ceremonies. If so, the valid certificate should be the one with the higher page reference on the basis that register office marriages are always at the end of the records for each district.

The booklet then goes on to deal with the quarterly returns, trying to deal with the problems of timings and overlaps.

It points out that Act 1 Vic c.22 (passed in 1838), specified that the Quarterly Certified Copies were to relate to quarters ending on the last day of March, June, September and December. Unfortunately we well know that the clergy continued to have difficulty with this for at least another two decades and probably very much longer.

> "On no account may a certified copy of an entry belonging to one quarter be included on the same sheet of certified copies with an entry belonging to another quarter". Again we know this was a major problem in the early records. This instruction might have avoided the Childerditch problem described earlier in this chapter.

Then we have another requirement that we look askance at, knowing what we do about the quarterly returns in practice. "The copies *must be literal transcripts* of the entries in the register book, reproducing even the inaccuracies which occur in the originals. If any name appears to have been misspelt in the register book, it must be spelt the same way in the copy".

Most genealogists would probably agree with this principle, if with some regret, and it clearly affects the legal standing of the record. Even so, it is a pity that there could be no provision for a marginal note in such a situation.

The real problem remains, however, that we have so much evidence from this research proving that the copying was often very bad, often easily misread, often with real mistakes, and we also know that there was no provision for the copying by the clergy to be verified in any way. Whatever the inaccuracies in the originals, we can be certain the inaccuracies in the quarterly copies were far greater. The very notion of asking the clergy to ensure that they made literal transcripts of visible errors when literal transcripts of perfectly good entries were often beyond them, this seems decidedly optimistic to say the least. It would have been far better to ask the clergy to take the greatest care in all their copying and then to arrange for their work to be checked by a trustworthy second person.

Some of the investigative proposals made in chapter 9, if they are pursued, will provide much more good evidence of the quality of the record system, from the registers to the final indexes, and in particular might give us even more evidence of the copying standards of the clergy.

The Registrar General's booklet makes the recommendation that clergy should adopt the practice of selecting one of the duplicate registers to be copied from, "keeping always to that one". This probably suggests that it wasn't a procedure in common practice. It also seems to show that there was no indication on the registers themselves that one was intended as an original and one as a copy.

The Registrar General's recommendation was explicitly based on the fact that as errors wouldn't necessarily match in the two copies, then the system of numbering errors throughout each register individually mightn't match in the quarterly copies and this could cause confusion when looking at them in succession. This was a finesse that was hardly a significant worry from what we now know of the quality of the quarterly copies in general and the apparent level of checking that took place.

There was no suggestion as to which register should be deposited with the Superintendent Registrar. In keeping with the legislation, the Registrar General simply said that "one of them" must be delivered and "the other" must be kept. It would have been logical that the one used for the quarterly copies should be the one deposited. In practice the two registers were probably used indiscriminately.

"The delivery of quarterly certified copies to the Superintendent Registrar is usually made through the Registrars of Births and Deaths in his district .....". (This was allowed for in the Act of 1838, so that some clergy wouldn't be legally obliged to travel great distances to deliver them). These district registrars were under instructions to apply for the copies each quarter within the first fifteen days of January, April, July and October. The dates that the quarterly returns were actually completed are entered by the clergy in the sign-off section at the foot of each page and most that I have seen were long after the prescribed fifteen days. Forty five days seems to have been rather more usual and many were far, far later, this despite the fact that 1 Vic. c 22 laid down a penalty of £10 for failing to provide the returns within a calendar month of being required to do so.

As we know from chapter 2, clergy were required to permit searches of their marriage register (but registers deposited with Superintendent Registrars were *not* available for such searches). Any certified copies supplied after such a search "must be written on forms procured by the clergyman at his own expense, or on plain paper - not upon any official forms supplied by the Registrar-General".

Such are the suggestions in the Registrar General's booklet that are relevant to this research. There are numerous other instructions relating to burials, baptismal certificates, and corrections to entries in registers.

We are indebted to John Harnden for discovering a copy of this booklet among the records in the Hereford Record Office. Copies may perhaps have found their way to other record offices.

In theory the marriage registration system set up by the 1836 legislation could have been a great success, provided that :

a)   The clergy had written their returns carefully, accurately, completely and on time

b)   Superintendent Registrars had set up systems to keep track of all quarterly returns, both from clergy and from registrars

c)   The GRO indexing rules had guarded against unnecessary variant indexing

d)   The GRO had introduced numerical controls to trap the many unindexed entries

e)   The GRO had set up numerical controls to record variant indexing and thus to be able to check numerically that all entries for each volume were actually indexed

f)   The GRO had set up controls to check visually the indexers' output for each volume indexed (which would have caught thousands of wrong references)

g)   The GRO had set up numerical controls to ensure that typed fiche yielded the same number of entries as counted in the manuscript pages

h)   The GRO had set up checks on the completeness of the microfiche and microfilm outputs.

In all these areas we have suffered hugely from errors and omissions. If any one of these weaknesses had been tightened up it is very likely that other problem areas would automatically have been improved at the same time.

The Registrar General's little booklet of "Suggestions for the guidance of the Clergy" was clearly a sign of recognition that things were not as they should be. One wonders what he might have written if the results of this current research had been available to him. We can be sure that no such in-depth study had been done at that time, this present research having been welcomed by ONS as a basis for learning more about the quality of the earlier records.

The legal position of the clergy vis-a-vis the General Register Office seems to reflect a little of the legal concept of "benefit of clergy". Under this, clergy had "the advantage of belonging to a privileged order which was exempted from the jurisdiction or sentence of the ordinary courts of law" (Shorter Oxford Dictionary). This makes it ironic that the original meaning of the word "benefit" was "a thing well done". If only their quarterly returns were entitled to this description ! Likewise the General Register Office was not given legal control over the operations of the Superintendent Registrars, beyond a right of appointment in certain circumstances.

No doubt there will be readers who remember Sir Alan Herbert and his novels on legal matters. There may even be some who recall his poem "The Piteous Ballad of Arabella Booley". Poor Arabella by mishap and by some manipulation of the church clock was actually married at half past four when the church clock said ten to three, making her marriage invalid.

There was a tragic outcome for Arabella that needn't concern us here, but it is a little surprising that our legal marriage record makes no mention of the time of a marriage. In view of what we now know about the erratic and unreliable performance of the clergy in practical matters we may well wonder whether all marriages were actually within the allowed legal times. After all, Rupert Brooke's "Grantchester" contains the well known line "Stands the Church clock at ten to three ?" Is there any significance, at a time when the legal marriage period ended at three o'clock, in two poems pointing to a rural church clock that was stopped at ten to three ? After all, Brooke did also claim to see "The sly shade of a Rural Dean".

This is an area of research beyond my scope but perhaps some one will come across some evidence one day in a court record or an ecclesiastical diary.

Chapter 8 - The Grass Roots

Up to this point the discussion has been based on comparing the marriage records in the General Register Office with the published index to those records, the GRO Marriage Index. It has been pointed out, however, not once but many times, that these marriage records are only copies of the originals and often poor copies at that.

The only total measure of quality in the GRO marriage index is its closeness to the primary marriage records as they exist in the Marriage Registers held in the offices of the Superintendent Registrars.

A good alternative to comparing the GRO marriage index with the local marriage registers is to compare the GRO index with *the local indexes to the marriage registers as created by Superintendent Registrars.* I have been able to make just such a comparison, using an index provided by the Superintendent Registrar for the district of Taunton in Somerset. This index covers all of 1844 with names of 852 brides and grooms. As a local index it is based on original registers, generally better written than quarterly copies, and local indexers must have more familiarity with local names and places.

Format of the local index for Taunton

The marriage records held by the Superintendent Registrars are organised quite differently from those in the General Register Office. They consist simply of a set of marriage registers, parish by parish, and each register will cover a different time span from every other register. For some large parishes there will be a succession of registers. On the other hand one register for a small parish may easily cover fifty or a hundred years. In the Taunton district around nine registers dating from 1837 are still in the parishes and still in use.

The GRO system of volumes in which district marriages are aggregated on a quarterly basis is a completely alien structure so far as the Superintendent Registrars are concerned.

Indexes first produced by Superintendent Registrars were for individual registers. They identify the contents by reference to the page number in the register or specify each marriage by its reference number within the register.

Thus to find a particular person it is necessary to know which parish register or registers are likely ones and then to search the corresponding indexes.

Many registrars have now found it worthwhile to begin building indexes for their holdings of registers on an annual basis and this is the type of index that I have been able to work from in the case of Taunton, one index covering all Taunton district marriages for the whole year of 1844.

Let us look at some extracts from the Taunton 1844 index.

Surname	Forename(s)	Register details
Arthers	George	CE62 1/243
Ash	Eliza	CE54 1/73
Ashton	William	CE10 1/8
Atton	Mary B	CE39 1/391
Ayres	Mary A	CE39 1/376
Gatter	John	CE28 1/29
Gear	Charles	CE39 1/376
Gent	Diana	RM 2/51
Gent	Thomas	CE9 1/50
Parsons	Thomas	CE27 1/44
Parsons	Thomas	CE36 1/13
Partridge	Mary A	CE39 1/376
Patton	Charlotte	CE42 1/217

These names are three short extracts from different parts of the alphabetical index, chosen to illustrate some aspects of the records.

The personal names need no explanation. The register details are readily explained. All the "CE" references are to Church of England parishes. CE62 is the parish of St John the Baptist in Wellington, CE54 is St Michael's in Milverton, CE9 is Stoke St Gregory, CE10 is St Michael's in Burrowbridge and CE39 is St Mary's in Taunton. RM relates to marriages registered by Registrars.

A number such as 1/376 identifies an entry as item 376 in the first register for that parish. No Taunton parish entries were in a second register in 1844.

When I first looked at this local index and compared it with my computer file of Taunton marriages for 1844/Q1 I immediately began to see differences. I decided to turn the Taunton index into a computer file as well and sort it to look at the parish structure. This was done by entering it into a spreadsheet and sorting it on the basis of the register references   This grouped all entries by parishes and confirmed the register references as the entry numbers for each marriage rather than the page numbers. In other words the index identifies each married couple. It also identifies the parish.

Brides and grooms came neatly together and also showed up another way in which the Taunton index differs from the GRO index. There were several groups of three, too many to represent "also known as" situations. Take for example three names in the selected extracts above. Mary A Ayres, Charles Gear and Mary A Partridge are all shown as item 376 in the first register book for CE39, St Mary's Taunton. There are 25 instances of one groom and two brides with the same given names and it is obvious that they are all widows remarrying. This has been confirmed by the Taunton registrar. The index doesn't say which name is the maiden name and which is the previous married name. That would be very helpful.

The Taunton index gives no indication of the quarter each marriage belongs to but there is really no reason why it should. It is purely an annual index.

Comparison of the Taunton index and the GRO index

To gain maximum value from this Taunton index, I needed to compare it with the GRO indexes for the full year, not just with the Q1 index that I'd already extracted. I therefore went through the GRO marriage indexes for the other three quarters to find all Taunton entries. I returned to the GRO index step by step to search for any names in the Taunton index that I failed to match in the first search. This showed that the Taunton index also included entries for parishes that were part of the Bridgwater and Wellington districts in 1844.

Equipped now with the entries in the Taunton local index and also with the entries in the GRO index that relate to Taunton and to the relevant parts of Bridgwater and Wellington, how do they compare ?

The comparison has proved startling to say the least.

a)   Of the 406 marriages in the Taunton index, 12 marriages (or 3%) are not found in the GRO index.

b)   There are 22 other individual names in the Taunton index that cannot be found in the GRO index. This raises the omissions to well over 5%.

c)   There are just over 60 names that vary in the two indexes, including several where the GRO index has variant entries because of bad quarterly returns.

d)   There are 21 entries in the GRO indexes (as Taunton entries) that fail to appear in the Taunton local index. Some may be from parishes that were in the Taunton district in 1844 but have since crossed boundaries to other districts. One is a bride unindexed in the Taunton list. Most omissions will be from 1837 registers not yet deposited in Taunton.

e)   The GRO index has several incorrect references. The Taunton index has only two.

Overall this level of differences between the two indexes is almost incredibly high. The Superintendent Registrar for Taunton has checked my preliminary report on differences and omissions, relating just to the March quarter. My later research has extended the comparison to the full year.

Omissions from the GRO indexes

Of the 12 marriages shown by Taunton but not in the GRO, eight are for Q1 in the parish of St John the Baptist in Wellington. Either they are further proof of entries missed from the quarterly returns or they were returned but simply not indexed. They are (as I showed on p95) :

> John Hammet and Jane B Sercombe
> James Marks and Elizabeth Manley
> John Hayes and Sarah Lane
> John Mayner and Mary A Dockings
> James Westcott and Maria Forward
> George Cavell and Mary A Baker
> James Keates and Susanna Wright
> John Burston and Mary A Stevens

These are items 208 to 215 in the parish marriage register. Marriages for St John the Baptist for the following three quarters are in both indexes.

If these eight marriages *had* been included in the quarterly return for 1844/Q1, then they would have occupied two sides of one sheet and would have been numbered recto/verso in the bundle for volume 10 (Devon and Somerset). Because I have the sorted index file for this volume I can say categorically that there is no evidence at all of a page or pages unindexed in the Wellington district entries. Wellington marriages occupy pages 737 to 760 in the volume 10 film and every recto page is present and fully represented in the index. I have no instances anywhere in this research of returns incorporated in the bundles yet missing the page numbering process.

The clear inference is that these eight marriages were not reported for 1844/Q1. They are a major loss to the Wellington record, eight marriages missed out of thirty five. I would have considered eight marriages a serious loss in the whole of volume 10, not just in one district out of twenty four.

But there are more to come. Two marriages from the parish of St Mary's, West Buckland, are in the Taunton index but not the GRO index. They are :

> Henry Marthawick and Jane Westcott
> Edward G Jenkins and Elizabeth Knight

Two marriages from St Nicholas in Kittisford are in the Taunton index but not the GRO index. They are :

> John Cridge and Ann Webber
> James Chick and Jane Webber

I suspect these *were* in the quarterly return but were missed by the GRO indexer. The page numbering of the GRO index references suggests that this may be one of the recto pages missed in the indexing.

Four marriages are in the Taunton index, shown as items 37 to 40 in the marriage register of the district registrar for Wellington, Somerset. They are :

> Robert Trenchard and Elizabeth Forbear
> James Lewis and Sarah Sparks
> Thomas Walker and Catharine Masey
> Joseph King and Betsey Nation

I can find no entries in the GRO index for Trenchard, Sparks or Walker. Based on the other five names that *do* appear in the GRO index, all four marriages should be on page 750a of the GRO marriage film for 1844/Q4.

You will recall seeing these names at the very beginning of Chapter 1. To lose three names in a group of four marriages seems to suggest some sort of slip by the indexer. Blaming the typists seems a little doubtful but there is certainly a hint in the index of a typing loss with Sarah Sparks.

The following nineteen names appear in the Taunton index but I cannot find them in the GRO indexes. Their spouses, identified via the Taunton index, *are* in the GRO index and their page references are therefore known.

Sarah Bodger	p771 in Q2	John Nurcombe	p855 in Q2
Thomas Fabret	p533 in Q1	James Parr	p783 in Q2
Robert Dinham	p789 in Q2	Catherine Pyne	p698a in Q3
Mary Hayes	p672 in Q3	William Shallis	p854c in Q2
John Hellings	p853 in Q2	Jane Shorland	p854 in Q2
Elizabeth Jenkins	p811 in Q2	William Smith	p826 in Q2
Robert Jenkins	p831 in Q2	Charles Verier	p603 in Q2
James Killand	p699 in Q3	William White	p709 in Q4
Jeremiah Leavens	p824 in Q2	Robert Yendall	p705 in Q4
Anna Lendell	p821 in Q2		

It isn't simply that I have failed to find these names in the GRO 1844 indexes exactly as shown. Having checked right through the GRO indexes for all Taunton entries and as far as possible for all relevant Bridgwater or Wellington entries, no names have turned up that are corruptions of these names. I am satisfied that all or virtually all these apparent omissions from the GRO indexes are indeed omitted. Of the 19 missing, 12 are from 1844/Q2, including two of the Jenkins clan. There is a strong suggestion that this quarter had more sloppy typing than most. If the typist was able to miss two whole pages of the Jenkins family in 1844, then it would have been all too easy to miss odd names or small groups of names. I was suspicious of such a happening with one or two of the Taunton problems. This could quite easily be the explanation for many of the isolated "non-indexed" names throughout the Essex/Suffolk files.

In total the missing marriages and missing individuals represent 5.6% of the persons in the Taunton index, a rate significantly higher than the omissions found in any of the previous studies.. It is a horrendously high figure

I also checked that wherever the Taunton local index seems to include both the maiden name and the previous married name of a widow, only one name is shown in the GRO index. This is to be expected. It identifies for me which name is which, something that the Taunton index doesn't do.

I increasingly feel that many of the nineteen missing *individuals* are very likely to be losses at the typing stage. We can be sure that this applies to Elizabeth and Robert Jenkins in 1844/Q2, victims of the Jenkins disaster.

The IGI has been of no help with any of the Taunton problems because Somerset seems to be another of the counties where the IGI has very few entries beyond the very early 1800s.

Variant indexing (TSR = Taunton Superintendent Registrar)

This illustrates how much variation arises once the GRO indexers have to struggle with the quarterly returns and the disastrous manuscript of some of the vicars.

TSR has Ann Corrick, GRO index has both Ann and Anne
TSR has Sparke, GRO index has Sparks* and Sparkes
TSR has Charles Dare*, GRO index has both Dare and Clare
TSR has John Saffin, GRO index has Jaffin and Taffin
TSR has John Keirle*, GRO index has both Keirle and Kearle
TSR has Ann Hodge, GRO index has Hodge and Hodges
TSR has Martha Palmer, GRO index has Palmer and Palmar
TSR has Caroline Sturley, Saterley and Saturley. GRO has Saturly
TSR has Mary Beadon Atton, GRO has Alton and Atton
TSR has John Farquhar, GRO has Farquhar and Farquher
TSR has James Owen and Owne, GRO just has Owen
TSR has John Lippiatt, GRO has Lippiatt and Luppiatt

(Asterisks are correct versions checked by the TSR for 1844/Q1)

Different indexing

Here we see how the GRO indexer can interpret differently what he sees in the Quarterly Returns, again a likely consequence of the writing of the clergy. One almost begins to wonder if the clergy were a little like general practitioners of today, experts in a writing style calculated to deceive ninety nine people out of a hundred.

> TSR has Mary Bromsgrove*, GRO has Broomsgrove
> TSR has William Cape, GRO has William Cafe
> TSR has Sarah Combes*, GRO has Combe
> TSR has Amelia Tristin, GRO has Triston*
> TSR has David Loud*, GRO has Lovel
> TSR has Charlotte* Greed, GRO has Charalotte
> TSR has Caroline Ball, GRO has Pratt*
> TSR has William Batstone*, GRO has Balstone
> TSR has Mary Hembrow*, GRO has Hemhow
> TSR has Patricia Shearn, GRO has Patience*
> TSR has Elizabeth Hoskins. GRO has Hopkins*
> TSR has Betsy Charles, GRO has Betty
> TSR has Edmond Wyatt, GRO has Edmund
> TSR has Betsy Bromgrove, GRO has Broomgrove

I can double this list from the Taunton results, but enough is enough. And, yes, Ball and Pratt are very possible alternative readings in terms of the writing style of the 1840s. Asterisks again indicate the correct readings checked by the Taunton registrar in the marriage registers (but again only for 1844/Q1). Taunton wins on points but the contest is not one-sided.

Other indexing errors

GRO errors include :
> Philip Francis in Q2 mis-indexed as page 191 for page 791
> Robert Gibbard in Q2 mis-indexed as page 851b for page 854b
> Robert Parsons (noted in Chapter 6) mis-indexed as *Wellingbro* page
> 698a in volume *15* instead of *Wellington* page 698a volume *10*
> Sarah Ross in Q3 mis-indexed as page 653 for page 655
> Henry Taylor in Q2 mis-indexed as page 797 for page 796

TSR errors include :
> Charles Knight and Mary Weston are mis-indexed as register CE2.
> The registrar writes that they should have been indexed to the
> parish of Durston, reference CE3.

Caroline King in the parish of St George's, Wilton, is not indexed. She
is the bride of Joseph Parish, who *is* indexed. This index omission
has been confirmed by the TSR.

Conclusion

All these examples illustrate the extent of differences between the Taunton
index and the GRO indexes. The comparisons seem to confirm my earlier
suppositions that the quality of the quarterly returns had a devastating effect
on the quality of the published GRO marriage indexes, aggravated by typing
problems. The Taunton exercise was initiated after I left Southport and has
added immensely to the scope and value of the whole investigation.

Taunton is simply one annual record from 62 years picked by chance from
over 600 possible Superintendent Registrars' districts, i.e. one annual record
from more than 30,000 possibles. There is no reasonable probability that I
could have picked the worst of all records by chance. There could be
hundreds or thousands of records that are worse. It just happened that I spent
a few days in Somerset as a break before flying home to New Zealand.

The most stirring thought is that if this sample is anywhere near average, then
an omission of 5.6% of marriage entries would mean over a million names
missed from the marriage indexes of the 1800s. It is not at all impossible that
there could even be names that have failed to be picked up both by the local
indexer and the GRO indexer. One lesson from these studies has been that
almost any imaginable error has happened from time to time.

The Taunton exercise also re-emphasises the value of the sorted index files in
these comparisons. They are the only suitable tool, to my mind, for
comparing the GRO marriage index against any of the other records, the
GRO marriage films, the local indexes and ultimately the local marriage
registers. As shown in the many examples in earlier chapters, they bring
together all that the marriage index has to say about every page in the
marriage films, or about every localised group of marriages in the local
indexes or local registers. The sorted files bring together the Jaffin and
Taffin to be compared with the Saffin. There is no other effective way.
Therein lies the uniqueness of the proposal that I was able to offer to ONS.

A comparison between the GRO marriage record and the local marriage
registers would reveal very little - it would largely evade the crucial quality
aspect of the legibility of the films as expressed in the indexes derived from
them. The comparison needs to be with the marriage index for it to mean
anything. The marriage index in its alphabetical sequence would be
impossible to handle as a tool for comparison. After all, if a marriage is badly

indexed because it was badly copied, where on earth do you find it in the index ? How do you discover if a name has generated two or more variant readings ? It is in fact the entries that *are* mis-indexed that one most needs to find in a study on indexing quality and they are the very ones hardest to find, or impossible to find, without an index sorted by page references.

Sorted index files are the *only* tools.

Despite errors and differences on this scale, one still has to say that the GRO record is correct and complete for the most part.

On the other hand the error levels, both in omissions and incorrect entries, seem so great that most researchers using the system are sure to be baulked at some point by them, quite apart from the difficulty in reading much of the fiche and film. It is like a bucket with a hole in it. However small the hole, the bucket is faulty. What the Taunton exercise seems to have shown is an alarmingly higher level of overall errors than I found in the Southport work.

As I pointed out in chapter 5, it is inevitable that the hand-written quarterly returns would have contained not just bad handwriting but also many actual transcription errors. Hence it is hardly surprising that the Taunton exercise has found a higher error rate by taking the comparison a step nearer to the original records. It all seems to show that the Southport exercise found only one part of the errors in the system.

As I also pointed out in chapter 5, the way that the registration system was set up was almost a guarantee that errors would occur and that they would be virtually impossible to check. It seems that no such checks have ever been made except for the occasional correction of a few particular entries that have come into question.

Further checking exercises are, I believe, very easily carried out and are included as final suggestions in chapter 9. However, ONS appear to feel that the comparisons made in this research have done enough to highlight the problems in the system, as indeed I feel they have, and that the need now is to consider what action may need to be taken.

My own thoughts in that respect will be found in Chapter 9. Understandably I would be very glad to see more research done because I can very clearly see many more nooks and crannies in the system that I would like to throw some light on.

Chapter 9 - Where next from here ?

Radical thoughts on future development

The conclusions

At the end (well, nearly the end) of this investigation, where do we stand ?

I believe we can be sure that tens of thousands of marriages, very probably hundreds of thousands, failed to reach the General Register Office via the quarterly returns. We have seen indications pointing to even larger figures.

Similarly large numbers of marriages and individuals are apparently missing from the indexes, through faulty indexing or faulty typing.

Even larger numbers of variant entries and incorrect entries in the indexes have resulted from the poor quality of the quarterly returns.

Significant numbers of other errors in the indexes exist by way of incorrect references, often too incorrect for the names to be discovered in the records.

There is evidence that errors in the system persisted to the end of the century and beyond, compounded by problems with the tiny and fragile typeface of the indexes, but it would take more years of work and further checking against the GRO films to assess the extent of errors in the later years.

There are many gaps in the published fiche of the GRO marriage index (as shown in Chapter 11, pages 142 onwards), running at least into thousands of names. These are not faults in the record system itself but they are major faults in the published form of it.

The proposals

If the conclusions of this study are valid, and I believe for the most part they are, then the study would be incomplete without taking a step into space and trying to define a pathway towards a better system. It is certain that a much better resource can be created from the marriage records of the 1800s. The benefits for genealogy at large and for the Office for National Statistics could be immense, all this at much less cost than has been sometimes suggested.

It is very clear that the existing GRO marriage records for the 1800s, i.e. the film records at the GRO, and the corresponding GRO marriage indexes are very seriously flawed.

I am also sure that the errors in the present system are so many that it is beyond the bounds of possibility and cost to consider any attempt to correct them. Even to set about identifying all errors and omissions would be an enormous task, not easy, and almost certainly a waste of valuable effort.

Much the most promising approach is to make use of modern technology to create a new marriage record for the GRO for the 1800s, at the same time creating a much better index and access system that could be a vast improvement for genealogists in general, for the GRO and for the Superintendent Registrars.

My proposals for a radically new marriage index for 1837/99 will be a very great jump forward in terms of access and effectiveness.

It is also very likely, though I will not expand on this here, that large benefits can be achieved for birth and death records through the same process, as copying and typing have demonstrably introduced errors into those systems too. It would not only be an opportunity for correction of errors but an opportunity for the creation of better and more informative indexes.

Filming the registers . . . .

All the results of this study point to the local marriage registers as very much the best data source in completeness and legibility. In fact I believe the local registers are the *only* valid basis for reforming the marriage record system.

I would argue first for a filming of all the *marriage registers* covering the 1800s. This would be a dispersed operation, working within the 600-plus Superintendent Registrars' offices, and hence relatively simple. It would also involve calling in any current marriage registers running since the 1800s, and setting up an inventory of registers for all parishes so that any lost or badly damaged registers can be covered in some way, from the existing GRO records or from County Record Offices or even from bishops' transcripts.

Not only will this create a total marriage record, removing the present gaps in the quarterly returns, but it will be based on a legible primary document (compared with the quarterly copies). With modern technology it should yield a high quality copy. It has the further benefit of producing a much smaller total output of film than the existing GRO films which typically have a data density varying from around 90% in main cities to 20% or less in rural volumes because of all the blank and partly used pages.

This filming is an operation in which the GRO has ample experience and it can easily be costed. The existing films also have many interleaved supplementary pages where entries have been corrected and many or most of these would be redundant in a record based on the original marriage entries.

Indexing . . . .

The existing local registrars' indexes are completely unsuitable for a national search system. This is reflected in the way that many registrars, as in Taunton, have been putting time into building their own indexes on a yearly or quarterly basis, simply to give better access to the registers. All local indexes, however, are either related to individual registers or to that local registration district. Their individual systems of reference to their own registers are unlikely to be compatible on a national basis. To use the local indexes as they stand is rather like looking for someone in the census. You need to know quite a lot about your family before you start.

The filming of the more accurate marriage registers, therefore, would make it essential to re-index from these new films. I realise that large sums have been quoted for such a project but it seems very hard to justify such a belief.

The arithmetic, which has no room for significant flaws, is approximately as follows. Total marriages in the period 1837 to 1899 are about 11.5 million, based on the Registrar General's statistics. (If the Quarterly Returns were significantly deficient, there could be 2-5% more marriages than the Registrar General would have known about). There are rather over 600 Superintendent Registrars' offices for England and Wales. Thus the average number of marriages for 1837/99 held at each is around 19000. This is *not* a large number. Some will be a great deal larger but many will be small. I believe I am right in recalling that the capacity of each of the GRO film reels is comfortably 3000 marriages, assuming all pages are full (as they are in the original registers), so we are looking at an average of some six films per Superintendent's district, or perhaps less than 4000 films in total to cover all marriages in the period 1837 to 1899.

I am convinced that creating a new index system for this 1837/99 information can be done easily and cheaply, even though aiming at a much better and fuller index than at present, and I have satisfied myself by simple experiment.

Using simple spreadsheet software rather than any form of specialised software, I have experimented with creating a new index from a collection of marriages mocked up to represent the situation of a marriage register book.

This new index has a content well beyond the scope of the existing marriage index. The items I included were :

> Surname of married person
> Given names of married person
> Surname of spouse
> Full date dd/mm/yyyy of the marriage
> Name of Superintendent Registrar's district
> Code number to show parish of the marriage)   required to access
> Reference no. in the marriage register   )   the new film record

It would also be necessary to add a sequence number for the register books, of which large parishes would have a good number. I also suggest that widows remarrying should be indexed under their maiden name and their last married name, with an identifying flag.

The significant result in this test exercise was that I created index material at the very comfortable rate of 500 marriages per modest working day. This implies that the material for the *average* Registry office (19000 marriages) should take no longer than 40 working days to index. Even allowing for double entry as a checking process, this is modest. A pattern of one person working for three months, or preferably two people to provide for checking processes, should be very comfortable indeed. This rate of data entry is very close to my findings when struggling with magnifying glass and page range table to work from the very poor print of the 1891 marriage index.

Britain now has a large pool of experienced volunteer workers who have achieved large amounts of data capture for the 1881 census project and for the ongoing 1851 projects. They are family history enthusiasts with a depth of knowledge that would be made available without reservation. It has been suggested to me that there would be no problem in securing a thousand or more volunteers via the Family History societies to re-index the 1837/99 marriages from films of the registers. At most register offices we would only be looking at 10 to 12 weeks of work on a generous assessment, and extra volunteers would materialise easily for the large registries. When I have voiced this suggestion it has been greeted with very positive enthusiasm.

It is by dividing the task between 600 local offices that an immense task becomes a small one. Carrying out the filming or scanning locally also means that registers wouldn't have to leave the local offices, a potential stumbling block in terms of the legislative obligations of the system.

I appreciate that ONS may have misgivings about using volunteer effort for the index operation but I hardly think that should be a real worry. These volunteers are experienced and they would be dedicated to such a project. If we try to associate a staff cost with it, and consider, say, 100 man-years in total at some £20k per head, then we are talking of £2 million. But if we are talking of volunteers then that figure doesn't arise. Direct GRO costs would be mainly for design and supervision, plus costs of actual filming or scanning.

We should be looking at very small costs for a major project.

Some of the benefits

There are significant bonuses in indexing from film of primary registers :

a)   Legibility will be much better than the quarterly returns.

b)   Handwriting will be consistent over much of any given register, giving benefits in familiarity and in resolving difficulties. Compare this with today's GRO films, each parish and often each page in a new hand.

c)   Local surnames will tend to be consistent in most registers.

d)   Computer checks of date order and register entry numbers for a whole register can be done instantly. Both should be in the same order.

e)   Files can be immediately sorted by surname, both for person married and for spouse, and quickly checked visually for likely errors.

f)   The indexing can easily be done on a dispersed, localised basis.

g)   All indexing would use the reference numbers in the registers and not page numbers, so that every marriage would be uniquely   identified.

h)   Maiden names of all widows can be included in the indexing.

Scanning

I have written here about filming, but clearly another option is scanning. A scanning option might make only limited sense if we were looking at the quarterly returns where handwriting is so variable from page to page, but the local registers would be far more consistent over long periods and this might make scanning a better option, with OCR as an aid in the indexing process. I know of other large projects where scanning and then conversion to CD-ROM has been found the cheapest and best option, with data entry from the CD-ROM as the OCR option was unjustified.

Multiple indexes

Having created new indexes to this newly filmed material, there is no technological problem whatsoever in creating two new index systems from it.

Firstly it is easy to break out the information by years and quarters and to produce a new national index looking superficially the same as the present marriage index but with at least the extra fields suggested. Secondly, any desired form of index can also be designed for the Superintendent Registrars themselves, which will immediately be a huge advance on their existing indexes that are on a register by register basis. They will be able to search their whole record as an entity.

Thirdly, this new index can be available on microfiche or film as a direct replacement for the existing systems, or even better can be available as a fully computer-searchable index system. For the GRO it would be a huge new marketable resource.

The GRO marriage records

The most radical part of this suggestion is that the existing GRO marriage films for the 1837/99 period would then be archived and replaced totally by the new films as a working source. The new films will be an assured and complete data source. They can be organised by years, or by districts, or whatever, but the new index system would be capable of giving total access to them. It should make no significant difference to GRO work in producing marriage certificates for this period except to improve it immensely in quality and completeness.

The way the new films are stored, identified and accessed in the GRO system would be very much a matter of system design within the GRO, just as it has always been since the system was first established.

Inevitably there would be many ifs and buts in a system design for such a project but the overall concept feels very simple. I have been involved in designing and developing computer projects over the years. There will be the occasional "special" entries over the years (I forget their official title) but these should all be part of the registers.

Design and planning for such a project could take six months to a year, implementation less than a year. There would be no need for changes in legislation for such a project. The GRO has already complied with the existing legislation and should be free to carry out this additional work.

Benefits for the researcher

These benefits would be substantial and could easily be available within a year of the project's being undertaken.

The updated index would be legible, in whatever form it is used. It should also be available in a machine-searchable form.

The upgraded system would provide completeness, i.e. the elimination of omissions in the system caused by the faulty quarterly returns or the faulty indexing.

Variant indexing, with all the large number of additional name entries resulting from it, would be largely eliminated.

The innumerable instances of marriages indexed in two consecutive quarters would be removed.

Spelling of names in the indexes would become far more accurate.

Indexing errors of the sort that have pervaded the system in the past should be generally eliminated.

Information in the index would be greatly enhanced, with exact dates, precise localities, spouses' surnames, widows' maiden names.

More certificates could be ordered and with great confidence of success.

Benefits for the GRO

a)   The GRO would be consciously providing a greatly enhanced
        reliability and completeness (in line with its mission statement)
b)   Restructured files would give easier and more reliable access to GRO
        data.
c)   Output of certificates would be easier and of higher quality.
d)   The growing pressure on the GRO services, which is a growth that is
        likely to continue, would be eased by a modernised system.

Transition

Introduction of a new marriage record system would co-exist with the existing system for some while because many researchers would still base requests on the old system. The GRO system of Customer Service Teams could easily cope with such a situation by a reallocation of some responsibilities.

Indeed it should be easy to develop a reasonably effective cross-reference system within the GRO so that certificate requests on the "old" basis could be translated into references to the new system.

Better access to GRO records

My belief is that these proposals for restructuring the record system must be seen as a far higher priority than any moves towards freer access to the existing records. Whatever may happen in that direction in the longer term, and I am not decrying that as an aim, it must now be obvious that the real benefits to genealogy will come from dealing with the manifold defects that this research has uncovered and this book has illustrated. My solutions, I believe, are feasible and are achievable within a reasonable time scale.

Further proof ? A few suggestions

If further evidence on the quality of the records is needed, I can see three other avenues of investigation open to the GRO. All are certain to yield a great deal of new information and are worthwhile in any event.

Proposal A

This is a proposal I have already advanced, namely a procedure for using my sorted index files of Essex/Suffolk entries to make a total comparison with marriage registers for all the corresponding Essex and Suffolk districts. This would be similar to the Taunton exercise but would use about 14,000 index entries instead of about 800. This would make a much more reliable measure of the quality of the records "ab initio ad finem", from the beginning of the records to their emergence in the marriage indexes. It would give a measure of omitted returns, copying errors, index errors either from copying or the quality of the handwriting, indexing omissions and typing omissions.

Visualise my sorted files for eight successive quarters for Essex and Suffolk as if they are eight vertical slices through those counties, district by district as illustrated for one year in the Page Range Table of Appendix 5.

My proposal is to make thin horizontal slices across these same eight files. Each such slice would represent a single parish's marriages and a contiguous group of such slices would represent all parishes and register offices in the district of a particular Superintendent Registrar.

This material would be a means of checking the entries from the marriage indexes (as recorded in my files) against the original marriage registers for all of those parishes, simply and efficiently. It would be a comparison of 13,900 names, a big advance on the 800 names compared in the Taunton exercise.

There would be some 700 thin slices, of which some twenty to forty would need to be checked against the registers in each of the register offices of the Superintendent Registrars. It might take me a month or two to prepare the slices. It might take a month to six weeks to tour the counties, and another month to prepare a full report. That would be my estimate if I was doing the work myself. Quicker, but perhaps less complete, would be to use registers held in the Essex/Suffolk record offices.

The results would be a comprehensive assessment of the performance of the system, measuring the extent to which names have been missed, altered or in any way corrupted in the copying, the indexing, the typing and the fiching.

Proposal B

My other and rather different proposal is for a random sample of, say, 100,000 entries to be made at the GRO from the first thirty years of the marriage indexes. These names would then be checked against the GRO marriage films to identify the parish or register office from which each entry came. The sample of names would then be broken down into batches according to Superintendent Registrar's districts. These would need to reflect the district *now* responsible for each parish (often different from the district responsible at the time the quarterly return was made, but which will be available at the GRO). This would give a batch of around 150 to 200 names on average for each Superintendent Registrar, some more, some less.

The Superintendent Registrars would compare these batches very carefully with the entries in the marriage registers and report back on all differences. The items in the sample would be single names rather than actual marriages.

This exercise would check the accuracy of entries that actually got as far as the published GRO index fiche. It would *not* cover problems that I was able to cover in respect of Taunton or that would be covered by proposal A, i.e. it wouldn't throw any light on the marriage items that failed any of the various hurdles on the way to the index.

All the same, it would be a comparatively simple and inexpensive exercise. The sample might take a couple of people two to three months to extract, check against the films, and allocate to districts. If registrars have insufficient staffing for this operation, then a GRO team could carry it out. Based on the number of entries, the same two people could visit perhaps one

Superintendent Registrar's office per working day on average and accomplish the whole check in about three years. Allowing for salaries and expenses, we are probably looking at under £100,000, probably very much less than the real value of the work put into my own study to date. For the project to succeed, the people involved would need to be enthusiastic, knowledgeable and well motivated.

Proposal C

This is a simple and inexpensive numerical check on numbers of marriages. If it hasn't been done before then I believe it is an immediate "must" and could be done very quickly.

Step 1. Tally the number of marriages in the 1837-1899 period from the marriage registers. Superintendent Registrars can quickly tally all registers in Register Offices (up to 31/12/1899). Actual counting isn't needed, the entries being numbered. Subtracting spoiled register entries would be worthwhile if possible. One of the district registrars can be deputed to visit parishes and tally the marriages for 1837-1899 in any registers outstanding.

Step 2. Compare this total of marriages with the Registrar General's figures for 1837-1899. Register numbers should be higher to the extent of marriages missed in the quarterly returns.

Step 3. Tally the number of entries in the marriage indexes for the 1837/99 period, based on the index registers in Southport. This is a longer job but can be expedited by using marked scales (different scales for different styles of register). We would expect this figure to be quite a lot higher than the Registrar General's figures, inflated by multiple indexing and only partly offset by the marriages missed in the indexing process.

The tallying in step 3 can and should be done by year so as to give an annual comparison with the published marriage totals. The tallying in step 1 should ideally be done by year but this would be far more difficult and time-consuming.

The results of this numerical check could be published by ONS and would contribute towards the public appreciation of the condition of the records.

Chapter 10 - Marriages, the numbers

Some of the basic figures of births, deaths and marriages are not readily available or easily found when you want them. They can reveal a few useful facts and ideas as general background for research.

The following table of births, deaths and marriages appears in "An abstract of UK Historical Statistics" quoting the Registrar General as the primary source. The figures relate to England and Wales taken together.

	Births	Deaths	Marriages		B	D	M
		(000s)				(000s)	
1838	464	343	118	1869	773	495	177
1839	493	339	123	1870	793	516	182
1840	502	359	123	1871	797	515	190
1841	512	344	122	1872	826	492	201
1842	518	350	119	1873	830	493	206
1843	527	347	124	1874	855	526	202
1844	541	357	132	1875	851	546	201
1845	544	350	144	1876	888	510	202
1846	573	390	146	1877	888	501	194
1847	540	419	136	1878	892	540	190
1848	563	398	138	1879	880	526	182
1849	578	441	142	1880	882	528	192
1850	593	369	153	1881	884	492	197
1851	616	396	154	1882	889	517	204
1852	624	407	159	1883	891	523	206
1853	612	421	165	1884	907	531	204
1854	634	437	160	1885	894	524	198
1855	635	426	152	1886	904	537	196
1856	657	391	159	1887	886	531	201
1857	663	419	159	1888	880	511	204
1858	655	449	156	1889	886	518	214
1859	690	441	168	1890	870	562	223
1860	684	422	170	1891	914	587	227
1861	696	435	164	1892	898	560	227
1862	713	437	164	1893	915	570	219
1863	727	474	174	1894	890	499	226
1864	740	496	180	1895	922	569	228
1865	748	491	185	1896	915	527	243
1866	754	500	188	1897	922	541	249
1867	768	471	179	1898	923	552	255
1868	787	481	177	1899	929	581	262

Totals 1838-1899   46625 29220 11235

The broad picture

It isn't really possible for this simple table of births, deaths and marriages (with its known deficiencies) to be closely analysed to produce precise results but perhaps we can extract a few possibilities.

With certain reservations, the BDM table does give us some hints of changes over the period. Birth data are too deficient to compare births and deaths.

The BDM table shows, when you double the marriage numbers to account for bride and groom, that exactly 30% more people were recorded as dying in the years 1838 to 1899 than are recorded as marrying. We tend to think from more recent times that life's typical pattern is to be born, to marry and to die. As genealogists, though, we are all too painfully aware of the high child mortality of past centuries. This 30% excess certainly suggests that many were born and died before reaching marrying age. My wife's families include one family of sixteen where ten lived only a few weeks or even days. We are thankful that she is safely descended from the sixteenth child.

In general terms those marrying are mainly those aged around their 20s. Those dying are of all ages but predominantly those in middle and old age and that very special group, the infants and young children.

We see from the table that 1838 deaths were 343,000 and 236,000 people married. The difference of 107,000 carries some indication of infant mortality and is 31% of the deaths. Deaths in that year were 2.2% of the population. By 1899 the deaths were 581,000 and 524,000 married. The figures have come much closer together. The difference of 57,000 is only 10% of all deaths. Deaths had fallen to 1.8% of the population. This is a big drop. In a static population a crude death rate of 1.5% represents an average life expectation of 67 years. 2.2% represents 45 years.

Even allowing that those marrying are a different generation from those dying, a different "cohort" in demographic terms, that common law marriages are ignored, and that there are deficiencies in the figures, the figures must reflect the large drop in infant child mortality. This was the period when Pasteur reported his discovery of germs (1864) and Joseph Lister was taking this discovery much further with his work in antisepsis (1860s and 1870s).

When similar calculations are made *annually* from the BDM table it appears that mortality gradually but irregularly fell between 1838 and about 1893 and then dropped very sharply for the final six years of the 1800s. Historians ascribe the sudden drop to improved knowledge and cleanliness practices among doctors and midwives, thanks largely to the work of Joseph Lister. Women's movements in the 1890s began to speak out against large families. Economic changes played a part. Several factors combined to bring about major change at this time, not only in Britain but in Europe and the USA.

Surprisingly the BDM table shows low points in deaths in 1845 and 1850 and one might be tempted to ask if these were particularly kind years. But no, they weren't. 1845 had an arctic spell of weather from 27th January to 21st March, with the coldest February for fifty years and 1850 was a wet, cold season with poor harvests. Knowing what we now do about omissions in the records, we could think that some of these bitter and snow-swept times led to under-registration of both births and infant mortality. If we had the birth and death registrations available in more detail, broken between urban and rural, it would be interesting to correlate the figures with severe and mild winters.

Births and deaths

The record of births is curious. They rose by 91% between 1838 and 1876, an average increase of 1.7% each year. Then growth suddenly and abruptly declined. Births in 1899 were only 4.4% higher than 23 years earlier in 1876, a tiny average increase of 0.19% each year. The steady rise in births up to 1876 was immediately followed by fourteen years in which the level of births was static. Average annual births for the years 1877 to 1890 was 888,000, exactly the same as in 1876 and 1877. This is clearly shown in the graph at the end of this chapter.

The sudden cessation of growth from 1876 seems very much at odds with the 1875 introduction of penalties for non-registration of births. One might have expected births to jump suddenly when the penalty was introduced rather than suddenly ceasing to grow at all. The continuity of the graph does seem to suggest that birth registration must have been largely total by the 1870s. A less charitable interpretation could be that the penalty for non-registration had no impact at all on peoples' failure to register.

It is said that births in some areas of the country were under-registered by around 15% between 1837 and 1860. If so, then the very steady line of births in the graph should perhaps start a little higher in 1838 and merge gradually with the existing line over 30 years or so. It is perhaps hardly surprising that some births went unregistered when there were costs for late registration (and some birth dates were "adjusted" to avoid the penalties).

Deaths are understandably more erratic than births, reflecting major epidemics and health problems. The graph shows a very decidedly ragged line for deaths compared with the smoother lines for births and marriages.

Deaths grew much more slowly than births, 71% overall in 61 years, or just under one percent per year. In the same period the total population rose by about 111% so that deaths steadily fell as a proportion of population, from about 23 per thousand of population to 18 per thousand in 1899.

There was so much migration, both within the British Isles as a whole and outside the country, that there is no simple relationship between births, deaths and population movement. These figures are quoted simply to give a very general impression. As it happens, adding the net increase from births and deaths for the period 1838-1899 to the estimated 1837 population produces a figure only about 700,000 higher than the census population in 1899.

If, however, we look at 10-year intercensal periods from 1841 to 1901 we do get a rather different picture. Intercensal growth is growth in population between two censuses (as shown in the table at the end of this chapter) and natural increase is the difference between births and deaths in the same period. It is the change in population you would expect if no one moved.

Population changes 1841 to 1901
(000s)

Period	Intercensal growth	Natural increase
1841-51	2013	1724
1851-61	2139	2261
1861-71	2646	2703
1871-81	3262	3412
1881-91	3028	3654
1891-1901	3525	3581

From 1851 onwards the figures suggest a steady drift of net migration out of the country, simply because total population failed to match the calculated natural increase. Between 1841 and 1851 we had the reverse, population growing faster than the apparent natural increase. This is where the probable under registration of births lies. It is very likely that births should have been at least 400,000 more in that period, perhaps as much as 500,000 more. This would increase births by some ten per cent and bring the apparent natural increase up to around 2.1 to 2.2 millions for that decade, enough to allow for some emigration to the antipodes.

Going back just a little further to 1837, it is clear from our table of births, deaths and marriages (and from the graph) that annual recorded births were only about 140,000 higher than recorded deaths between 1837 and 1841, yet the population rose by 840,000 in those four years, an increase of 210,000 a year. We can reasonably suppose that births may have been under-registered by 70,000 to 100,000 a year. This could bring the total shortfall in the recorded births for the period 1837 to 1851 to between 700,000 and 900,000. It is probably reasoning along these lines that lies behind the official statement about births being under-recorded, though net migration into and out of England and Wales makes any such estimates very uncertain.

If the proposals for filming original registers are adopted by ONS it will be interesting to see how far some of the BDM statistics may alter.

Marriages

Marriages grew quite slowly and steadily from 1838 to 1879 (including a small decline in the later 1870s so that in 1879 there were the same number as in 1870). This was an overall growth in marriages of 54 per cent in those 41 years, only just over 1% a year. Then to 1899 the numbers grew faster, another 44% in 20 years, or about 1.85% a year. This brought total growth to about 120% for 1838 to 1899, just a little more than the growth in population, reflecting an age structure becoming a little younger.

Those who have read and absorbed Chapters 1 to 9 may be asking just how accurate the Registrar General's marriage statistics could have been. After all, we know that many marriages were not in the quarterly returns so that the Registrar General can hardly have been aware of them. Many marriages were submitted twice and arrived in the records for two quarters and in the indexes without apparent detection. Many marriages are in the record and in the index twice in a single quarter. Many marriages failed to be indexed, as did many individuals. Many other individuals were indexed twice or more.

Consider this table :

Marriages 1838 to 1844		(000s)
	Published	Indexed
1838	118	124
1839	123	128
1840	123	128
1841	122	125
1842	119	124
1843	124	127
1844	132	135

By way of comparison with the official figures for marriages I have tried to make an approximate count of the number of entries recorded in the marriage index for a short series of years, 1837 to 1844. For the purpose of this comparison I have simply divided the index entries by two to make them equivalent to notional married couples, creating the foregoing table. In the table the index entries are compared with the Registrar General's figures of marriages from the table at the start of the chapter.

The index-derived figures are consistently higher than the Registrar General's figures, by some 3.5% over the seven year period, or the equivalent of about 30,000 marriages. We know that there could easily be at least 1000 to 2000 marriages a year that failed to get into the quarterly returns. Equally we know that large numbers of marriages or individuals failed to be indexed or were lost from the indexes in the typing process. Thus the GRO figures should be higher because of the missing quarterly returns but the index figures should be even higher as the result of all three factors. The difference between the resulting figures would be greater than shown and this should be some mix of marriages submitted twice and individuals indexed twice.

When we come to 1891 we find that the index-based estimate is equivalent to just over 228,000 marriages, compared with 227,000 in the table of births, deaths and marriages. My files suggest that index entries are probably still inflated by at least 1% by way of variant indexing. Removing these would give an estimate of about 225,500 marriages recorded in the 1891 indexes. There is reason to believe that the Registrar General's estimate of the number of marriages is based on a count of the marriages in each bundle, quite independently of the indexing operation. Therefore these figures could imply that around 1500 marriages are in the bundles for the 1891 marriages but have somehow been lost in the indexing or typing processes. At the same time it is also possible that the quarterly returns have continued to be deficient. In fact it would be surprising if they were perfect. Therefore the gap in our knowledge could be the greater to that extent.

I hasten to say that all this is highly speculative. I have not carried out the same analysis for the 1890s as for the 1840s. It would take at least another year or two of work and another visit to Southport to make a more informed judgement possible.

Seasonal patterns

Chapter 4 commented on the seasonal pattern found in East Anglian marriages in 1843 and 1844. Counting the early index entries for comparison with the Registrar General's statistics was a good excuse for looking at seasonal patterns again. Counting was done on the basis of surnames starting with each letter of the alphabet. Not surprisingly, the patterns were almost identical for each letter. One of the graphs at the end of this chapter shows the distinctive patterns that emerged for 1838 to 1842, quarter by quarter, for those initials yielding large numbers of surnames. Patterns for the other surnames have been omitted to avoid cluttering the graph but all were similar.

There is a clearly repeating annual pattern, few marriages in the March quarter, a peak in the June quarter, a small drop to the September quarter and a very strong peak in the December quarter. The graph extends to 1842 but the same pattern certainly continues for a good while after that. The average pattern of marriages by quarter for the five-year period 1838 to 1842 is as follows :

March quarter	20.6%
June quarter	25.6%
September quarter	23.6%
December quarter	30.2%

I traced this same pattern through to 1844 and then picked up the quarterly figures again in 1891. *By that time the early pattern had disappeared.* Two elements remained, March as the lowest quarter and December the highest, but there was now a smooth curve joining the two. The distinctive and repeating ups and downs of the early pattern had gone by 1891 and the overall seasonality was also rather less. Economic and social development must have reduced the pressures that dictated the pattern in earlier days. The pattern shown by 1891 is as follows :

March quarter	21.7%
June quarter	23.3%
September quarter	25.9%
December quarter	29.1%

As marriages were growing at 1.85% a year over this period, the December quarter would be expected to be 1.5% higher than the March quarter even if there was no seasonality as such. Here, however, the December quarter has some 34 per cent more marriages than the March quarter. This is less marked than the 46% difference in the early years but there' is still a very strong seasonal peak in the fourth quarter.

Notice from the graphs that surnames beginning with B, H, W, C, M, P, G, R occupy virtually the same relative positions in these two periods. There has been no change in the pattern of names in that respect over a 50-year period. The same is broadly true of surnames beginning with the other letters of the alphabet. The same is definitely *not* true of given names, as Chapter 14 shows.

The total population

The total population of England and Wales rose from a little over eight millions in 1801 to exceed thirty millions by the end of the century. I have interpolated the approximate figures for 1837, 1838, 1876 and 1899, years needed in the discussion. It is a sobering thought that when civil registration began in 1837 the population of England and Wales was only about fifteen millions and when we take our researches back beyond 1800 we come to a country peopled by eight millions and less.

Population of England and Wales

Census year	Date	Population	Day
1801	March 10	8,892,536	Tuesday
1811	May 27	10,164,256	Monday
1821	May 28	12,000,236	Monday
1831	May 30	13,896,797	Monday
1837 est		15,074,257	
1838 est		15,279,980	
1841	June 7	15,914,148	Monday
1851	March 31	17,927,148	Monday
1861	April 8	20,066,224	Monday
1871	April 3	22,712,266	Monday
1876 est		24,288,647	
1881	April 4	25,974,439	Monday
1891	April 6	29,002,525	Monday
1899 est		31,790,062	
1901	April 1	32,527,843	Monday

The estimates for 1837, 1838, 1876 and 1899 are interpolated on the basis of the average growth rate within the decade concerned.

The population of Greater London was 1.1 million in 1801 and by 1901 it was 6.6 million, an increase of 500%. The population of England and Wales as a whole grew by 266% in the same period. The cities were growing fast.

A sidelight on regional change

The first table in this chapter shows that marriages in England and Wales rose by 43% in the thirty five years from 1856 to 1891. This hides a very uneven pattern of change in different areas. The page range tables in appendices 3 and 4 are limited to the *March* quarters of 1856 and 1891 but they do give a hint of regional differences through the changes in the number of pages taken up by each GRO volume.

They suggest that marriages were largely unchanged in these thirty five years in East Anglia (volumes 4a and 4b) and in the whole of the West Country (volumes 5a, 5b, 5c and 6a). North Wales (vol 11b) declined in this period.

Even in the London area the change seems very uneven, with much the greatest change being seen in the Surrey corner.

The strongest growth in marriages seems to have been in the industrial areas covered by volumes 8, 9 and 10, plus very strong growth in South Wales (volume 11a). Even in the north the change seems to have been patchy. In volume 9d, for example, all the growth seems to have been accounted for by Hull, Sculcoates and Middlesborough.

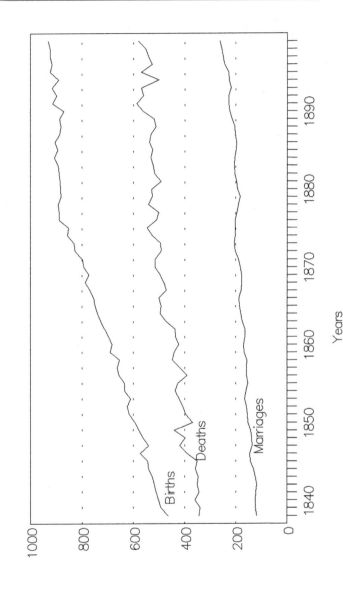

Births, deaths and marriages 1838 to 1899

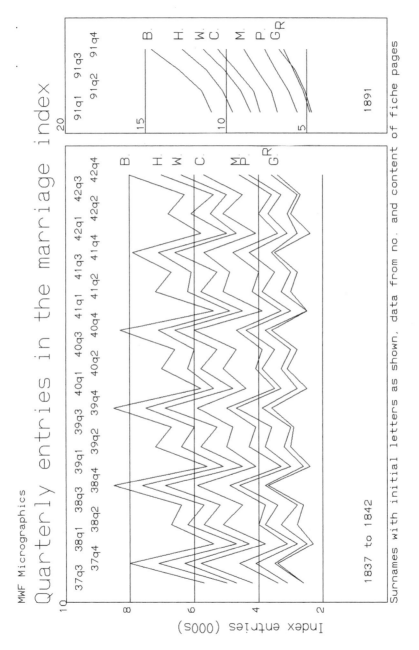

Chapter 11 - Quality and Completeness
of fiche and film

Most users of the births, deaths and marriages indexes make use of them in the form of microfiche and microfilm, the form held in libraries and family history centres around the world. Problems of quality and completeness are outlined in this chapter. There are also in Chapter 12 some hints that may help solve some of the problems.

Parts of the indexes are in the original handwritten form. Other parts are in typescript, in formats and type sizes that have varied over the years.

The handwritten index

The handwritten index can present some beautifully written clear text but it also has some horrifyingly difficult material, arising almost entirely from the process of filming it. There are great differences in legibility between the formats that can be found. Sometimes one can read parts in one format that are illegible in the other.

The most widely used form of the fiche/film is the index published by the General Register Office, a negative print in which the writing is a white text on a dark background. Some of it is excellent but it is also possible to meet frames (i.e. the picture of one index page) in which the white image is so faint or fuzzy that little can be read. Fragments of text can be visible but names and references may be impossible to decipher. In such problem areas it is often found that the upper half of a frame is much worse than the lower half. There is also a tendency for the column of page references on the right hand side of the frame to be particularly hard to read, especially the final digits.

Film or fiche with a positive print, black or dark text on a white or light ground, is also found. This is not the GRO fiche but a filming of the index by the LDS. For the most part the LDS fiche is very sharp and clear, showing text in much finer detail than the GRO fiche. Any bad pages in this format seem to have a black smoke screen over parts of a frame. This can sometimes be the more frustrating of the two problems because you can see there is some text but it simply can't be read.

It seems to be the negative fiche that can provide some of the worst problems in identifying page references, reasons for this being firstly the style of script of some of the clerks, secondly the difference in contrast between bold strokes of the pen and finer strokes and thirdly a difference in procedure when the photography was carried out. The photographic process in the negative fiche can sometimes miss the finer strokes completely and make a figure look like something different. This can make it extremely hard to pick a 3 and a 5, and sometimes an 8. Sometimes an 8 looks like a 1 because the strongest stoke is vertical and the rest of the figure is invisible.

Often it is only the downstroke of a 7 or 9 that is seen, or maybe the downstroke of a 9 is invisible and the remainder looks like a 0. Sometimes a 0 is written with almost no fullness and therefore looks like a 1. Sometimes the cross-stroke of a 4 is bold but the rest is faint and the bold stroke is then shown up as a 1. Sometimes the downstroke of a 7 or 9 can only be picked up as a bold segment at the tip of its tail, easily missed because it looks more like part of the following page reference, but the figure is unable to be identified as a 7 or a 9. Sometimes the downstroke can only be detected because its interference with the following page number gives it away.

With the greatest difficulty I have been able to resolve some uncertainties only after a compilation of a whole quarter has shown pages with an uneven gender balance. Then a careful recheck of references for those particular index entries can sometimes (but not always) allow a figure to be altered and pages rebalanced. This is not a remedy open to a normal user of the index but it has made some of my files much more accurate than the published index material. After all, I was sometimes looking at, say, five particular names in the index knowing that one reference must be wrong, and often with a good idea of what that reference might be. Sometimes all five names have still looked much I first read them, but perhaps now four of them are undoubtedly right and one offers the smallest ground for suspicion and must be wrong. As a result my files have proved to be surprisingly accurate.

The biggest surprise in making some of these checks has been the contrast in legibility at times between the two different sources. One entry was almost unbelievable. It is from the 1849/Q1 fiche. The entry for Hannah Valentine was sharp and clear in the GRO fiche as Manchester vol 20 page 44. It was a certain error in the page number because it put the entry in the Ashton section of volume 20 and the Manchester entries are from page 315 upwards. When I checked some of these entries in the black-on-white film at a Family History Centre of the Latter Day Saints it was startling to see the page reference very clearly as 448. This put Hannah neatly in a waiting gap. The negative fiche entry was sharp and clear and without the slightest hint or trace to show that a third figure had been missed, yet the black-on-white film showed a 3-digit figure that was sharp, clear and complete. It is hard to see how any photographic process could have been capable of such different results.

It was tempting to feel that these filmings were of two copies of the original registers. One register is held in London and one in Southport. A careful check of some frames from the GRO index with the matching frames in the LDS index has made it quite clear that they are from the same original. There are marks in both versions that clearly make them identical The LDS version is generally very much clearer and sharper and shows the script in all its detail. There is evidence by way of annotations on the original that the LDS filming is later than the GRO filming so it may well have benefited from later technology. Nevertheless the LDS film does have its bad patches, some smudges of sooty darkness and some loss of definition where the GRO image is actually sharper. All the same, the parts that I could check are clearly from the same source.

A very distinctive feature of the LDS filming is the wide gutter between the pairs of pages, i.e. the wide space on the inner edge of the leaves. The GRO index has very little gutter and this is a reason for the poor quality of many page references. The register was opened out very fully for the LDS filming, apparently almost back to the inner edges of the leaves. Therefore the page references on the verso pages were based on the filming of paper lying flat, unlike the GRO filming where the inner edges of the verso pages disappear back into the spine. Another difference is that the GRO filming was of each page separately. The LDS filming was of the entire two-page opening of the register, lying almost perfectly flat. The LDS filming used better procedures and almost certainly had better technology.

Which register was filmed ? There is a little definite evidence by way of pencil markings in the original registers held at Southport that confirm them as the source of the filming. These same markings can be seen in the fiche copies. This is not proof that the Southport copies are the source of *all* the fiche and film, but certainly of some of it.

Some questions on the original index registers remain unanswered (or incompletely so) and they are questions well worth asking. Of these two vast sets of register books, one must surely be a copy of the other. This book has already shown only too clearly the extent of the errors and omissions in the copying processes elsewhere in the system. Which of the two primary registers (assuming that there are just two) is the original and which is the copy ? How many errors or omissions may there be in the copy ? What might readily be found by taking a few of the Southport volumes down to Myddelton House in London and reading them through in parallel with the other set ? It would take time but I believe it could be well worth while. I know that some corrections (not always successfully) have been made to the registers at Southport. Have all the same alterations been made to the London copies ? Have the over-inked amendments (page 79) been made in both copies ? Because they were restoring worn figures they wouldn't be needed in both - when sometimes "restored" in error, the other copy would have shown up the error. Some of the GRO fiche is clearly filmed from the Southport register but some of the manuscript fiche very clearly shows the tattered and worn corners of pages that must surely have been in long use in the public search room in London. Is this so ? Questions, more questions.

Perhaps the one interpretative advantage of the manuscript index over the typed version is that the surnames are all written out, not just the first occurrence of a particular name but all of them. Otherwise there would be large groups of names that you could never identify at all.

The typewritten index

The typewritten index on fiche and film has at least three or four different layouts.

The earliest typing of parts of the index in the 1830s and 1840s was in a large type that is very readable even in fiche and film. As already described, the typing created additional errors in the index but in terms of legibility it is good. Frames are not consistent but are generally around 76 lines to the frame, two columns of typescript to a frame.

The slightly tighter format adopted in the 1840s has 84 lines to the frame. Most is still very readable although there are occasional spots where there is some loss of focus and text may blend together and be hard to be sure of.

The typing in the later years of the 1800s became much tighter and much harder to read. The layout changed from two columns to three on a page and the number of lines to a frame increased to 125 giving 375 entries on each fiche or film frame. The quality of reproduction is often much poorer and a fiche reader can sometimes be refocussed fruitlessly in trying to get a clearer image. Either the filming or the printing is not sharp.

Some of the type-face in this later material seems fragile, a little like some of the rub-down lettering systems in that some parts of a character seem to break and move. It recreated some of the problems in distinguishing between particular digits. Even with long experience it can be almost impossible to distinguish 1 and 4, the latter being virtually a straight line with often the barest projection to hint that it may be a 4. Sometimes there is nothing whatever in shape or size to suggest a 4. It is often very easy to mistake a 5 for a 6. Sometimes a 3 is quite well formed but often the bicuspid form is scarcely suggested. If there is any deformation of figures like 8 and 0 they can be very hard to distinguish. A badly focussed page can be very hard indeed. My page range table has often been the only way to make a decision.

In my 18000 entries extracted for 1891/Q1, over 400 have had to be noted as queries, page references unable to be read with certainty. This number is conservative. Some references were taken for what I thought they were but may yet prove otherwise. I always hope to resolve some of the options when an extraction exercise is completed. If the queries are too numerous it can become impossible. With this uncertainty and possible error, between ten and twenty percent of all pages in my 1891/Q1 marriage record may not show up on completion as balanced pages in my files, i.e. as pages having exactly one or two marriages. This would be a much higher level of doubt than in any of the other exercises, whether from manuscript or typed indexes.

As earlier chapters have made clear, the typed indexes are also, and not surprisingly so, much more error-laden than the handwritten indexes.

Because of some of the discoveries of errors in the typing, I've now become more suspicious of possible gaps. In 1891/Q1, for example, there is a jump from Mary Emma Williamson to Richard Eldred Williamson. A surname such as Williamson tends to have around a hundred entries in the index and you might well expect a few names such as Matthew, Peter, Philip and Phoebe, perhaps a few Mary combinations higher than Mary Emma. But suspicion is one thing, proof is another thing altogether. Proof involves entering the rest of the 99,000 1891/Q1 names and then checking the sorted names against the thirty three GRO marriage films for the quarter. The effort is huge, another year's work overall, the outcomes may well be revealing but they are uncertain. That is the nature of this sort of research. It can't be comprehensive. It is based on samples. This is the practical reason why the GRO can have little real idea of the true quality of the records or the indexes.

Missing Fiche

The published fiche of the BDM indexes in libraries is unfortunately not complete. Either in the filming process or in the printing process some frames of the material have failed to appear. Thanks to the efforts of Philip Jones in Nottinghamshire we now have in Wellington some thirty four photocopied pages of the marriage index for 1856/Q4, 1858/Q4 and 1861/Q2, and the New Zealand National Library has also been able to obtain similar copies of some further pages that were later discovered to be missing.

These omissions alone amount to nearly 1600 names. Are there likely to be many more ? The answer is "undoubtedly yes". The evidence seems to point to a decided lack of quality control in the production of the GRO fiche.

Take as an example the marriage indexes for 1864. In this part of the index we are dealing with the handwritten version, with forty names to each handwritten index page and thus to each frame of the fiche.

In 1864/Q1 the production seems to have been in rather cautious hands. Eight fiche frames are printed twice without any apparent need or difference in quality. Sheet no.1691, covering names from Thomas Weaver to John Wood, has been reprinted identically as sheet no.1692, all 98 frames of it.

In 1864/Q2 the fiche is perfectly regular and complete until it starts the names that begin with S. The frame between Ellen Salisbury and Ann Salt is missing. Names like Salmon will be fished for in vain in Q2.

In 1864/Q3 the situation is sadly deficient. No less than fourteen frames fail to appear in the fiche as published, scattered from the beginning to the end of the alphabet. This means approximately 560 names, perhaps a few more if they include late insertions. The missing frames are shown below, identified by the names immediately overlooking both ends of the gaps so that you can see if any of your families are among the victims. The gaps lie between :

> Nora Conway and David Cook
> Jane Gates and Anne Gauntley
> William Stephen Harry and James Hart
> Emma Meredith and William Merry (two frames missing)
> Mary Moore and Sarah Ann Moore
> Ps up to Paddison (e.g. Pace, Pacey, Packer, Packham etc)
> James Potter to Lucy Potton
> William Reeves to William Reiley
> Charles Scoffield to Charles Dalrymple Scott
> Albert George Sharpe to Ann Shaw
> Margaret Sherman to Hannah Shevvein
> Emily Soames to William Somerfield
> Esther Tuckey to Frederic Tull

The fiche for 1864/Q4 is fairly uneventful. Two frames are included twice but there are no omissions.

The total number of names missing from the 1864 marriage fiche is therefore about 600. With 180,000 marriages in the year (see chapter 10), or about 360,000 persons, the omissions amount to one for every 600 names. In terms of my checking against GRO film, these would all be missing individuals.

Very often it is far from obvious that material is missing from the fiche. Take the 1864 gap between Emma Meredith and William Merry as an example. One fiche frame ends with :

| Meredith | Emma | Ross | 6a | 795 |

and the next begins with :

| Merry | William | Liverpool | 8b | 612 |

Here there is gap of two frames or eighty names but both names begin with Mer.. and the gap isn't as obvious as one might expect. The page numbering shows Emma on p178 and William on 181. Neighbouring fiche shows that the gap probably held another 15-20 Meredith entries, followed by names such as Merrall, Merrell, Merrells, Merrett, Merrick, Merrill, Merriman and perhaps another ten Merrys.

What about another year ? What about 1865 ? 1865/Q1 shows three frames printed twice. 1865/Q3 shows complete regularity. 1865/Q2 has no less than 21 fiche frames printed twice and one frame printed three times. Three frames have been missed, lying between :

> Isaac Philip Adams and Rachel Adams (one frame)
> John Innoles and Andrew Little Irving (two frames)

1865/Q4 has three repeated frames, plus a batch of three frames repeated as a group, but also has three missing frames, lying between :

> Maria Shiner and Cord Shlobohn (two frames)
> James Wells and Sarah Wells (one frame)

Thus we have at least another 240 names missing from the 1865 index.

Some of these examples of gaps would have been impossible to spot without the aid, not always present, of page numbering in the index register. Sometimes each page is numbered. Sometimes only recto pages are numbered 1, 2, 3, 4 etc leaving verso pages unnumbered. Sometimes every other recto page is numbered 1, 2, 3, 4 etc, leaving three pages unnumbered. When some of the numbering is so faint that it is invisible on a fiche reader it is very hard to follow the sequence well enough to pick up gaps in pages.

I had expected that omissions would be few and far between and that a long day of searching might have nothing to show for it but the search has proved rather more eventful. Nevertheless it is still another tedious process.

Third time lucky ? Perhaps trying a third year from the marriage index might find a fault-free fiche ? How about changing direction, back to 1863 ?

Yes, the checks started well. Q1 and Q2 were trouble-free, just a couple of harmless repeat frames. Q3, though, turned out to be hard work. Only the recto pages, i.e. the odd-numbered pages, are numbered and very faintly.

Much care was needed, a lot of counting of pages, quite a lot of back-tracking, sometimes a run of ten or twenty pages between legible page numbers. The page numbering of the index register is also erratic in places, jumping forward ten numbers, jumping back in another place. If I had started this little checking exercise with 1863 instead of 1864 I might well have given up at this point. The legibility of the fiche is so poor in some places that it was hard to be sure if a page might be missing or not.

Identifiable gaps have nevertheless been found, between :

> John Fennel and Ann Fenwick (Fenner, Fenton etc ?)
> Elizabeth Jane Green and Henry Green
> Catherine Hughes and Emma Hughes (all those Davids and Edwards)
> "I" entries up to Mary Iley (Ibbotson, Iken etc)
> Mary Johnston and William Jolley
> William Stewart and Henry James Stillwell (missing Stiles, Still etc)
> William Whittaker and Richard Whittington (missing several Whitt names)

The fiche for Q4 proved better in many respects, more legible, better numbered, but it still had two examples of missing fiche frames, between :

> Elizabeth Freebury and James Freeman
> William Henry Murrey and James Musselwhite

Thus we have at least nine frames missing from the fiche and therefore at least another 360 names

Just for good measure, I happened to notice a gap in the marriage index fiche for the March quarter of 1862 when looking for something else. This is a gap of one frame lying between :

> Hannah Gepps and John Gibbons.

This would cover names like Gerrard and the earlier Gibbons. I decided to check the rest of 1862/Q1 but found no more problems. Likewise 1862/Q2 was troublefree, apart from some erratic page numbering. 1862/Q3 proved to be another scene of desolation. Not only is the page numbering erratic but a total of eleven frames are missing from the fiche. They lie between :

Frederick Bland and Eliza Blayney
The Ds before Sarah Dagnall
Eliza Mallett and Betsey Malpus (such as Mallinson
    and Malone)
Timothy Murphy and Jane Murray
The Ps before John Paddison (Pace, Pacey, etc)
William Rhoades and Mary Frost Rich
Hannah Robson and Christopher John Rodgers
    (two frames)
John Wallis and Elizabeth Walmsley
William Harrison Wilson and Sophia Sarah Winch
    (names such as Wilton and Wiltshire)
Sarah Winter and Richard Wippell

In the last-named gap there are names like Winterbottom rather aptly left out in the cold. It is also unfortunate that the first frame of surnames beginning with "P" is missing, as it is from the fiche for 1864/Q3, a double injury for those looking for Pace and Pacey and similar names. All the Packers have been sent packing from both fiche.

A novel and successful technique was used in 1877 to achieve the loss of forty five names from the marriage index. This must have involved misplacing the negative during printing, or perhaps masking part of it. This part of the index has three columns of 125 names and the lower fifteen names in each column of one page have been blocked out. The three missing groups of fifteen names lie between :

Schlerer (very hard to read) and Arthur Schofield
Andrew Scott and Eliza Matilda Scott
Anna Elizabeth Scotts and William Scrivener

From the point of view of researchers, these numerous large gaps in the fiche have to be added to gaps in the typing of the indexes, gaps in the primary indexing, and gaps in the quarterly returns from the parishes. I have a beautifully preserved Victorian penny dated 1864. Would Her Majesty have been amused or otherwise if she knew what was happening to her records ?

Fiche of index material where the original register pages are not numbered is really impossible to check. Each pair of pages have to be checked and every possible or probable gap has to be checked against other fiche to see that enough names would be in that space to confirm an actual gap. It would be a long slow process. The 1857 marriage index is such a case, with no page numbering in the March and June quarters. The September and December quarters do have page numbers, faintly and with several aberrations. From these quarters we can note four more gaps between frames :

Q3   K surnames before John Kavanagh (1 frame)
        Ann Nicholls to Susan Nicholls
        Joseph Smith to Maria Henderson Smith
Q4   John Boyce to Mary Emily Boyle

All these gaps show that no checking took place when fiche were produced. It is also strange that with these indexes in constant use right round the world there has been no apparent detection of many of the gaps or only very limited action to repair some of the gaps that have been found. The indexes are also in constant use in the GRO, checking requests for certificates, and one could wonder at the absence of action there. The explanation for that situation may simply be that little checking at the GRO is needed for names in the missing fiche frames because requests for those names would be few and almost all would arise from researchers using the original registers in London. As those are more legible there would rarely be a need to check the references given in applications.   The resemblance to a "comedy of errors" appears to have grown another facet.

The patchiness of the gaps and duplications in the fiche frames suggests very strongly that at least two or three clerks were involved in the filming process and that they were not equally reliable.

There are reports that the positive-print microfilm, black text on white ground, filmed by the LDS, contains entries omitted from the film and fiche that have been bought by libraries in general. I have not been able to check any specific examples because I have had no access to films corresponding to fiche with known omissions but it is now obvious that the proposition is bound to be true, if only because it would be impossible for two different products to omit the same frames. The more gaps one finds in the GRO fiche, the more certain the proposition becomes.

How could we reliably detect all omitted frames ? Much of the fiche has no page numbering and it is hard to find gaps without it. It would be simple for the ONS to make a direct comparison of the physical index registers and the GRO fiche. Where the register sheets are numbered and the numbers are visible in the fiche it is a quick process, between one and two hours to check the fiche for a year. If page numbers are not available the time would expand at least 10-fold or 20-fold, each fiche frame having to be checked.

Gaps in fiche would surely occur for births and deaths as well as marriages. All would need to be checked As readers will appreciate, the amount of work that could potentially be put into examining the indexes for errors is almost unlimited.

I had not put any time into checking the fiche for births and deaths but my conscience finally pricked me. There could be a sceptical reader doubtful about accepting such assertions without some positive evidence. Having an hour or so to spare, I picked the deaths index for 1860 out of the fiche drawer at the library and worked through it.

Past half way through the March quarter and the sceptical reader might perhaps be right after all. Then I found a gap of one frame between :

Charles Read and John Read

Charles from Norwich and John from Mutford in Suffolk were not too far apart in terms of distance but they are certainly forty names apart in the index.

The June quarter proved to be complete, apart from some erratic page numbering of the index pages.

The September quarter revealed another gap, the frame between :

Edna Johnson and Frederick Johnson

a space normally occupied by Eliza, Elizabeth, Ellen, Emily, Fanny, Frances and Francis. Then came a gap of four frames, lying between :

Sarah Ann Salt and John Sanderson.

It is only when you look at the fiche for other quarters that you realise the extent of such an innocuous looking gap. It would normally contain large numbers of names such as Salter, Sambrook, Sampson, Samuel, Samuels and Sanders, plus the early Sandersons. Gaps in the fiche are not at all obvious unless you are deliberately looking for them.

The December quarter was complete, but we have 240 missing names for the year as a whole. In total, for five years of the marriage index and one year of the deaths index we have over three and a half thousand omissions, plus two punctured quarters of 1857. It would look conservative to say there may be at least 300 names missing annually from all fiche of hand-written indexes.

Of all the years' indexes that I have checked for possible gaps, *not one single year* has come up with a clean bill of health. If an official check is made on the completeness of all the GRO fiche, it would then be possible for ONS to make up a set of a few fiche with the missing frames for the benefit of the thousands of customers worldwide who have copies of the material.

Chapter 12 - Hints for the reading of
difficult fiche and film

There are techniques that can help with some of the problems in reading handwritten parts of the index and one that can help in the typewritten parts.

The Page Range Table

Appendices 1 - 4 present four tables based on the main segments of this marriage index study, namely the first (March) quarters of 1844, 1849, 1856 and 1891. They show the page ranges occupied by the marriages for each Superintendent Registrar's district. In other words they show the page ranges of marriages from those districts in the GRO marriage films for those quarters. They display the structure of the record system. The table for 1891 is incomplete, based on less than twenty percent of index entries for that quarter. Therefore there are small discontinuities between some of the page ranges. These will gradually fill up as the entries are completed.

The tables show very clearly the alphabetical arrangement of districts within their county groups in the 27-volume structure, and the new arrangement based more on contiguity in the 33-volume structure.

The tables were built up gradually within this project as index entries were captured. They were invaluable in deciphering bad page references. Usually they can narrow your options for an indistinct page reference. Sometimes they can answer a question completely. For example a Peterborough entry in 1856/Q1 beginning with a 2 must be in the narrow range 297 to 299. More often they will give you at least a clue but a less precise one.

You won't normally be able to apply these particular tables exactly because page ranges vary from quarter to quarter but if you need to decide an indistinct page reference for a particular index entry then the table can often give you a good guide. It is easy to look quickly around the nearby fiche/film for a few readable page numbers for the same district. These should suggest an approximate range. The very fact that you have seen and appreciated the significance of the Page Range Tables can help in working with the index.

As chapter 10 shows, marriages were seasonal, highest in Q4 and lowest in Q1. This makes the GRO films longer in Q4 than in Q1 and extends all the page ranges. Appendix 5 illustrates this by showing Essex/Suffolk page ranges for the four quarters of 1844. Notice that although Q4 marriages were about 124% more than in Q1, the page range itself was only 56% greater.

Many of the extra marriages mean more entries per page rather than a simple increase in the number of pages.

Sometimes you will find you can read the page number in the marriage index, more or less, but the district name escapes you. There may be a visible hint of a letter or two in the name but little more. You may perhaps be fairly certain that the volume number ends in "c". Look through the district names in volumes 1c, 2c, 5c, 6c, 8c and 9c (these are the only "c" volumes) and you may then be able to decide on some possible districts. Now the page number may help you eliminate one or two. The Page Range Table is a detective device. It won't always give you a precise answer but you can use it intelligently to improve your chances.

It has only been possible to build up these few tables from the laborious extraction of index material, the work of many years. It is easy to see that such tables could be written out for every quarter of the system by taking the information straight from the original records of births, deaths and marriages. Complete tables, probably on microfiche, would be an asset in family history workplaces worldwide and would go a very long way, very easily, in helping users of the GRO index material. This suggestion has been put to ONS and is a small project that could be developed there quickly and cheaply.

The Page Range Tables are relevant to all the index material, whether hand-written or in typed form, and equally to births, deaths and marriages.

A marginal peephole

The quality problems with the fiche of the handwritten indexes come from the standard of the copying process. Different versions of the material show text that is wholly illegible in one copy but totally clear in another. The original index registers are very readable for the most part (though not entirely so).

There is a thin ray of hope in some of the fiche, however.

Visualise, if you will, one of the original index registers lying open on a table. The index was written continuously on the back and front of each page. The open register shows two pages, running alphabetically down the left-hand page and then down the right-hand page, the verso and the recto pages.

The filming process for the GRO index would have copied the verso page and then the recto page. The centre line of the register would have been a problem as the edges of the pages dipped into it. This seems to be the main reason for the poor quality of many of the columns of page references, especially the final digits. Our help lies in the fact that the copying sometimes took in a little of the right-hand page when copying the left-hand page and a little of the left-hand page, particularly those vital page references, when copying the right-hand page.

The peephole only helps you with the left-hand page and is found on the left-hand edge of the corresponding recto page. Remember that the peephole will therefore be on the frame *after* the one you are struggling with, if it is there at all. There is obviously no peephole for badly copied right-hand pages. It is usually perfectly clear from the fiche whether you are looking at a picture of a left-hand or of a right-hand page.

Sometimes the little peephole is tantalisingly narrow. It may only allow you to see a trace of a faint line distinguishing a five from a three, or enough of a loop to suggest that a three is actually an eight. Often the peephole is wider at the bottom of the frame and quickly peters out as you move up the page. Sometimes you can read the final digit clearly, sometimes even two and rarely three digits. These peepholes have been invaluable in my research as I have needed to read every reference as well as possible.

Some areas of fiche are well endowed with these helpful embellishments, others are not. The 1856/Q1 marriage index has some good examples in the area of the Barnes entries.

The peephole figures are another proof, if one is needed, that the quality problem lies in the filming. Some peephole figures are crystal clear whereas the primary copy is illegible.

The peephole does not exist in the LDS filming, where the index register was spread virtually flat and both pages were photographed as a single shot.

Prints from the fiche

The legibility problem with the negative fiche is very often that the text can be too faint to be read. Often large parts of a page are very black and the text is either completely invisible or too fragmentary to be read.

One attack that has often yielded amazing results is to make a print of a bad page, using a fiche printer set to produce a positive black on white print. To maximise your chances it is often necessary to set the tone control to produce the darkest possible print. There is then a very good chance that some of the faintest parts of the text will emerge well enough to be read or at least to be guessed at. Some fiche is too faint even for this technique but I have succeeded with hundreds of thin images. The lamp used in the printing process is usually far stronger than the lamp used for simply reading the fiche.

This technique can normally only help with handwritten parts of the indexes. Obscure parts of typewritten indexes are more often caused by bad focus or blurry typescript and fiche prints are often harder to read than reading the fiche itself on a good reader.

Lateral thinking

Sometimes the handwritten fiche is so bad that surnames and given names are no more than a few incompletely visible letters. When all else fails, it can be well worth while to try looking at the same alphabetical section in other fiche to find names that are fully readable. Often this gives you valuable clues for the surnames. If you finish up by deciding that there is a run of the same surname, remember that the most common given names are the most likely and see if you can pin down a hint of even one or two. That may help with a few more because they will be in alphabetical order. It may even help you in deciphering district names if think you have a very localised surname. All this is still fairly marginal but it does improve your chances of success. I have sometimes spent an hour on one frame, with a magnifying glass and the best and brightest fiche reader in the row, and all the logical aids including a Page Range Table, and have read more than one might ever think possible.

So you can't find Great Aunt Emily at all ?

We have seen that many marriages failed for a variety of reasons to traverse the path from the marriage register to the GRO index. Some partnerships, of course, failed to get even as far as the marriage register but that is outside the scope of this discussion, save to say that the "marriage" you are looking for may never have taken place at all.

Sometimes the omission in the index is just the bride or just the groom, either not indexed or missed by the typist.

In rather more cases the loss of an individual is not an actual loss by omission, it is a loss because the index entry is wrong. It is more likely that Great Aunt Emily is mis-indexed in some way than that she isn't in the index at all. This can have happened because :

a)   The information given to a vicar or registrar was not what you think it was or what it should have been.

b)   The quarterly copies were either wrong or were so badly written that the name is unrecognisable for what it really is.

c)   The indexing clerk misread the handwritten copy of the marriage entry.

d)   The indexing clerk wrote the name badly in extracting it from the quarterly return so that it became mis-sorted and then mis-entered in the final index.

e)   The indexing clerk made an error in the district name or volume reference so that the entry became one you dismissed as irrelevant.

f)   The index entry may have been mistyped in some way so that you failed to identify it.

When we say that Great Aunt Emily may be mis-indexed, we are not thinking simply or even mainly of names with variant versions like Nicols, Nichols and Nicholls. We need to consider complete transformations of the name.

The name variants discussed in Chapter 6 are useful examples because they can give us an idea of the dramatically different ways in which a name can be mis-read. Here is a small selection :

Crane and Ware (to mention our old friend once again)
Saffin, Jaffin and Taffin (from Taunton)
Pratt and Ball (from Taunton)
French and Trench (from my own research)
Barber and Barker (again mine)
Foster and Poster (again mine)

Huffer and Buffer	Self and Jelf
Hall and Hill	Leney and Seney
Pitt and Tilt	Parritt and Pawitt
McDonald and McDowell	Lard and Law
Hirst and Host	Hatcher and Slatcher
Prue and True	Weekley and Wickley
Butt and Rutt	Linfield and Tinfield
Able and Orble	Land and Laud
Baker and Maker	Jarvis and Tarvis
Flatt and Platt	Howe and Stowe

Most of these examples are taken from just a few of my large collection of sorted index files. I could multiply them very many times. None are in any way conventional variations. They all arise from attempts to interpret badly written names. The indexes are full of highly improbable names. Some are no doubt correct. Many are probably valiant but unsuccessful interpretations.

Initial capital letters were a big problem. Many capitals were written in an elaborate style and were very easily mistaken. Quite often it is hard to decide between, say, "H" and "Sl". It is easy to misread B P and R. Lower case "t" was often not crossed or hardly so and it could be hard to choose between Barrett and Barrell. Lower case "u" and "n" were very often confused.

You will be forced to use your own imagination. One useful technique is to look in a handwritten index at the name you are trying to trace, looking in several indexes to get variations in the script. Even try writing out the name yourself in a similar style, preferably with some sort of broad-nibbed pen. Even try writing it a little carelessly. Try to imagine other letters or letter combinations that could appear similar. Ask someone else to read what you have written. This isn't necessarily going to be easy and it may not succeed but keep in mind that Great Aunt Emily may very well be hiding there somewhere. I have tried this and I have found people.

Some genealogical societies, as in New Zealand, are lucky to have dedicated members who provide an outstanding look-up service for members who can't reach the major libraries themselves. They become very skilled in this work and get the greatest satisfaction from tracking down some of the badly garbled index entries.

Some of the earlier indexes are full of mistyped district names. There is Stow for Stone. There is Ludbury for Sudbury. Not just once but many times. Errors like this have clearly arisen because the handwriting was misread.

It has been one of the advantages of my sorted index files that they have brought all these variant versions of names together, often from the furthest reaches of the alphabetical indexes. It shows that Great Aunt Emily can be far away from where you have been looking (see, too, pages 171-173).

The homophones

Some of the name variants that I have found have been homophones, often very striking. They have happened right through the 1800s.

A few examples are :
>   Hobrow and Hobraugh
>   Clarke and Clerk
>   Knighter and Nighter
>   Shoe and Shew
>   Bowditch and Beauditch

They could perhaps indicate that clerks sometimes worked in pairs, one reading and one writing, but it would be valuable to go back to the original marriage registers in these cases to see just how these variations arose.

For Great Aunt Emily you may do well to try possible homophone versions of her surname.

My files as a research resource

Because of the way my sorted indexes have been built up they have become a research resource in their own right that is often superior for particular segments of time to anything officially published.

- The sorting process has led to the correction of many hard or impossible readings in the index on fiche or film.

- Likewise this process has corrected many errors in index references.

- The use of the page range tables has also resolved many entries that are unreadable in fiche or film.

- The use of both GRO and LDS filmings of the 1849/Q1 index has produced better results than either alone can provide.

- The resolution of some of the very worst index entries by friends visiting London has been a source of further improvements.

- Some of the omissions and errors in the index have been resolved by the research work in Southport.

- The sorted indexes identify thousands of marriage partners immediately and can help with identifying many thousands more.

A few of these files are available as resources on Bulletin Boards but copyright problems can obviously arise with more formal publication. If the proposals of chapter 9 for upgrading the 1800s records are adopted, then that is the ultimate way of achieving a vast improvement in research material. If not, then I will endeavour to explore means of publishing this laboriously constructed and valuable collection of processed indexes.

Whether or not you are fortunate enough to find an objective of your own in these files, they will be a contribution in terms of resolving at least some of the existing problems of legibility and accuracy.

Chapter 13 - Changing district names

The early district names

The first years of civil registration show us a picturesque collection of district names in the indexes, many of which quickly changed or disappeared. Some were perhaps temporary districts that the 1836 legislation made provision for in the setting up of the system. By early in the 1840s the structure of the districts seems to have settled down. If you come across one of the early names with a page reference it may be fairly easy to locate it approximately from the range tables in this book. In many instances the name is related to one of the established districts.

1837 and 1838 offer the largest collection of names that have now changed or have disappeared

St Matthew Bethnal Green	Vol 1
St George Bloomsbury	Vol 1
St Giles in the Fields	Vol 1
Bishopsgate	Vol 2
St Giles Camberwell	Vol 4
St Mary Newington	Vol 4
Wandsworth and Clapham	Vol 4
Gravesend and Milton	Vol 5
Buntingford	Vol 6
Tring	Vol 6
Brighthelmston	Vol 7 (later Brighton)
Chailey	Vol 7
Newhaven	Vol 7
Winchester and Mursley	Vol 7
West Firle	Vol 7
Cricklade and Wootton Bassett	Vol 8
Swindon and Highworth	Vol 8
Westbury and Worwhellsdown	Vol 8
Bosmere and Clayton	Vol 12
Lexden and Winstree	Vol 12
Mitford and Launditch	Vol 13
Loddon and Clarering	Vol 13 (Clavering, dear typist)
Mutford and Lothingland	Vol 13
Tunstead and Happing	Vol 13
Caxton and Arrington	Vol 14
Selsdon	Vol 17
Matlock	Vol 19
The High Peak	Vol 19
Kingston on Hull	Vol 22
Durham and Darlington	Vol 24

Durham and Lanchester	Vol 24
Sedgefield	Vol 24
Alston and Garrigill	Vol 25
Bridgend and Cowbridge	Vol 26
Presteigne and Kington	Vol 26
Newtown and Llanidloes	Vol 27

The names above were found from a brief inspection. No doubt there are many others to be found. Certainly all these names had disappeared or been shortened before 1844, my first countrywide index capture. However the disappearance was often only in terms of the names written in the GRO indexes. The full name of the Superintendent Registrars' districts was still often written in the headings of the quarterly returns, a part of the record that you never see when getting a certificate.

To paint a complete picture of these early district names and how they changed would be a big job. It would be hard to justify building computer files from the 380,000 names in the marriage indexes for 1837 and 1838 simply to satisfy a curiosity. The full picture will emerge, of course, if ONS takes up the suggestion of producing page range tables for the whole system.

The name Swindon-and-Highworth became Swindon but was later replaced by Highworth. The name of Kington disappeared and then reappeared much later in the century as a small district in its own right in volume 6a. Durham and Darlington became two separate districts. The name of Lanchester came into use again later in the 1800s.

In 1839 and 1840 it appears that the marriage records for Bloomsbury and for St George Hanover Square were mixed together. Their page references are not in separate ranges. By 1841 it seems that they may have been separated.

Some old district names do seem to be very durable. The district name of High Peak in Derbyshire is now the title for one of the British Telecom telephone directories. Some of the old county hundreds have taken on a new life in local government, such as Uttlesford as the name for the district council centred on Saffron Walden in Essex.

If the proposals for creating a new record system are adopted, then many of these old district names would probably disappear from the index system altogether. A new index based on a filming of the original registers may have to adopt a reference system based on the Superintendent Registrars' districts in which those registers are now held rather than the districts to which they may have originally belonged.

Errors in passing

Even in this very cursory survey of the first few indexes there were spelling errors or indexing errors to be noticed in passing and a very liberal sprinkling of typing errors (there are more and more indications that the early typed indexes are badly flawed). A few examples are :

> Ronbridge in vol 5, an error for Tonbridge
> Seisdon in vol 17, an error for Selsdon
> Ongag in vol 12, an error for Ongar
> Glendall in vol 24, an error for Glendale
> Horley in vol 16, an error for Henley
> Bishop Strotford in vol 6, an error for Stortford
> Newth Tyne in vol 24, an error for the usual Newtle Tyne

A Manchester entry in 1837 was indexed to volume 19 instead of 20. As the typing was from early manuscript, this is possibly a mistype of XIX for XX and is a more likely error on that basis. The spelling of Clavering (above) was a certain slip, probably in the later typing. We see Wemborne for Wimborne, Medhurst for Midhurst, Erpenham for Erpingham. These typing slips in the early material are more significant than they appear. Typing errors in district names should never really happen. They create fears for the quality of the typing in general and I do intend some more work in this area of the indexes. Further, the evidence of errors points all the time to a lack of checking procedures in the system.

Other changes in the 1840s

Even between 1844/Q1 and 1849/Q1 there were a few changes in districts, as shown by the Page Range Tables in Appendices 1 and 2. Districts found in 1849 but not in 1844 are Hampstead (volume 3), Farnborough (volume 4), Fleggs (volume 13) and Hunslet (volume 23). The district of Fleggs is to be found in the 1837 indexes.

Hampstead is still only a tiny district in 1849 and the page numbers suggest that the Registrar General probably divided it off from Edmonton. In general, though, one can't read too much into the numbers of marriages for individual quarters. The statistics are too variable and many of the Superintendent Registrars' districts are really very small. There are many with a range of ten pages or less and this often implies that the quarterly return would have consisted of four or five sheets with only one or two marriages on each.

Although most of the volumes in 1849 are distinctly longer than in 1844, a few are shorter and it is quite a surprise that Manchester, the largest of all the districts, grew very little. As we can see from the figures in chapter 10, marriages nationally in 1849 as a whole were just 7.5 per cent higher than in 1844.

Changes by 1856

There was no great change of districts in 1852, simply a major reorganisation into a very different pattern of volumes. We no longer see districts arranged within volumes in alphabetical order but on the basis of proximity to each other. At the upper end of volume 2a in Appendix 3, for example, you can see all the districts in the eastern end of Kent grouped together.

Several districts changed the spelling of their names. Alstone became Alston, Tonbridge went to Tunbridge (though it was firmly Tonbridge when I lived there in 1960), Thrapstone seemed to settle down as Thrapston. Fleggs seems to have varied constantly between Fleggs, Fleggs E & W, E & W Fleggs. Wimborne became generally Wimbourne (but has today reverted). Wetherby was a new district name.

Changes by 1891

In the thirty five years between 1856 and 1891 the system of districts remained largely stable. I show 621 districts in 1856/Q1. By 1891/Q1 it appears that some 33 of these had been withdrawn or renamed and about 27 new names had appeared. In addition to the renaming of a district, such as East Preston in place of Worthing, Strood for North Aylesford, Smallburgh for Tunstead, Barton Regis for Clifton, Cannock for Penkridge, Chester for Great Boughton and Wharfedale for Otley, no doubt there were boundary changes as well. The work on the Taunton index (chapter 8) showed changes in the boundaries of the Taunton, Bridgwater and Wellington districts, with parishes moving from one district to the other.

The lists of districts that appear in the Page Range Tables are based on my files of particular quarters. Remember that some of the small districts are so very small that there can be quarters without a single marriage. Therefore they can miss a table based on a particular quarter.

What is perhaps remarkable is that five of the thirty three volumes remained completely unchanged in terms of the district names they contained from 1856/Q1 to 1891/Q1. Volume 4b, Norfolk and Suffolk, was not only unchanged but the density of marriages was much the same in 1891 as in 1856. Devon and Cornwall are similar, actually having a slight reduction in the number of marriages. They are not areas affected greatly by industrialisation and growth of towns was probably offset by migration to other districts.

In this period, however, the population of the country as a whole grew steadily and marriages grew accordingly. The number of entries in the marriage index in 1856/Q1 was approximately 57800 and by 1891/Q1 it had risen to about 99100, an increase of about 71%. Thus the average number of entries per district in that quarter rose from 93 to 159. Remember though that these figures relate only to March quarters. The increase in total marriages from 1856 to 1891 was only 43%, as shown in chapter 10. There was a marked change in seasonality as the character and living standards of the population changed. The March quarter was a very low quarter for marriages in the earlier part of the 1800s but it had clearly risen by the 1890s.

The growth of London is demonstrated vividly. The number of London districts in the four GRO volumes 1a, 1b, 1c and 1d fell from 36 in 1856 to 30 in 1891 but the total range of pages within the four volumes increased from 3064 to 4607. This increased the average range of pages per district from 85 to 154. St Saviour, for example, spanned 36 pages in 1856/Q1. In 1891/Q1 the range was 369 pages. West Ham, over the border in Essex, rose from 26 pages to 269 pages. Such figures bring urban growth to life.

The changes make one realise the magnitude of the changes that were happening in Victorian Britain, and at the same time the lack of change in the more rural parts of the country.

But to me one of the more surprising district changes evident in 1891/Q1, though only based on a sample of 18% of the quarter, was that no entries appeared for the district of Shrewsbury. This is a district with a hundred or more entries for the corresponding quarters of 1844, 1849 and 1856.

Shrewsbury appears to be the only county town to have disappeared in the 1891 sample. I checked my 1881 work and found it absent then as well. It falls in volume 6a in the GRO filing system, lying between the districts of Atcham and Oswestry. The Page Range Table for 1891/Q1 (in Appendix 4) shows no space at all in that area of volume 6a for any batch of entries for Shrewsbury. Is it remotely possible that Shrewsbury entries somehow went astray ? This might seem a preposterous question but we have already seen that much larger blocks of information have dropped out of the system in various ways, apparently without being noticed. With about 465,000 bundles of births, deaths and marriages being created in the 1837/1899 period, might a few have gone astray or have not been sent ?

No, this doesn't seem to be the explanation here.

The present Superintendent Registrar for the Shrewsbury Registration District is unaware of any reason for the absence of Shrewsbury marriages in the indexes for the late 1800s and has suggested that they may be listed under Atcham, the neighbouring district. Based on the numbers of entries in my samples this does seem to be the most probable explanation. It is another signal that the handling of material in the GRO is completely independent of the BDM organisation at a local level.

This sort of situation does raise questions for researchers using the indexes. As the arrangement of the GRO volumes and the way they are indexed is entirely at the discretion of the GRO, then the Shrewsbury registry office wouldn't have any concern, or even any knowledge, of the way that Shrewsbury returns might be filed and indexed by the GRO from time to time. This particular example suggests the probability that the Shrewsbury district may have continued to function in all respects as a Superintendent Registrar's District but that the returns may have simply been handled and indexed as though they were from Atcham.

If this sort of thing has happened very often, and especially if it can happen for a district such as a county town, then the researcher who is looking for index entries for a particular district may easily be put off the scent. Some of the apparent changes in the system that we have seen may not have been real changes, simply a change in GRO procedures. There is no official information readily accessible to researchers to tell them exactly what changes of this sort have happened in the system, or when. Such information would be valuable background information in research and it is rather surprising that it isn't available.

There must remain the possibility, as I rather hypothetically suggested, that a few bundles of returns out of the hundreds of thousands could have gone astray. Undocumented changes to the system just make it much more difficult to check for them. It would take an impossible amount of work on the indexes to uncover even a hint of any such problems.

An official reference book from ONS to document all the changes in district structures that have taken place would be a valuable asset in family history libraries.

Chapter 14 - "Name this child"

The marriage index isn't the best place to go looking for naming patterns but it seems a pity to have a large resource without learning a little more from it.

A sample of 250,000 names from those married between 1839 and 1891 is a basis for looking at patterns of given names for births taking place between roughly 1815 and 1870, twenty years or so before the majority of the marriages. I have taken two time slots, 1844 & 1891, giving some 70,000 names as a main source, supported by about 60,000 names in 1844 & 1881. As with so much in this book, readers will have to be content with selected illustrations from the research material. There is no room for more.

The 1800s are a period when many of the old favourites like John and Mary, William and Sarah and the like became gradually less dominant and some of the more "modern" names began to appear in significant numbers. It is worth glancing at the bottom end of the scale too, at changes in the use of the less common Old Testament names like Nehemiah, Hezekiah, Eli and the like.

There are names like Victoria and Albert to be noticed. Diminutives like Annie and Lizzie became more frequent, as well as short forms such as Fred and Tom. Preferred spellings seem to have changed as well, especially for names such as Ann and Catherine. It is impossible to report with confidence on spellings such as Harriet and Harriot, Elizabeth and Elisabeth, because film and fiche of later indexes are often so fuzzy that it is virtually impossible to distinguish them. One name combination is in a class of its own, good old Mary Ann (or Mary Anne) which often appears as Marianne as an indexing variant. Mary Ann deserves a spot on her own apart from the other varieties of Mary. I then have "Mary other" to include Mary with any other second name(s).

There are some discernible local features, names especially popular in some localities, other localities where some popular names are almost non-existent.

Spelling errors and variants have to be watched for and often discounted, not to mention some of the improbable variants. We wouldn't consider that name variants in the index such as Ann and An, Thomas and Tom, William and Wm, Avis and Evis, are distinct names. There are plenty of such situations. William must be William whether indexed as William, Willm or Wm. Allice and Alice are probably one name for this purpose, likewise Margaret and Margreat and Margerat. In many or most such cases the doubt has been created by the poor quarterly copies. Some names are too illegible in the indexes to be counted at all.

To make more sense of the tables I have grouped some names. For example Betsy is taken to include Betsey and Bessie. The various versions of Harriet are taken as one. Lilian is taken to include Lillian, Lilly, Lily and Lilley, all of which appear. Frederic and Fredrick are taken as Frederick. Occasional Henery is taken as Henry. Susanna and Susannah are taken as Susanna. Eleanor is taken to include Ellinor and Elinor. Catharine and Catherine are taken together, Catharines being generally rather few.

There are differences between the patterns of English and Welsh names so there is a benefit in looking at the Welsh volumes separately. Places such as Liverpool tend to be richer in names like Patrick and Bridget but even these large samples are not big enough to allow too much to be deduced from localising the figures in fine detail. I decided to break the country down into five blocks for purposes of broad illustration, taking particular groups of GRO volumes according to the volume structures applying up to 1851 :

> London   The rest of southern England   East Anglia and fenland
> Midlands and northern England   Wales

In terms of the GRO volumes these are 1-4, 5-11, 12-14, 15-25 and 26-27.

The advantage of having marriage indexes on computer files is again demonstrated. They were sorted once to take them from an alphabetical basis to a page-by-page order. They are now sorted again by given names, or at least by the first of such names where there are two or more. On the other hand it takes more than simply pressing a button to get the answers. A lot of checking back is needed in order to get results. A small computer program to count the different names has helped but only does part of the work. I have taken only the first given name where there are two or more, except for showing Mary, Mary Ann, Mary Anne and other Mary combinations as four separate categories.

1844 March quarter

The first two tables of Appendix 10 show the patterns of names of bridegrooms and brides for this March quarter. The names are shown in order of overall frequency. The tables are necessarily incomplete. There are certainly a few other names that could justify inclusion and there are hundreds more that appear only once or twice in the whole quarter. Adding a name to a table because it is strong in Wales but appears nowhere else can look like ignoring other minor names in the other areas.

Don't expect the totals of brides and grooms to agree. With so many errors and omissions and so many duplicate entries, not to mention names that can't be read properly at all, differences in tables such as these can be substantial.

The pattern in years gone by was for the dominance of a few principal names. The top four male names of John, William, Thomas and James accounted for half of all the grooms in this quarter (except narrowly for London).

Running an eye down the columns will show some regional differences. David and Edward rank much higher in Wales than elsewhere. Joseph is more prominent in the midlands and north than elsewhere. My groupings conceal some very localised differences. Within the group of volumes 15-25 there are very few Samuels in the far north-east, in volumes 24 and 25. Lawrence and its variants are names I haven't shown in the table. There were 18 in the 1844/Q1 marriages and 15 of them were in Lancashire (volumes 20 and 21).

Among the brides the top four names of Elizabeth, Mary, Ann and Sarah are not quite enough to amount to 50%, even with the Mary combinations. The pattern of women's names is that at one end of the scale there is less concentration on the few most popular names but at the other end of the scale there is not the huge range of names found just once in the quarter among the men.

"Oncer" names that can be spotted among the women include Aminda, Bernice, Comfort, Euphimia, Justina, Melinda, Perseverance, Petronella, Pleasant, Temperance, Unity, Virtue and Zenobia. The oncers among the men seem to have a large proportion of family names as given names, such as Bateson, Bolland, Bradford, Bristow, Branwhite, Duckworth, Gooby, Holgate, Jugg, Snowden and Teesdale. These lists could be expanded to pack a page with names.

Women's names seem to have more regional variation than men's. The impression is that some names might have taken time to spread from the centres of fashion. Some names popular in general are sometimes virtually absent from some of the GRO volumes.

Ann outnumbers Anne by about 6 to 1 in general in 1844 but in Wales the numbers are much more even. Mary Ann heavily outnumbers Mary Anne almost everywhere. Margaret is a rare name in East Anglia and many Midlands areas but there are 504 in Lancashire, Wales and the North East in 1844/Q1 and 533 in 1849/Q1, out of 1550 in the whole of England and Wales in those two quarters combined. Lancashire is also very strong in the names of Alice, Ellen, Nancy and Nanny. Lancashire and the two GRO volumes in the far north east (24 and 25) are also the stronghold for Isabella, with 68% of those appearing in 1844/Q1 and 70% of those in 1849/Q1. Names such as Elizabeth, Harriet and Caroline are correspondingly fewer in those districts.

1849 March quarter

I have used my 1849/Q1 files as a check on the 1844 data, to make sure that the patterns shown by the 1844 data are not mere random variations. It is a relief to find that much the same patterns appear in both quarters. There are inevitably some variations but little real change.

In Wales, for example, we still see John as 18.6% in 1849, William 14.9%, Thomas down a little to 12.4%, Edward 3.4% and David 8.5%.

It was a relief to find that even the detailed patterns, volume by volume, remain surprisingly similar. The third table in Appendix 10 picks six names, three men and three women, and compares the frequencies for all the GRO volumes for the two quarters. The patterns are remarkably alike despite occasional divergences.

The patterns are then shown as bar graphs in the next page and the similarities become even more obvious. The graphs have bars in pairs for each GRO volume, the left-hand bar showing the names in 1844/Q1 and right-hand bar the names in 1849/Q1. The display panels are automatically sized to keep the same scale for each panel. There are more similarities in this detail than I would have expected, yet each name has a distinct pattern.

Grace and Isabella are also compared in detail in this same 1844/1849 table. As my mother's name was Grace I have tended to accept it as a very normal name and it was a surprise to find the particular importance of the name in Devon and Cornwall. It is good to find something unexpected.

1891 March quarter

My sample for 1891 is far smaller and therefore less reliable. Even so there are large and obvious changes. Because the sample is smaller there are some quite small figures for some occurrences and these can only be seen as indicative.

Pages 5 and 6 in Appendix 10 show bridegrooms and brides for 1891/Q1, as for 1844/Q1. I have tried to make the geographical groupings as similar as possible. To achieve this I took the entries for Herefordshire from volume 6a and included them with those for volume 11a (where they belonged in 1844).

In the table for bridegrooms we now need to use the top six names to reach 50%. The two top names (William and John) have dropped from one in three grooms in 1844 to one in four in 1891. The popular names have lost ground. David remains virtually unchanged and still very popular in Wales.

The other side of the coin is the rise of other names. Frederick has risen from 15th in 1844 to 9th in 1891, with many more names in this small sample of 9000 names than in the 1844 sample of 26600, up from 0.8% to 3.3%.

Other names to rise or to appear from nowhere are Arthur, Alfred, Albert, Walter, Harry, Herbert, Frank and Ernest. Frederick and Alfred together were 1.2% in 1844, the rest hardly existed. Even in the 1881 sample these new names were much less significant, suggesting that the pace of change was fast in the last decades of the century.

The popularity of Albert is understandable. The 1891 sample shows even more of them than the 1881 sample. It is clear that Albert's popularity was not shared by Victoria. There are 159 Alberts in the 1891 sample but only three Victorias. The 1881 sample shows 15 Alberts and one Victoria.

Together these nine new or improved names account for 15.7% of the entries for 1891. The top names have had to give way.

The 1891 sample is still too small to be taken as reliable, especially in detail. The main changes are no doubt fairly accurate. Many of the smaller figures may well be validated but some are sure to change.

One of the real curiosities of the men's names is that volume 9, covering Yorkshire, seems to be unique within the system in 1891/Q1 in having a very large number of index entries for Ben, Fred, Jim, Jimmy, Joe, Sam and Tom. Other volumes have one or two. Volume 9 has large numbers. This could be a characteristic of Yorkshiremen, or of the vicars in Yorkshire. Perhaps it was rather more likely that one clerk working on the indexing of volume 9 was a shortener of names, possibly corrected when it was realised what he had been doing.

A quick answer might well be possible. It took an hour or so with the marriage indexes for 1892 and 1893 to gather a sample of index entries for Fred, Joe, Sam and Tom. I built up two hundred entries and *over half came from volume 9*. There were just 94 entries for all the other ten volumes. Every single one of the index entries for Joe came from volume 9. This isn't the whole answer and doesn't tell us enough to suggest an explanation - a visit to the Southport films might provide more clues. Some research in the birth indexes around 1870 might also be a help. Two small conclusions come from this little story. Firstly, that any concentrated local phenomenon that we can find is valuable as a potential research pointer. Secondly, that even small questions can easily take a great deal of work to resolve.

What of the brides ? The story is not so very different. The top names have lost numbers and newer names have moved up the ladder.

Alice, like Frederick, shows more names in 1891 than in the much larger 1844 sample and has moved up from 1.4% to 3.7%. Other names to jump up the ladder are Emily, Ada, Florence and Clara. We now have to use ten names to fill the top 50% and Alice is up in that top ten from her 20th position in 1844.

The use of diminutives in the records has developed by 1891. We see Minnie and Lizzie in the table, and it is possible to find a few examples of Maggie, Lillie, Lottie, Katie, Susey and Rosie (or Rosey).

Major changes in usage are in the treatment of Ann and Mary. In our tables for 1844/Q1 and 1849/Q1 we have the following results :

	Ann and Mary in	
	1844/Q1	**1891/Q1**
Ann *	12.2 %	2.2 %
Anne *	2.1 %	0.2 %
Annie *	0.0 %	4.8 %
Mary #	15.4 %	4.1 %
Mary Ann	7.4 %	4.5 %
Mary Anne	0.7 %	0.1 %
Mary other	1.0 %	5.5 %
* with or without second names	# plain Mary	

Annie swept into favour by 1891 at the expense of Ann and Anne. Annie had little impact on Mary Ann and Mary Anne. Perhaps Mary Annie didn't have a convincing ring to it. The "Mary other" names in 1891 number 491 in my sample but only contain 10 examples of Mary Annie.

In 1844/Q1 the traditional plain Mary, Mary Ann and Mary Anne were a very solid 23.5% of all the brides in the index. By 1891/Q1 they were down to 8.7%. Mary with other given names went up from 1% to 5.5%, part of the general trend towards two or more given names but not enough to save Mary from a big fall overall.

The tabulations are too sparse to say much about detailed regional changes. Some of the earlier patterns do seem to have persisted. Margaret seems to have remained well out of favour in East Anglia. Wales continued to show little interest in Agnes, Betsy, Charlotte, Emily and Fanny. Isabella has clearly remained very strong in the North Eastern counties.

And what about those Old Testament names ? As individual names they are often quite rare. The 1844 sample has only one each of Laban, Mordecai, Zachaeus and Lot over the whole country. In total, however, they were quite numerous. It is a little difficult to know where to draw the line, exactly which to take as Old Testament names, but a scan through my listings of men's names for 1844 gives me a total of nearly 50 different names and about 220 men who rejoiced in those names in their lifetimes, just under one per cent of all the men. Names like Aaron, Joel, Elijah, Jeremiah, Abel and Moses are the most common.

Women were more often presented with names hopefully extolling their future virtues, such as Charity, Mercy, Temperance, Unity, Comfort and Pleasant. Patience and Prudence were not uncommon, and there was even a Perseverance in 1844. They were all virtues valuable in marriage. The Old Testament wasn't resorted to in the same degree. I have listed some 15 different names (of which the most numerous in 1844/Q1 were Leah, Keturah, Zillah and Lois), some 40 women with Old Testament names in total.

My impression, without a thorough search, is that these names were rather less common by the 1881/1891 period.

   * * * * * * * * * * * * *

It hasn't proved possible to write as convincingly on name patterns as I would have liked but I hope that the tabulations and some of the comments may prove useful.

Chapter 15 - The GRO marriage indexes and the IGI

In chapter 6 we saw that the IGI (the International Genealogical Index) contains two marriages from Northumberland that were missed by the indexer of the GRO's quarterly returns for 1849/Q1. The marriages were present on the GRO marriage film but were simply not indexed. Is it likely that the IGI will have many marriages that have slipped through one of the several cracks in the GRO system ?

Unfortunately the IGI only contains a fairly small number of marriages since 1837. For some counties there are very few indeed. Therefore at best only a minor proportion of marriages missed from the GRO indexes are likely to be found in the IGI.

A measure of the relationship between the two systems can be looked for by examining a sample of marriages recorded in the IGI and testing them to see if they can be found in the corresponding GRO indexes. (A little reflection will show that working in the opposite direction would do no more than confirm that the GRO record is larger than the IGI record).

The GRO indexes, as we know, were constructed from hand-written copies of the original marriage registers, i.e. the quarterly returns. The IGI record is constructed from two sources, firstly from a filming of the original marriage registers, secondly from information provided to the LDS by relatives.

The filming from the original registers should be inherently better as a source than the quarterly returns. On the other hand we have to remember that the quarterly returns were indexed by clerks who, whatever their other shortcomings, were at least more familiar with contemporary writing styles. This can put modern indexers at something of a disadvantage.

The information supplied by.relatives could be of variable quality. It is possible that relatives may even have tended to supply information that the official record appeared to have missed or partly missed. In other words there could be a direct "cause and effect" situation inherently more likely to show up omissions in the GRO indexes. It does seem that more of the post-1837 marriages in the IGI are those from relatives than those from the filming of registers.

All this, however, is speculation and needs to be checked and quantified.

To use this approach to throw some different light on the quality of the GRO index we need to take a large sample of marriages from the IGI. In fact we need two large samples, one for marriages indexed from the filming of registers and one for marriages supplied by relatives. Each of the marriages in each of these samples then has to be checked against the corresponding GRO marriage indexes to see whether the names are in the indexes and whether they are the same or different.

Each sample should include marriages more or less at random around the country and over the period 1837 to 1899 (though there will tend to be more from the earlier years). If the samples are fairly large, they may well give some indication of changes in the GRO system over time, particularly if some sort of steady pattern of change emerges. For example, more differences could possibly appear for earlier marriages than for later ones.

An indication

I have initiated a project to create two samples of five thousand marriages each, i.e. twenty thousand names in total.

The first few names in these samples can give us a hint of what can perhaps be expected.

Firstly I have a small sample of 25 marriages in the IGI derived from films of the registers. All the names do appear in the GRO indexes but there are small differences :

An Adelaide Laiender in the IGI appears in the GRO as Adelaide Lavender, much more likely to be correct.

An Elizabeth Reeves in the IGI appears in the GRO index as Elizth. This is probably the way the vicar copied the name from his register.

There is a GRO indexing error, Ann Brown of Alverstoke in the index as vol 12 p38 instead of vol 7. Obviously a typing error of XII for VII.

One Harriet Ford appears twice identically in the GRO index for no reason.

An Elizabeth Wood in the IGI appears as Eliza in the GRO index.

Roseann Bragg in the IGI is Rose Ann Bragg in the GRO index.

An Emily Buckenham in the IGI is out of sequence in the GRO index (and I nearly missed her).

Agnes Faarin in the IGI is in the GRO index as Farrin (certainly correct).

Secondly I have a sample of 25 marriages in the IGI supplied by relatives. Here we have fewer differences but they are more significant :

William John Brown in the IGI is in the GRO index as Wm. John Brown.

Harriet Barrett in the IGI is given as Harriet Barnett in the GRO index.

Joseph Lefe Bure appears in the IGI index but is found, with some difficulty, as Joseph Lefebure in the GRO index.

A marriage of George Everitt and Rachel Townsend appears in the IGI for 1857 in Ampthill, Bedfordshire. George is in the GRO index, but Rachel cannot be found, even after trying Townsend, Townend and Townshend.

Henry Broomfield in the IGI index (married in Southampton) became Bromfield in the GRO index.

John Thorne in the IGI is given as Thorn in the GRO.

Altogether we have fourteen differences of some kind between the two records in 100 names. These particular differences can be ignored for what they actually are but they are significant in being there at all.

This is a very small sample but it does tend to suggest that two large samples are likely to reveal a great deal by way of differences between the two records and it will be interesting to see if any definite message emerges from the exercise.

It is quite a slow process, firstly the sampling and secondly the succession of checks against different GRO index fiche, constantly taking fiche from storage, checking and replacing.

On a personal note

The certificate for the birth of my great-grandmother Mary Maria Barber in Brighton in 1847 shows her parents as George Barber and, on my reading of it, Elizabeth Haines or perhaps Staines. I wasn't able to find such a Barber/Haines/Staines marriage in the GRO index for the preceding few years and put the problem on one side.

Later I betook myself to the IGI for Sussex and almost immediately found an entry for a George Barber marrying an Elizabeth Starnes in the parish of Laughton on 6 July 1839. This was a little earlier than I had previously searched and, yes, Mary's birth certificate could well show her mother as Elizabeth Starnes. In fact, as often happens, it becomes obvious once you realise what it is.

Back to the GRO marriage index for 1839 and there, sure enough, is Elizabeth Starnes whose marriage is registered at Hailsham, volume 7, page 349. Laughton is a village just a few miles out of Hailsham. But where is George Barber in the index ? He is certainly not among his fellow Barbers. After a short search of likely alternatives I found him lurking as George *Barker*, registered in Hailsham exactly as is Elizabeth.

Though I am fully confident that this Barber/Barker/Starnes marriage is the one I was looking for, the point of this story is that it seems to be a certain case in my own family history where the IGI entry, based on film of the original register, is correct as Barber but where the GRO index, based on a handwritten quarterly copy, is incorrect as Barker.

The error may be as simple as a careless guess by the indexing clerk, or may be a poorly written quarterly copy with which the clerk then did his best, or may be an actual error in the copying by the clergyman. A certificate for this marriage will establish which answer is right.

In this particular example, with uncertainty about the names of Haines and Staines, and with Barber entered incorrectly in the GRO index, this is a marriage I would probably never have found in the GRO index. Therefore I am fortunate that it is one of the comparatively few to appear in the IGI. With indications that indexing errors are perhaps of the order of one in every twenty marriages or so (as shown in the detailed Essex and Taunton research), most researchers will be blocked in their research at some points. Unfortunately it only takes one broken bridge to make a road impassable.

Buried in a trench

Sometimes the IGI can be used obliquely to help to solve a problem.

Via a Fidonet bulletin board message I heard about an 1848 marriage where the husband James Clemas appears in the GRO index but the bride (identified from the marriage certificate as Emma Thomas French) is not to be found. The bulletin board correspondence revolved around the possibility that the bride had been omitted from the index. This research has established that comparatively few individuals fail to appear in the index but that errors in entries are common, reflecting careless indexing or bad copying. Therefore I went to work to look for possible variants of French in the index. After several attempts I found the missing young lady as Emma Thomas Trench, matching the entry for James in volume 8, registered in the district of Poole. Once again an indication that errors are more common than omissions.

Which was right, French or Trench ? The IGI shows clearly that there are plenty of French entries in Dorset but not a single Trench. French therefore looked to be virtually certain.

Why was the GRO wrong ? The Fidonet correspondent later told me that the name of French was perfectly clear and easy to read on the marriage certificate. The indexer perhaps guessed wrongly or carelessly, or perhaps more probably he read French correctly in extracting the name from the quarterly return but then wrote it badly, thus creating the wrong index entry when the names were sorted and the index itself was written. As I said early in Chapter 6, there are many ways to be wrong (but only one way to be right). When the poor quarterly copies presented so many chances for errors in the indexing, it is rather distressing when an error is made from a very legible entry.

Chapter 16   In conclusion . . . . . . in brief

For the benefit of those who have travelled these fifteen chapters, and for the stimulation of those who, like my wife, have an inclination to read the last chapter of any book first, what do we conclude ?

- The system of civil registration from 1837 was designed and developed in such a way that verification of its contents was made virtually impossible.

- The central national record of births, deaths and marriages consists entirely of hand-written copies rather than original entries.

- For marriages in particular there was no provision in the legislation for checking the accuracy of the copies and there is great doubt whether much of any checking that was done was effective.

- The filing systems and indexing systems at local and national levels are entirely different in structure and lend themselves neither to checking of content nor even numerical checking of recorded events.

- The evidence is overwhelming that omissions and errors occurred at all levels of the system. That most went apparently unnoticed and certainly uncorrected is further evidence of the lack of checking and probably of the impossibility of checking.

- The rules, if any, for indexing led to unjustified and confusing duplication of index entries on a very large scale.

- The large number of manual copying processes between the original entries and the final published indexes was an assurance of a high level of errors, starting with the very poor quality of many of the quarterly returns.

- The typing and filming processes were final manual copying stages that have taken a heavy toll of the accuracy and completeness of the already defective indexes.

- The findings of this research are based on the partial checking at the General Register Office of a *one per cent sample of the marriage material*. It can only be expected that the untouched ninety nine per cent and more, not to mention the birth and death records, will conceal much more of the same and undoubtedly some that is much worse. Here are very round figures based on findings from different parts of the research.

Omitted quarterly returns could well be between 50,000 and 350,000 marriages, based on findings from the Essex and Somerset analyses.

Marriages missed in the indexing process could be at least some 15,000

Individual entries missing from the index could be around 20,000

Variant/duplicate indexing could amount to 250,000 to 500,000 names

Errors in names as indexed are many and could rival the variant names

Names lost from the indexes through the typing process are certainly significant and impossible to quantify at this stage

Names lost from at least the handwritten fiche and film of all three indexes are of the order of 25,000 through frames missed in their production

Errors of indexing (in volume/page numbers and district names), both in original indexing and through later typing, could range from 50,000 to 200,000

There are many other errors in great variety, witnesses indexed, fathers indexed instead of sons, brides indexed with new names

These estimates of errors may well be conservative. A million errors in the 1837/99 period are very probable.

- Recommendations are made in this book for a complete overhaul of the 1800s records to overcome most of these deficiencies and to produce a new record system and a computer-searchable index system at both local and national levels.

- This is the only effective and comparatively low-cost path towards a complete and dependable record of births, deaths and marriages for England and Wales in the 1800s (and perhaps some way beyond).

- These conclusions in no way detract from a sense of our good fortune in possessing such a huge and invaluable resource as the GRO record system.

- Recommendations are also made for some further investigations that could improve the estimates of errors in the system.

*   *   *   *   *   *   *   *   *

What will really happen ?

Having spent nearly sixteen chapters in the past, so to speak, what view can we take of the future ? What may the findings of this research achieve ?

First and foremost, I hope and believe they will awaken the genealogical world as never before to an awareness of the status of at least the 19th century records. This research has never been done before and the findings are new, both inside and outside the General Register Office.

Second, I hope the findings and recommendations will be enough to convince all readers, and ultimately government as the source of funds, that the situation is such that renewal and correction of the records is essential and economically feasible. These records are the basis of Britain's vital statistics. Shouldn't this mean that the records themselves are fundamentally vital ?

What could be more appropriate than looking towards the year 2000 as the launch date for the revitalised marriage records of England and Wales (with births and deaths to follow) ?

I am only too well aware that funding is the most likely snag in the political field of vision and that this is a constraint that can so easily prevent movement of any sort. The task has been seen as too big and too expensive. I can only emphasise that Chapter 9 has shown that it is *emphatically not* as big as has been thought, nor expensive, if the army of available, willing and skilled voluntary resources is brought to bear on it.

Let us recall what we read on page 43, those rediscovered and prophetic final words of the 1837 letter from the Registrar General to the clergy. The letter called for the exact fulfilment of their civil duties assigned by law, *especially as by neglecting them there might be an injury, one knew not how serious, inflicted on the descendants of those who had received the holy ordinance of matrimony.* Those words of the first CEO of the General Register Office should now be echoing down the long elegant corridors of Smedley Hydro in Southport, urging and compelling the repair of past faults. The Registrar General was right in what he was calling for. The clergy to a large extent seem to have failed him. After more than 150 years it is surely time that his words were heeded and acted upon.

If Great Aunt Emily of Chapter 12 is still languishing lost and undetected in some unfamiliar part of the alphabet, then she may well be reflecting on those well-known words from the Book of Common Prayer "Those whom God hath joined together let no man put asunder". She and her countless friends will surely be solidly behind my proposals for an overhaul of the marriage records.

It is the support of the living that is now needed in order to satisfy Aunt Emily. I hope this book will secure that support and that Emily, her friends, and all who have laboured in the past to create this record system may finally breathe a sigh of relief.

Sharing with Admiral Nelson a slight optical deficit, I now clap my telescope to my non-seeing eye and cry "full steam ahead and all hands on deck".

T H E   E N D

(except for the appendices)

Page Range Table for 1844 March Quarter

This table shows the range of page references for each Superintendent
Registrar's district within each of the 27 volumes of the GRO records

Volume 1	St George Han Sq	1	42	Marylebone	131	211
	Bloomsbury	43	71	St Pancras	213	274
	St James	73	97	Strand	275	299
	St Martin	99	130	Westminster	301	327
Volume 2	Bethnal Green	1	29	St Luke's	233	252
	St George East	31	49	Poplar	253	268
	Holborn	51	65	Shoreditch	269	333
	London City	67	168	Stepney	335	385
	East London	169	195	Whitechapel	387	417
	West London	197	231			
Volume 3	Brentford	1	17	Hendon	133	139
	Chelsea	19	35	Islington	141	175
	Clerkenwell	37	73	Kensington	177	250
	Edmonton	75	95	Staines	251	263
	Hackney	97	131	Uxbridge	265	273
Volume 4	Bermondsey	1	11	Kingston	129	145
	Camberwell	13	29	Lambeth	147	241
	Chertsey	31	40	Newington	243	289
	Croydon	41	49	Reigate	291	303
	Dorking	51	59	Richmond	305	313
	Epsom	61	69	Rotherhithe	315	324
	Farnham	71	87	St Geo Southwark	325	351
	Godstone	89	93	St Olave	353	358
	Guildford	95	117	St Saviour	359	375
	Hambledon	119	127	Wandsworth	377	393
Volume 5	E Ashford	1	9	Hollingbourne	255	273
	W Ashford	11	23	Hoo	275	277
	Blean	25	43	Lewisham	279	301
	Bridge	45	67	Maidstone	303	325
	Bromley	69	81	Malling	327	337
	Canterbury	83	104	Medway	339	359
	Cranbrook	105	115	Milton	361	369
	Dartford	117	142	N Aylesford	371	383
	Dover	143	163	Romney Marsh	385	391
	Eastry	165	185	Sevenoaks	393	411
	Elham	187	204	Sheppey	413	416
	Faversham	205	219	Tenterden	417	423
	Gravesend	221	227	Thanet	425	441
	Greenwich	229	253	Tonbridge	443	461

Volume 6	Ampthill	1	29	Amersham	385	401
	Bedford	31	78	Aylesbury	403	431
	Biggleswade	79	95	Buckingham	433	451
	Leighton Buzzard	97	111	Eton	453	477
	Luton	113	133	Newport Pagnell	479	509
	Woburn	135	145	Winslow	511	521
	Abingdon	147	171	Wycombe	523	549
	Bradfield	173	199	St Albans	551	568
	Cookham	201	209	Barnet	569	581
	E Hampstead	211	215	Berkhampstead	583	595
	Farringdon	217	237	Bps Stortford	597	611
	Hungerford	239	259	Hatfield	613	615
	Newbury	261	286	Hemel Hempstead	617	628
	Reading	287	299	Hertford	629	645
	Wallingford	301	319	Hitchin	647	671
	Wantage	321	351	Royston	673	715
	Windsor	353	369	Ware	717	733
	Wokingham	371	383	Watford	735	745
Volume 7	Alresford	1	11	Brighton	334	358
	Alton	13	29	Chichester	359	370
	Alverstoke	31	47	Cuckfield	371	391
	Andover	49	83	Eastbourne	393	397
	Basingstoke	85	103	East Grinstead	399	401
	Catherington	105		Hailsham	403	421
	Droxford	107	117	Hastings	423	433
	Fareham	119	127	Horsham	435	443
	Hartley Wintney	129	135	Lewes	445	485
	Havant	137	145	Midhurst	487	507
	Kingsclere	147	153	Petworth	509	514
	Petersfield	155	165	Rye	515	525
	Portsea	167	205	Steyning	527	547
	Romsey	207	217	Thakeham	549	561
	Southampton	219	244	Ticehurst	563	575
	South Stoneham	245	255	Uckfield	577	591
	Stockbridge	257	267	Westbourne	593	597
	Whitchurch	269	274	Westhampnett	599	623
	Winchester	275	311	Worthing	625	637
	Battle	313	333			
Volume 8	Beaminster	1	19	Amesbury	359	371
	Blandford	21	43	Bradford Wilts	373	387
	Bridport	45	67	Calne	389	397
	Dorchester	69	111	Chippenham	399	417
	Poole	113	124	Cricklade	419	427
	Shaftesbury	125	141	Devizes	429	451
	Sherborne	143	160	Swindon	453	463
	Sturminster	161	165	Malmsbury	465	485
	Wareham	167	193	Marlborough	487	497

Volume 12	Colchester	77	97	Witham	373	393
continued	Dumow	99	124	Bosmere	395	415
	Epping	125	143	Cosford	419	441
	Halstead	144	167	Ipswich	443	476
	Lexden	169	201	Plomesgate	477	505
	Maldon	203	235	Risbridge	507	535
	Ongar	237	249	Samford	537	557
	Orsett	251	271	Stow	559	591
	Rochford	273	289	Sudbury	593	625
	Romford	290	303	Woodbridge	627	653
Volume 13	Aylsham	1	33	Swaffham	467	484
	Blofield	35	59	Thetford	485	511
	Depwade	61	99	Tunstead	513	549
	Docking	101	127	Walsingham	551	583
	Downham	129	153	Wayland	585	604
	Erpingham	155	189	Yarmouth	605	617
	St Faith's	191	215	Blything	619	659
	Forehoe	217	235	Bury St Edmunds	661	667
	Freebridge Lynn	237	257	Hartismere	669	699
	Guiltcross	259	281	Hoxne	701	719
	Henstead	283	309	Mildenhall	721	731
	King's Lynn	311	323	Mutford	733	757
	Loddon	325	347	Thingoe	759	789
	Mitford	349	395	Wangford	791	807
	Norwich	397	466			
Volume 14	Cambridge	1	23	Bourn	325	347
	Caxton	25	41	Caistor	349	387
	Chesterton	43	73	Gainsborough	389	415
	Ely	75	94	Glanford Brigg	417	451
	Linton	95	123	Grantham	453	486
	Newmarket	125	157	Holbeach	487	503
	N Witchford	159	167	Horncastle	505	531
	Whittlesea	169	173	Lincoln	533	592
	Wisbeach	175	205	Louth	593	625
	Huntingdon	207	229	Sleaford	627	659
	St Ives	231	249	Spalding	661	679
	St Neots	251	281	Spilsby	681	705
	Boston	283	324	Stamford	707	729
Volume 15	Ashby de la Zouch	1	26	Oundle	407	423
	Barrow on Soar	27	43	Peterborough	425	455
	Billesdon	45	67	Potterspury	457	473
	Blaby	69	81	Thrapstone	475	495
	Hinckley	83	93	Towcester	497	508
	Leicester	95	131	Wellingborough	509	541
	Loughborough	133	156	Basford	543	586
	Lutterworth	157	175	Bingham	587	613

Volume 15	Mkt Harborough	177	199	East Retford	615	653
continued	Mkt Bosworth	201	225	Mansfield	655	677
	Melton Mowbray	227	257	Newark	679	718
	Brackley	259	279	Nottingham	719	747
	Brixworth	281	299	Radford	749	766
	Daventry	301	333	Southwell	767	809
	Hardingstone	335	351	Worksop	811	822
	Kettering	353	373	Oakham	823	839
	Northampton	375	406	Uppingham	841	865
Volume 16	Banbury	1	33	Birmingham	261	323
	Bicester	35	55	Coventry	325	349
	Chipping Norton	57	81	Foleshill	351	364
	Headington	83	107	Meriden	365	377
	Henley	109	118	Nuneaton	379	385
	Oxford	119	137	Rugby	387	401
	Thame	139	157	Solihull	403	411
	Witney	159	183	Southam	413	429
	Woodstock	185	212	Stratford on Avon	431	451
	Alcester	213	229	Tamworth	453	471
	Aston	231	253	Warwick	473	500
	Atherstone	255	259			
Volume 17	Burton on Trent	1	27	Stoke on Trent	129	156
	Cheadle	29	45	Stone	157	173
	Leek	47	57	Uttoxeter	175	201
	Lichfield	59	82	Walsall	203	217
	Newcastle L	83	97	Wolstanton	219	237
	Penkridge	99	111	Wolverhampton	239	291
	Stafford	113	128			
Volume 18	Atcham	1	23	Wem	245	261
	Bridgnorth	25	45	Bromsgrove	263	275
	Church Stretton	47	53	Droitwich	277	297
	Cleobury Mortimer	55	63	Dudley	299	337
	Clun	65	80	Evesham	339	363
	Ellesmere	81	93	Kidderminster	365	377
	Ludlow	95	119	Kings Norton	379	404
	Madeley	121	135	Martley	405	427
	Market Drayton	137	151	Pershore	429	440
	Newport Salop	153	171	Stourbridge	441	461
	Oswestry	173	194	Tenbury	463	469
	Shiffnal	195	203	Upton on Severn	471	483
	Shrewsbury	205	222	Worcester	485	511
	Wellington Salop	223	243	West Bromwich	513	546
Volume 19	Altrincham	1	23	Ashborne	259	291
	Great Boughton	25	67	Bakewell	293	323
	Congleton	69	89	Belper	325	367
	Macclesfield	91	121	Chapel en le Frith	369	377

Volume 19 continued	Nantwich	123	155	Chesterfield	379	407
	Northwich	157	174	Derby	409	435
	Runcorn	175	193	Hayfield	437	447
	Stockport	195	235	Shardlow	449	481
	Wirral	237	257			
Volume 20	Ashton	1	71	Prescot	587	612
	Chorlton	73	121	Salford	613	617
	Liverpool	123	315	Warrington	619	641
	Manchester	317	585	West Derby	643	697
Volume 21	Blackburn	1	49	Haslingden	271	297
	Bolton	51	109	Lancaster	299	319
	Burnley	111	153	Leigh	321	331
	Bury	155	194	Ormskirk	333	363
	Chorley	195	223	Preston	365	415
	Clitheroe	225	243	Rochdale	417	467
	Fylde	245	260	Todmorden	469	481
	Garstang	261	269	Wigan	483	525
Volume 22	Dewsbury	1	31	Pontefract	259	291
	Doncaster	33	63	Rotherham	293	329
	Ecclesall Bierlow	65	69	Sculcoates	331	362
	Ecclesfield	71	99	Sheffield	363	431
	Halifax	101	163	Skirlaugh	433	445
	Huddersfield	165	220	Wakefield	447	483
	Hull	221	257	Wortley	485	495
Volume 23	Beverley	1	27	Otley	413	430
	Bridlington	29	49	Pateley Bridge	431	435
	Driffield	51	81	Ripon	437	454
	Howden	83	99	Saddleworth	455	459
	Patrington	101	113	Sedbergh	461	467
	Pocklington	115	139	Selby	469	477
	Bradford Yks	141	232	Settle	479	489
	Goole	233	243	Skipton	491	515
	Keighley	245	265	Tadcaster	517	535
	Knaresborough	267	303	Thorne	537	551
	Leeds	305	411	York	553	619
Volume 24	Auckland	1	17	Easingwold	273	279
	Chester le Street	19	27	Guisborough	281	295
	Darlington	29	46	Helmsley	297	309
	Durham	47	79	Leyburn	311	321
	Easington	81	93	Malton	323	353
	Gateshead	95	120	Northallerton	355	375
	Houghton le Spring	121	129	Pickering	377	393
	South Shields	131	157	Reeth	395	403
	Stockton	159	194	Richmond	405	423
	Sunderland	195	230	Scarborough	425	451
	Teesdale	231	248	Stokesley	453	463

Volume 24	Weardale	249	254	Thirsk	465	475
continued	Askrigg	255	263	Whitby	477	492
	Bedale	265	271			
Volume 25	Alstone	1	5	Bellingham	203	206
	Berwick	7	17	Castle Ward	207	213
	Bootle	19	25	Glendale	215	221
	Brampton	27	37	Haltwhistle	223	225
	Carlisle	39	56	Hexham	227	249
	Cockermouth	57	87	Morpeth	251	259
	Longtown	89	93	Newcastle on T	261	329
	Penrith	95	119	Rothbury	331	335
	Whitehaven	121	144	Tynemouth	337	367
	Wigton	145	165	East Ward	369	385
	Ulverstone	167	193	Kendal	387	411
	Alnwick	195	199	West Ward	413	423
	Belford	200	201			
Volume 26	Abergavenny	1	36	Crickhowell	385	402
	Chepstow	37	55	Hay	403	419
	Monmouth	57	77	Bridgend	421	449
	Newport Mon	79	108	Cardiff	451	482
	Pontypool	109	129	Merthyr Tydfil	483	524
	Bromyard	131	147	Neath	525	550
	Hereford	148	205	Swansea	551	582
	Ledbury	207	221	Carmarthen	583	630
	Leominster	223	248	Llandilofawr	631	651
	Ross	249	271	Llandovery	653	671
	Weobly	273	293	Llanelly	673	689
	Knighton	295	309	Haverfordwest	691	752
	Presteign	311	337	Narberth	753	793
	Rhyader	339	353	Newcastle Emlyn	795	823
	Brecknock	355	369	Pembroke	825	847
	Builth	371	383			
Volume 27	Aberayron	1	15	Festiniog	221	235
	Aberystwith	17	39	St Asaph	237	263
	Cardigan	41	66	Llanrwst	265	279
	Lampeter	67	85	Ruthin	281	295
	Tregaron	87	99	Holywell	297	325
	Llanfyllin	101	121	Wrexham	327	365
	Machynlleth	123	133	Bangor	367	396
	Montgomery	135	151	Carnarvon	397	411
	Newtown	153	178	Conway	413	423
	Bala	179	185	Pwllheli	425	459
	Corwen	186	199	Anglesea	461	501
	Dolgelly	201	219			

Page Range Table for 1849 March Quarter

This table shows the range of page references for each Superintendent
Registrar's district within each of the 27 volumes of the GRO records

Volume 1	St George Han Sq	1	54	Marylebone	147	232
	Bloomsbury	55	83	St Pancras	233	290
	St James	85	107	Strand	291	317
	St Martin	109	145	Westminster	319	340
Volume 2	Bethnal Green	1	52	St Luke's	233	259
	St George East	53	69	Poplar	261	284
	Holborn	71	81	Shoreditch	285	362
	London City	83	159	Stepney	363	415
	East London	161	195	Whitechapel	417	466
	West London	197	231			
Volume 3	Brentford	1	30	Hendon	155	173
	Chelsea	31	53	Islington	175	220
	Clerkenwell	55	89	Kensington	221	300
	Edmonton	91	113	Staines	301	313
	Hackney	115	150	Uxbridge	315	325
	Hampstead	151	153			
Volume 4	Bermondsey	1	21	Kingston	193	211
	Camberwell	23	49	Lambeth	213	303
	Chertsey	51	61	Newington	305	351
	Croydon	63	83	Reigate	353	366
	Dorking	85	95	Richmond	365	375
	Epsom	97	115	Rotherhithe	377	387
	Farnborough	117	128	St Geo Southwark	389	415
	Farnham	129	139	St Olave	417	424
	Godstone	141	145	St Saviour	425	441
	Guildford	147	173	Wandsworth	443	461
	Hambledon	175	191			
Volume 5	E Ashford	1	19	Hollingbourne	289	305
	W Ashford	21	38	Hoo	307	311
	Blean	39	57	Lewisham	313	337
	Bridge	59	71	Maidstone	339	370
	Bromley	73	93	Malling	371	385
	Canterbury	95	117	Medway	387	406
	Cranbrook	119	129	Milton	407	421
	Dartford	131	149	N Aylesford	423	434
	Dover	151	174	Romney Marsh	435	445
	Eastry	175	197	Sevenoaks	447	465
	Elham	199	221	Sheppey	467	473
	Faversham	223	245	Tenterden	475	484
	Gravesend	247	257	Thanet	485	505

Vol 5 ctd	Greenwich	259	288	Tonbridge	507	527
Volume 6	Ampthill	1	21	Amersham	369	380
	Bedford	23	63	Aylesbury	381	407
	Biggleswade	65	93	Buckingham	409	431
	Leighton Buzzard	95	113	Eton	433	447
	Luton	115	134	Newport Pagnell	449	476
	Woburn	135	157	Winslow	477	491
	Abingdon	159	179	Wycombe	493	533
	Bradfield	181	203	St Albans	535	551
	Cookham	205	215	Barnet	553	563
	E Hampstead	217	221	Berkhampstead	565	577
	Farringdon	223	237	Bps Stortford	579	599
	Hungerford	239	259	Hatfield	601	609
	Newbury	261	282	Hemel Hempstead	611	617
	Reading	283	296	Hertford	619	635
	Wallingford	297	320	Hitchin	637	671
	Wantage	321	339	Royston	673	705
	Windsor	341	355	Ware	707	727
	Wokingham	357	367	Watford	729	743
Volume 7	Alresford	1	11	Brighton	339	362
	Alton	13	25	Chichester	363	379
	Alverstoke	27	43	Cuckfield	381	390
	Andover	44	67	Eastbourne	391	399
	Basingstoke	69	95	East Grinstead	401	415
	Catherington	97	101	Hailsham	417	433
	Droxford	103	113	Hastings	435	449
	Fareham	115	127	Horsham	451	465
	Hartley Wintney	129	137	Lewes	467	499
	Havant	139	151	Midhurst	501	513
	Kingsclere	153	163	Petworth	515	521
	Petersfield	165	175	Rye	523	535
	Portsea	177	217	Steyning	537	557
	Romsey	219	229	Thakeham	559	563
	Southampton	231	261	Ticehurst	565	575
	South Stoneham	263	279	Uckfield	577	593
	Stockbridge	281	287	Westbourne	595	601
	Whitchurch	289	293	Westhampnett	603	631
	Winchester	295	319	Worthing	633	653
	Battle	321	337			
Volume 8	Beaminster	1	21	Amesbury	357	379
	Blandford	23	43	Bradford Wilts	381	395
	Bridport	45	61	Calne	397	407
	Dorchester	63	105	Chippenham	409	429
	Poole	107	119	Cricklade	431	445
	Shaftesbury	121	137	Devizes	447	477
	Sherborne	139	162	Swindon	479	497
	Sturminster	163	169	Malmsbury	499	519

Volume						
Volume 8	Wareham	171	187	Marlborough	521	537
continued	Weymouth	189	212	Melksham	539	555
	Wimborne	213	235	Mere	557	571
	Christchurch	237	243	Pewsey	573	595
	Fordingbridge	245	255	Salisbury	597	602
	Lymington	257	269	Tisbury	603	611
	New Forest	271	287	Warminster	613	631
	Ringwood	289	295	Westbury	633	645
	Isle of Wight	297	333	Wilton	647	667
	Alderbury	335	355			
Volume 9	St Austel	1	27	Scilly Isles	281	282
	Bodmin	29	56	Stratton	283	301
	Camelford	57	71	Truro	303	336
	St Columb	73	87	East Stonehouse	337	351
	Falmouth	89	109	Holsworthy	353	379
	St Germans	111	120	Kingsbridge	381	407
	Helston	121	150	Plymouth	409	441
	Launceston	151	168	Plympton St Mary	443	465
	Liskeard	169	204	Stoke Damerel	467	498
	Penzance	205	243	Tavistock	499	522
	Redruth	245	280	Totnes	523	546
Volume 10	Axminster	1	23	Axbridge	477	514
	Barnstaple	25	75	Bridgwater	515	555
	Bideford	77	102	Chard	557	589
	Crediton	103	129	Frome	591	607
	Exeter	131	165	Langport	609	637
	Honiton	167	199	Shepton Mallett	639	655
	Newton Abbott	201	261	Taunton	657	695
	Okehampton	263	305	Wellington Som	697	718
	South Molton	307	331	Wells	719	739
	St Thomas	333	396	Williton	741	771
	Tiverton	397	445	Wincanton	773	817
	Torrington	447	475	Yeovil	819	853
Volume 11	Bath	1	51	Newent	377	385
	Bedminster	53	84	Northleach	387	409
	Clutton	85	117	Shipston	411	443
	Keynsham	119	131	Stow in the Wold	445	459
	Bristol	133	207	Stroud	461	505
	Cheltenham	209	239	Tetbury	507	511
	Chipping Sodbury	241	255	Tewkesbury	513	539
	Cirencester	257	283	Thornbury	541	551
	Clifton	285	320	Westbury	553	573
	Dursley	321	333	Wheatenhurst	575	587
	Gloucester	335	376	Winchcombe	589	591
Volume 12	Billericay	1	17	Saffron Walden	319	347
	Braintree	19	52	Tendring	349	375

Volume 12	Chelmsford	53	73	West Ham	377	397
continued	Colchester	75	103	Witham	399	417
	Dumow	105	135	Bosmere	419	451
	Epping	137	159	Cosford	453	485
	Halstead	161	184	Ipswich	487	520
	Lexden	185	221	Plomesgate	521	550
	Maldon	223	251	Risbridge	551	573
	Ongar	253	269	Samford	575	589
	Orsett	271	285	Stow	591	625
	Rochford	287	299	Sudbury	627	672
	Romford	301	317	Woodbridge	673	711
Volume 13	Aylsham	1	31	Norwich	415	487
	Blofield	33	52	Swaffham	489	515
	Depwade	53	87	Thetford	517	551
	Docking	89	125	Tunstead	553	591
	Downham	127	147	Walsingham	593	627
	Erpingham	149	175	Wayland	629	651
	St Faith's	177	201	Yarmouth	653	669
	Fleggs	203	231	Blything	671	712
	Forehoe	233	243	Bury St Edmunds	713	720
	Freebridge Lynn	245	265	Hartismere	721	749
	Guiltcross	267	291	Hoxne	751	770
	Henstead	293	313	Mildenhall	771	775
	King's Lynn	315	330	Mutford	777	807
	Loddon	331	365	Thingoe	809	845
	Mitford	367	413	Wangford	847	871
Volume 14	Cambridge	1	29	Bourn	351	375
	Caxton	31	49	Caistor	377	407
	Chesterton	51	89	Gainsborough	409	441
	Ely	91	107	Glanford Brigg	443	495
	Linton	109	127	Grantham	497	549
	Newmarket	129	163	Holbeach	551	569
	N Witchford	165	175	Horncastle	571	595
	Whittlesea	177	180	Lincoln	597	659
	Wisbeach	181	217	Louth	660	687
	Huntingdon	219	247	Sleaford	689	721
	St Ives	249	275	Spalding	723	746
	St Neots	277	305	Spilsby	747	786
	Boston	307	349	Stamford	787	812
Volume 15	Ashby de la Zouch	1	31	Oundle	429	455
	Barrow on Soar	33	59	Peterborough	457	485
	Billesdon	61	73	Potterspury	487	499
	Blaby	75	95	Thrapstone	501	519
	Hinckley	97	113	Towcester	521	543
	Leicester	115	146	Wellingborough	545	569
	Loughborough	147	169	Basford	571	628
	Lutterworth	171	189	Bingham	629	649

Volume 15	Mkt Harborough	191	219	East Retford	651	683
continued	Mkt Bosworth	221	251	Mansfield	685	714
	Melton Mowbray	253	290	Newark	715	740
	Brackley	291	309	Nottingham	741	779
	Brixworth	311	331	Radford	781	794
	Daventry	333	357	Southwell	795	838
	Hardingstone	359	373	Worksop	839	859
	Kettering	375	399	Oakham	861	872
	Northampton	401	427	Uppingham	873	901
Volume 16	Banbury	1	38	Birmingham	281	373
	Bicester	39	57	Coventry	375	399
	Chipping Norton	59	78	Foleshill	401	413
	Headington	79	97	Meriden	415	423
	Henley	99	115	Nuneaton	425	436
	Oxford	117	141	Rugby	437	465
	Thame	143	165	Solihull	467	477
	Witney	167	191	Southam	479	491
	Woodstock	193	207	Stratford on Avon	493	513
	Alcester	209	229	Tamworth	515	529
	Aston	231	268	Warwick	531	567
	Atherstone	269	280			
Volume 17	Burton on Trent	1	39	Stoke on Trent	181	221
	Cheadle	41	65	Stone	223	251
	Leek	67	87	Uttoxeter	253	273
	Lichfield	89	123	Walsall	275	295
	Newcastle L	125	141	Wolstanton	297	321
	Penkridge	143	153	Wolverhampton	323	383
	Stafford	155	179			
Volume 18	Atcham	1	33	Wem	267	281
	Bridgnorth	35	47	Bromsgrove	283	295
	Church Stretton	49	61	Droitwich	297	315
	Cleobury Mortimer	63	73	Dudley	317	376
	Clun	75	95	Evesham	377	407
	Ellesmere	97	107	Kidderminster	409	424
	Ludlow	109	127	Kings Norton	425	455
	Madeley	129	145	Martley	457	471
	Market Drayton	147	165	Pershore	473	493
	Newport Salop	167	187	Stourbridge	495	523
	Oswestry	189	204	Tenbury	525	527
	Shiffnal	205	219	Upton on Severn	529	549
	Shrewsbury	221	240	Worcester	551	572
	Wellington Salop	241	265	West Bromwich	573	610
Volume 19	Altrincham	1	23	Ashborne	277	315
	Great Boughton	25	70	Bakewell	317	339
	Congleton	71	95	Belper	341	385
	Macclesfield	97	131	Chapel en le Frith	387	395

Volume 19	Nantwich	133	159	Chesterfield	397	432
continued	Northwich	161	181	Derby	433	469
	Runcorn	183	201	Hayfield	471	481
	Stockport	203	253	Shardlow	483	533
	Wirral	255	276			
Volume 20	Ashton	1	41	Prescot	607	635
	Chorlton	43	93	Salford	637	651
	Liverpool	95	313	Warrington	653	673
	Manchester	315	606	West Derby	675	729
Volume 21	Blackburn	1	43	Haslingden	293	324
	Bolton	45	110	Lancaster	325	358
	Burnley	111	159	Leigh	359	380
	Bury	161	203	Ormskirk	381	412
	Chorley	205	233	Preston	413	474
	Clitheroe	235	258	Rochdale	475	525
	Fylde	259	280	Todmorden	527	543
	Garstang	281	291	Wigan	545	592
Volume 22	Dewsbury	1	37	Pontefract	275	311
	Doncaster	39	73	Rotherham	313	351
	Ecclesall Bierlow	75	80	Sculcoates	353	403
	Ecclesfield	81	107	Sheffield	405	481
	Halifax	109	177	Skirlaugh	483	497
	Huddersfield	179	233	Wakefield	499	537
	Hull	235	274	Wortley	539	553
Volume 23	Beverley	1	29	Otley	455	476
	Bridlington	31	47	Pateley Bridge	477	483
	Driffield	49	85	Ripon	485	499
	Howden	87	102	Saddleworth	501	503
	Patrington	103	119	Sedbergh	505	511
	Pocklington	121	147	Selby	513	523
	Bradford Yks	149	251	Settle	525	535
	Goole	253	269	Skipton	537	569
	Hunslet	271	301	Tadcaster	571	596
	Keighley	303	322	Thorne	597	611
	Knaresborough	323	351	York	613	686
	Leeds	353	453			
Volume 24	Auckland	1	22	Easingwold	355	371
	Chester le Street	23	34	Guisborough	373	383
	Darlington	35	59	Helmsley	385	397
	Durham	61	105	Leyburn	399	405
	Easington	107	125	Malton	407	445
	Gateshead	127	149	Northallerton	447	459
	Houghton le Spring	151	165	Pickering	461	475
	South Shields	167	196	Reeth	477	487
	Stockton	197	246	Richmond	489	503
	Sunderland	247	301	Scarborough	507	529

Volume 24 continued	Teesdale	303	323	Stokesley	531	543
	Weardale	325	335	Thirsk	545	557
	Askrigg	337	341	Whitby	559	579
	Bedale	343	353			

Volume 25	Alstone	1	7	Bellingham	235	243
	Berwick	9	21	Castle Ward	245	249
	Bootle	23	31	Glendale	251	258
	Brampton	33	41	Haltwhistle	259	261
	Carlisle	43	70	Hexham	263	287
	Cockermouth	71	111	Morpeth	289	305
	Longtown	113	119	Newcastle on Tyne	307	380
	Penrith	121	134	Rothbury	381	391
	Whitehaven	135	166	Tynemouth	393	434
	Wigton	167	187	East Ward	435	455
	Ulverstone	189	209	Kendal	457	483
	Alnwick	211	225	West Ward	485	489
	Belford	227	233			

Volume 26	Abergavenny	1	33	Crickhowell	375	392
	Chepstow	35	49	Hay	393	407
	Monmouth	57	77	Bridgend	421	449
	Newport Mon	87	122	Cardiff	443	472
	Pontypool	123	149	Merthyr Tydfil	473	524
	Bromyard	151	157	Neath	525	558
	Hereford	159	216	Swansea	559	587
	Ledbury	217	233	Carmarthen	589	635
	Leominster	235	255	Llandilofawr	637	655
	Ross	257	277	Llandovery	657	677
	Weobly	279	291	Llanelly	679	698
	Knighton	293	303	Haverfordwest	699	755
	Presteigne	305	323	Narberth	757	787
	Rhyader	325	335	Newcastle Emlyn	789	813
	Brecknock	337	353	Pembroke	815	843
	Builth	355	373			

Volume 27	Aberayron	1	22	Festiniog	241	264
	Aberystwith	23	47	St Asaph	265	293
	Cardigan	49	75	Llanrwst	295	308
	Lampeter	77	95	Ruthin	309	321
	Tregaron	97	113	Holywell	323	351
	Llanfyllin	115	139	Wrexham	353	389
	Machynlleth	141	157	Bangor	391	428
	Montgomery	159	176	Carnarvon	429	459
	Newtown	177	198	Conway	461	479
	Bala	199	207	Pwllheli	481	519
	Corwen	209	224	Anglesea	521	579
	Dolgelly	225	239			

Page Range Table for 1856 March Quarter

This table shows the range of page references for each Superintendent
Registrar's district within each of the 33 volumes of the GRO records,
as the GRO records were re-arranged from 1852

Volume 1a	Kensington	7	179	St Martin's	405	457
	Chelsea	181	237	St James	459	514
	St George Han Sq	239	341	Marylebone	515	699
	Westminster	343	403	Hampstead	701	707
Volume 1b	Pancras	1	177	Strand	459	513
	Islington	179	306	Holborn	515	541
	Hackney	307	385	Clerkenwell	543	607
	St Giles	387	458	St Luke's	609	643
Volume 1c	East London	1	77	Whitechapel	583	671
	West London	79	145	St George East	673	714
	London City	147	258	Stepney	715	863
	Shoreditch	259	422	Poplar	865	930
	Bethnal Green	423	581			
Volume 1d	St Saviour	3	36	Lambeth	251	500
	St Olave	37	53	Wandsworth	501	545
	Bermondsey	55	102	Camberwell	547	599
	St Geo South'k	103	161	Rotherhithe	601	617
	Newington	163	249	Greenwich	619	709
	Lewisham	711	784			
Volume 2a	Epsom	5	15	Sevenoaks	411	431
	Chertsey	17	39	Tunbridge	433	464
	Guildford	41	72	Maidstone	465	507
	Farnham	73	79	Hollingbourne	509	531
	Farnborough	81	91	Cranbrook	533	551
	Hambledon	93	111	Tenterden	553	561
	Dorking	113	121	W Ashford	563	581
	Reigate	123	139	E Ashford	583	601
	Godstone	141	149	Bridge	603	617
	Croydon	151	178	Canterbury	619	650
	Kingston	179	211	Blean	651	673
	Richmond	213	223	Faversham	675	709
	Bromley	225	247	Milton	711	733
	Dartford	249	269	Sheppey	735	748
	Gravesend	271	288	Thanet	749	781
	N Aylesford	289	317	Eastry	783	815
	Hoo	319	321	Dover	817	852
	Medway	323	380	Elham	853	879
	Malling	381	407	Romney Marsh	881	893
Volume 2b	Rye	1	20	Worthing	339	359

Volume 2b	Hastings	21	44	W Hampnett	361	397
continued	Battle	45	64	Chichester	399	419
	Eastbourne	65	72	Midhurst	421	433
	Hailsham	73	91	Westbourne	435	445
	Ticehurst	93	105	Havant	447	454
	Uckfield	107	129	Portsea	455	613
	East Grinstead	131	139	Alverstoke	615	650
	Cuckfield	141	155	Fareham	651	665
	Lewes	157	207	Isle of Wight	667	737
	Brighton	209	273	Lymington	739	753
	Steyning	275	297	Christchurch	755	764
	Horsham	299	319	Ringwood	765	773
	Petworth	321	327	Fordingbridge	775	783
	Thakeham	329	337	New Forest	785	797
Volume 2c	Southampton	1	65	Kingsclere	293	305
	S Stoneham	67	83	Newbury	309	331
	Romsey	85	97	Hungerford	333	353
	Stockbridge	99	113	Farringdon	355	375
	Winchester	115	159	Abingdon	377	407
	Droxford	161	169	Wantage	409	429
	Catherington	171		Wallingford	431	443
	Petersfield	173	183	Bradfield	445	471
	Alresford	185	191	Reading	473	507
	Alton	193	213	Wokingham	509	521
	Hartley Wintney	215	231	Cookham	523	533
	Basingstoke	233	261	E Hampstead	535	543
	Whitchurch	263	269	Windsor	545	565
	Andover	271	292			
Volume 3a	Staines	1	11	Amersham	321	343
	Uxbridge	13	35	Eton	345	371
	Brentford	37	75	Wycombe	373	419
	Hendon	77	91	Aylesbury	421	457
	Barnet	93	103	Winslow	459	469
	Edmonton	105	141	Newport Pagnell	471	502
	Ware	143	157	Buckingham	503	523
	Bps Stortford	159	183	Henley	525	545
	Royston	185	223	Thame	547	569
	Hitchin	227	248	Headington	571	595
	Hertford	249	257	Oxford	597	629
	Hatfield	259	263	Bicester	631	655
	St Albans	265	286	Woodstock	657	681
	Watford	287	301	Witney	683	715
	Hemel Hempstead	303	311	Chipping Norton	717	737
	Berkhampstead	313	319	Banbury	739	792
Volume 3b	Brackley	1	21	Bedford	435	492
	Towcester	23	41	Biggleswade	493	527
	Potterspury	43	62	Ampthill	529	559

Volume 3b						
Volume 3b continued	Hardingstone	63	75	Woburn	561	571
	Northampton	77	125	Leighton Buzzard	573	591
	Daventry	127	164	Luton	593	618
	Brixworth	165	193	Caxton	619	635
	Wellingbro	195	225	Chesterton	637	689
	Kettering	227	248	Cambridge	691	717
	Thrapston	249	271	Linton	719	741
	Oundle	273	296	Newmarket	743	775
	Peterborough	297	343	Ely	777	801
	Huntingdon	345	371	N Witchford	803	817
	St Ives	373	405	Whittlesey	819	825
	St Neots	407	433	Wisbeach	827	866
Volume 4a	West Ham	1	34	Risbridge	457	483
	Epping	35	62	Sudbury	485	525
	Ongar	63	81	Cosford	527	551
	Romford	83	101	Thingoe	553	587
	Orsett	103	121	Bury St Edmunds	589	604
	Billericay	123	143	Mildenhall	605	619
	Chelmsford	145	179	Stow	621	655
	Rochford	181	201	Hartismere	657	688
	Maldon	203	237	Hoxne	689	723
	Tendring	239	275	Bosmere	725	753
	Colchester	277	306	Samford	755	773
	Lexden	307	344	Ipswich	775	824
	Witham	345	361	Woodbridge	825	862
	Halstead	363	385	Plomesgate	863	903
	Braintree	387	407	Blything	905	938
	Dunmow	409	437	Wangford	939	956
	Saffron Walden	439	456	Mutford	955	997
Volume 4b	Yarmouth	1	34	Depwade	373	415
	Fleggs	35	47	Guiltcross	417	437
	Tunstead	49	77	Wayland	439	471
	Erpingham	79	126	Mitford	473	528
	Aylsham	127	151	Walsingham	529	563
	St Faith's	153	173	Docking	565	599
	Norwich	175	281	Freebridge Lynn	601	623
	Forehoe	283	302	Kings Lynn	625	646
	Henstead	303	321	Downham	647	671
	Blofield	323	337	Swaffham	673	691
	Loddon	339	371	Thetford	693	717
Volume 5a	Highworth	3	25	Wilton	283	299
	Cricklade	27	45	Tisbury	301	321
	Malmsbury	47	68	Mere	323	340
	Chippenham	69	91	Shaftesbury	341	351
	Calne	93	101	Sturminster	353	366
	Marlborough	103	115	Blandford	367	383
	Devizes	117	145	Wimbourne	385	418

Volume 5a	Melksham	147	161		Poole	419	436
continued	Bradford Wilts	163	179		Wareham	437	461
	Westbury	181	191		Weymouth	463	499
	Warminster	193	211		Dorchester	501	544
	Pewsey	213	231		Sherborne	545	569
	Amesbury	233	245		Beaminster	571	583
	Alderbury	247	269		Bridport	585	619
	Salisbury	271	281				
Volume 5b	Axminster	1	39		Stoke Damerel	539	640
	Honiton	41	66		Tavistock	641	675
	St Thomas	67	129		Okehampton	677	705
	Exeter	131	202		Crediton	707	735
	Newton Abbot	203	277		Tiverton	737	793
	Totnes	279	333		South Molton	795	834
	Kingsbridge	335	373		Barnstaple	835	887
	Plympton	375	401		Torrington	889	915
	Plymouth	403	497		Bideford	917	948
	East Stonehouse	499	537		Holsworthy	949	973
Volume 5c	Stratton	1	19		Wellington Som	519	547
	Camelford	21	37		Taunton	549	597
	Launceston	39	67		Bridgwater	599	664
	St Germans	69	85		Langport	665	695
	Liskeard	87	125		Chard	697	739
	Bodmin	127	164		Yeovil	741	779
	St Columb	165	191		Wincanton	781	813
	St Austell	193	232		Frome	815	854
	Truro	233	281		Shepton Mallet	855	879
	Falmouth	283	311		Wells	881	908
	Helston	313	348		Axbridge	909	959
	Redruth	349	411		Clutton	961	979
	Penzance	413	469		Bath	981	1067
	Scilly Is.	471	472		Keynsham	1069	1090
	Williton	473	507		Bedminster	1091	1138
	Dulverton	509	517				
Volume 6a	Bristol	3	145		Weobly	679	687
	Clifton	147	217		Bromyard	689	707
	Chipping Sodbury	219	239		Leominster	711	729
	Thornbury	241	256		Ludlow	731	753
	Dursley	257	266		Clun	755	769
	Westbury	267	285		Church Stretton	771	778
	Newent	287	301		Cleobury Mortimer	779	791
	Gloucester	303	349		Bridgnorth	793	811
	Wheatenhurst	351	359		Shiffnal	813	835
	Stroud	361	403		Madeley	837	867
	Tetbury	405	413		Atcham	869	884
	Cirencester	415	459		Shrewsbury	885	917
	Northleach	461	477		Oswestry	919	953

Volume 6a	Stow in the Wold	479	495	Ellesmere	955	968
continued	Winchcomb	497	507	Wem	969	985
	Cheltenham	509	557	Whitchurch	987	999
	Tewkesbury	559	575	Market Drayton	1001	1021
	Ledbury	579	595	Wellington Salop	1023	1049
	Ross	597	612	Newport Salop	1051	1071
	Hereford	613	678			
Volume 6b	Stafford	1	29	Burton on Trent	349	394
	Stone	31	61	Tamworth	395	413
	Newcastle L	63	93	Lichfield	415	450
	Wolstanton	95	166	Penkridge	451	471
	Stoke on Trent	167	255	Wolverhampton	473	630
	Leek	257	281	Walsall	631	689
	Cheadle	283	313	West Bromwich	691	792
	Uttoxeter	315	347			
Volume 6c	Dudley	1	168	Upton on Severn	339	371
	Stourbridge	169	234	Evesham	373	395
	Kidderminster	235	262	Pershore	397	421
	Tenbury	263	273	Droitwich	423	445
	Martley	275	297	Bromsgrove	447	465
	Worcester	299	338	Kings Norton	467	524
Volume 6d	Birmingham	1	206	Rugby	401	427
	Aston	207	287	Solihull	429	446
	Meriden	289	299	Warwick	447	497
	Atherstone	301	309	Stratford on Avon	499	521
	Nuneaton	311	325	Alcester	523	543
	Foleshill	327	349	Shipton on S	545	577
	Coventry	351	400	Southam	579	585
Volume 7a	Lutterworth	1	33	Bourn	409	435
	Mkt Harborough	35	57	Spalding	437	457
	Billesdon	59	77	Holbeach	459	477
	Blaby	79	95	Boston	479	519
	Hinckley	97	115	Sleaford	521	557
	Mkt Bosworth	117	139	Grantham	559	598
	Ashby de la Zouch	141	175	Lincoln	599	674
	Loughborough	177	203	Horncastle	675	721
	Barrow on Soar	205	229	Spilsby	723	776
	Leicester	231	299	Louth	777	839
	Melton Mowbray	301	332	Caistor	841	879
	Oakham	333	353	Glanford Brigg	881	922
	Uppingham	355	377	Gainsborough	923	971
	Stamford	379	407			
Volume 7b	East Retford	3	44	Shardlow	389	425
	Worksop	45	71	Derby	427	503
	Mansfield	73	103	Belper	505	576
	Basford	105	186	Ashborne	577	607

Volume 7b	Radford	187	216	Chesterfield	609	675
continued	Nottingham	217	292	Bakewell	677	720
	Southwell	293	329	Chapel en le Frith	721	735
	Newark	331	369	Hayfield	737	765
	Bingham	371	387			
Volume 8a	Stockport	1	114	Congleton	265	303
	Macclesfield	115	171	Nantwich	305	343
	Altrincham	173	201	Gt Boughton	345	415
	Runcorn	203	231	Wirral	417	464
	Northwich	233	263			
Volume 8b	Liverpool	1	457	Prescot	615	685
	West Derby	459	614	Ormskirk	687	722
Volume 8c	Wigan	1	105	Bury	337	424
	Warrington	107	149	Barton	425	465
	Leigh	151	191	Chorlton	467	503
	Bolton	193	336			
Volume 8d	Salford	1	45	Ashton	495	632
	Manchester	47	494	Oldham	633	715
Volume 8e	Rochdale	1	104	Preston	465	574
	Haslingden	105	183	Fylde	575	598
	Burnley	185	282	Garstang	599	614
	Clitheroe	283	312	Lancaster	615	661
	Blackburn	313	423	Ulverstone	663	699
	Chorley	425	463			
Volume 9a	Sedbergh	1		Wetherby	129	142
	Settle	3	19	Otley	143	181
	Skipton	21	59	Keighley	183	226
	Pateley Bridge	61	64	Todmorden	227	245
	Ripon	65	85	Saddleworth	247	255
	Great Ouseburn	87	101	Huddersfield	257	369
	Knaresborough	103	128	Halifax	371	508
Volume 9b	Bradford Yorks	1	206	Leeds	259	448
	Hunslet	207	257	Dewsbury	449	555
Volume 9c	Wakefield	3	59	Rotherham	407	454
	Pontefract	61	101	Doncaster	455	513
	Hemsworth	103	111	Thorne	515	537
	Barnsley	113	146	Goole	539	557
	Wortley	147	175	Selby	559	573
	Ecclesall	177	188	Tadcaster	575	603
	Sheffield	189	405			
Volume 9d	York	1	104	Thirsk	517	531
	Pocklington	105	137	Helmsley	533	555

Volume 9d continued	Howden	139	162	Pickering	557	575
	Beverley	163	191	Whitby	577	610
	Sculcoates	193	251	Guisborough	611	635
	Hull	253	335	Stokesley	637	655
	Patrington	337	349	Northallerton	657	671
	Skirlaugh	351	371	Bedale	673	683
	Driffield	373	405	Leyburn	685	703
	Bridlington	407	427	Askrigg	705	710
	Scarborough	429	461	Reeth	711	719
	Malton	463	498	Richmond	721	741
	Easingwold	499	515			
Volume 10a	Darlington	1	33	Easington	315	347
	Stockton	35	119	Houghton le Spring	349	363
	Auckland	121	177	Chester le Street	365	388
	Teesdale	179	212	Sunderland	389	523
	Weardale	213	231	South Shields	525	579
	Durham	233	314	Gateshead	581	643
Volume 10b	Newcastle on Tyne	1	175	Penrith	379	403
	Tynemouth	177	265	Brampton	405	407
	Castle Ward	267	279	Longtown	409	417
	Hexham	281	308	Carlisle	419	454
	Haltwhistle	309	313	Wigton	455	481
	Bellingham	315	325	Cockermouth	483	513
	Morpeth	327	337	Whitehaven	515	554
	Alnwick	339	348	Bootle	555	559
	Berwick	349	362	East Ward	561	579
	Glendale	363	367	West Ward	581	587
	Rothbury	369	373	Kendal	589	622
	Alston	375	377			
Volume 11a	Chepstow	1	23	Swansea	559	611
	Monmouth	25	51	Llanelly	613	645
	Abergavenny	53	136	Llandovery	647	665
	Pontypool	137	183	Llandilofawr	667	689
	Newport Mon	185	243	Carmarthen	691	745
	Cardiff	245	329	Narberth	747	767
	Merthyr Tydfil	331	468	Pembroke	769	805
	Bridgend	469	502	Haverfordwest	807	877
	Neath	503	558			
Volume 11b	Cardigan	1	27	Llanfyllin	363	388
	Newcastle Emlyn	31	47	Holywell	389	433
	Lampeter	49	62	Wrexham	435	493
	Aberayron	63	87	Ruthin	495	510
	Aberystwith	89	125	St Asaph	511	543
	Tregaron	127	148	Llanrwst	545	558
	Builth	149	153	Corwen	559	575
	Brecknock	155	185	Bala	577	579
	Crickhowell	187	213	Dolgelly	581	593

Volume 11b	Hay	215	235	Festiniog	595	617
continued	Presteigne	237	259	Pwllheli	619	647
	Knighton	261	279	Carnarvon	649	687
	Rhyader	281	285	Bangor	689	747
	Machynlleth	287	299	Conway	749	765
	Newtown	301	328	Anglesey	767	811
	Montgomery	329	361			

Provisional Page Range Table for 1891 March Quarter

This table shows the range of page references for each Superintendent Registrar's district within each of the 33 volumes of the GRO records, based on a sample of 18200 entries from the 1891 marriage index

Volume 1a	Paddington	1	138	St George Han Sq	605	781
	Kensington	139	327	Westminster	785	839
	Fulham	329	498	Marylebone	847	1031
	Chelsea	503	603	Hampstead	1033	1097
Volume 1b	Pancras	1	267	St Giles	775	823
	Islington	269	567	Strand	827	889
	Hackney	569	769	Holborn	895	1039
Volume 1c	London City	1	108	St George East	539	582
	Shoreditch	117	243	Stepney	589	631
	Bethnal Green	247	470	Mile End	633	838
	Whitechapel	473	534	Poplar	839	986
Volume 1d	St Saviour	1	369	Camberwell	995	1164
	St Olave	373	469	Greenwich	1167	1287
	Lambeth	471	726	Lewisham	1291	1376
	Wandsworth	731	987	Woolwich	1385	1485
Volume 2a	Epsom	1	38	Tunbridge	925	968
	Chertsey	39	63	Maidstone	973	1023
	Guildford	81	109	Hollingbourne	1029	1037
	Farnham	113	170	Cranbrook	1039	1060
	Hambledon	173	198	Tenterden	1067	1071
	Dorking	201	223	W Ashford	1073	1100
	Reigate	225	265	E Ashford	1107	1113
	Godstone	269	282	Bridge	1125	1127
	Croydon	289	422	Canterbury	1133	1151
	Kingston	425	524	Blean	1161	1177
	Richmond	533	567	Faversham	1179	1203
	Bromley	569	633	Milton	1209	1234
	Dartford	635	687	Sheppey	1235	1247
	Gravesend	693	729	Thanet	1255	1296
	Strood	731	771	Eastry	1303	1327
	Medway	775	849	Dover	1333	1377
	Malling	853	887	Elham	1381	1438
	Sevenoaks	891	923	Romney Marsh	1439	1447
Volume 2b	Rye	1	20	East Preston	507	536
	Hastings	31	78	W Hampnett	537	564
	Battle	79	93	Chichester	567	583
	Eastbourne	97	134	Midhurst	585	593
	Hailsham	141	149	Westbourne	601	608
	Ticehurst	153	175	Havant	615	617

Volume 2b	Uckfield	183	199	Portsea	621	795
continued	East Grinstead	203	216	Alverstoke	799	811
	Cuckfield	217	235	Fareham	817	832
	Lewes	247	279	Isle of Wight	833	912
	Brighton	281	383	Lymington	921	940
	Steyning	395	447	Christchurch	943	988
	Horsham	455	475	Ringwood	995	998
	Petworth	479	488	Fordingbridge	1001	
	Thakeham	491	503	New Forest	1007	1027
Volume 2c	Southampton	1	70	Kingsclere	367	375
	S Stoneham	75	115	Newbury	377	407
	Romsey	129	130	Hungerford	409	434
	Stockbridge	139	149	Farringdon	461	463
	Winchester	151	201	Abingdon	465	490
	Droxford	203	207	Wantage	493	515
	Petersfield	223	229	Wallingford	525	545
	Alresford	233	247	Bradfield	551	575
	Alton	257	278	Reading	577	631
	Hartley Wintney	285	305	Wokingham	637	649
	Basingstoke	311	335	Cookham	661	677
	Whitchurch	339	341	E Hampstead	679	689
	Andover	345	361	Windsor	695	729
Volume 3a	Staines	1	33	Amersham	731	757
	Uxbridge	35	62	Eton	767	784
	Brentford	65	174	Wycombe	785	831
	Hendon	177	253	Aylesbury	835	865
	Barnet	263	289	Newport Pagnell	879	918
	Edmonton	295	456	Buckingham	925	939
	Ware	457	475	Henley	955	969
	Bps Stortford	485	510	Thame	975	981
	Royston	511	545	Headington	985	1020
	Hitchin	551	576	Oxford	1021	1044
	Hertford	583	601	Bicester	1049	1065
	Hatfield	603	615	Woodstock	1068	1091
	St Albans	617	644	Witney	1103	1111
	Watford	645	682	Chipping Norton	1117	1135
	Hemel Hempstead	687	703	Banbury	1139	1168
	Berkhampstead	707	726			
Volume 3b	Brackley	1	19	Bedford	499	556
	Towcester	25	37	Biggleswade	557	587
	Potterspury	41	55	Ampthill	589	611
	Hardingstone	63	82	Woburn	619	627
	Northampton	89	159	Leighton Buzzard	633	643
	Daventry	161	181	Luton	645	689
	Brixworth	187	215	Caxton	691	
	Wellingborough	217	273	Chesterton	697	736

Volume 3b continued	Kettering	277	319	Cambridge	741	780
	Thrapston	323	354	Linton	783	789
	Oundle	355	379	Newmarket	801	836
	Peterborough	383	429	Ely	841	864
	Huntingdon	435	453	N Witchford	867	873
	St Ives	465	469	Whittlesey	885	
	St Neots	473	497	Wisbeach	887	924
Volume 4a	West Ham	1	295	Sudbury	829	851
	Epping	301	323	Cosford	853	873
	Ongar	325	333	Thingoe	877	903
	Romford	341	380	Bury St Edmunds	909	922
	Orsett	385	410	Mildenhall	929	935
	Billericay	413	421	Stow	937	956
	Chelmsford	439	487	Hartismere	959	979
	Rochford	491	521	Hoxne	981	997
	Maldon	523	553	Bosmere	1001	1021
	Tendring	557	606	Samford	1025	1029
	Colchester	607	643	Ipswich	1041	1086
	Lexden	647	690	Woodbridge	1089	1123
	Halstead	697	717	Plomesgate	1127	1156
	Braintree	719	758	Blything	1159	1188
	Dunmow	761	777	Wangford	1191	1201
	Saffron Walden	783	799	Mutford	1205	1336
	Risbridge	809	823			
Volume 4b	Yarmouth	1	34	Depwade	339	368
	Fleggs	37	45	Guiltcross	377	381
	Smallburgh	59	63	Wayland	391	407
	Erpingham	69	85	Mitford	411	438
	Aylsham	87	115	Walsingham	439	457
	St Faith's	125	137	Docking	463	480
	Norwich	139	247	Freebridge Lynn	487	503
	Forehoe	251	263	King's Lynn	505	527
	Henstead	269	285	Downham	529	555
	Blofield	287	307	Swaffham	563	575
	Loddon	309	331	Thetford	587	593
Volume 5a	Highworth	1	44	Wilton	323	339
	Cricklade	47	57	Tisbury	349	
	Malmsbury	63	89	Mere	Not found	
	Chippenham	97	119	Shaftesbury	373	387
	Calne	127	133	Sturminster	389	393
	Marlborough	139		Blandford	409	431
	Devizes	147	175	Wimborne	432	457
	Melksham	185	201	Poole	463	488
	Bradford Wilts	209	223	Wareham	491	517
	Westbury	229	238	Weymouth	521	558

Volume 5a continued	Warminster	243	257	Dorchester	563	610
	Pewsey	269	271	Sherborne	615	633
	Amesbury	285	286	Beaminster	635	643
	Alderbury	293	319	Bridport	655	
Volume 5b	Axminster	1	27	Stoke Damerel	511	591
	Honiton	33	72	Tavistock	597	625
	St Thomas	75	127	Okehampton	631	659
	Exeter	129	176	Crediton	667	685
	Newton Abbot	179	271	Tiverton	689	716
	Totnes	277	327	South Molton	719	744
	Kingsbridge	337	345	Barnstaple	745	798
	Plympton	355	383	Torrington	805	824
	Plymouth	389	490	Bideford	833	852
	East Stonehouse	493	508	Holsworthy	861	872
Volume 5c	Stratton	1	13	Wellington Som	461	483
	Camelford	25		Taunton	485	543
	Launceston	29	46	Bridgwater	545	598
	St Germans	59	65	Langport	605	635
	Liskeard	71	104	Chard	641	668
	Bodmin	107	123	Yeovil	671	719
	St Columb	131	149	Wincanton	723	756
	St Austell	151	176	Frome	759	782
	Truro	179	223	Shepton Mallet	789	799
	Falmouth	225	244	Wells	801	829
	Helston	253	291	Axbridge	831	875
	Redruth	293	356	Clutton	881	920
	Penzance	361	410	Bath	927	995
	Scilly	Not found		Keynsham	999	1035
	Williton	419	450	Bedminster	1039	1110
	Dulverton	451	457			
Volume 6a	Bristol	1	133	Weobly	785	789
	Barton Regis	135	284	Bromyard	803	812
	Chipping Sodbury	287	319	Leominster	817	827
	Thornbury	321	327	Kington	837	839
	Dursley	335	347	Ludlow	841	865
	Westbury	353	377	Clun	873	883
	Newent	385	393	Cleobury Mortimer	899	900
	Gloucester	395	466	Bridgnorth	905	920
	Wheatenhurst	471	472	Shiffnal	923	935
	Stroud	477	509	Madeley	941	959
	Tetbury	515	518	Atcham	967	1015
	Cirencester	519	545	Shrewsbury	Not found	
	Northleach	555	561	Oswestry	1019	1060
	Stow in the Wold	579	583	Ellesmere	1063	1069
	Winchcomb	595		Wem	1081	1099
	Cheltenham	605	644	Whitchurch	1101	1115
	Tewkesbury	651	667	Market Drayton	1117	1140

Volume 6a	Ledbury	673	683	Wellington Salop	1145	1175
continued	Ross	691	716	Newport Sal	1177	1204
	Hereford	729	777			
Volume 6b	Stafford	1	43	Burton on Trent	507	590
	Stone	51	89	Tamworth	593	617
	Newcastle L	93	127	Lichfield	619	683
	Wolstanton	131	228	Cannock	687	735
	Stoke on Trent	231	373	Wolverhampton	737	890
	Leek	381	423	Walsall	893	1007
	Cheadle	427	473	West Bromwich	1009	1145
	Uttoxeter	481	499			
Volume 6c	Dudley	1	162	Upton on Severn	423	453
	Stourbridge	171	273	Evesham	463	475
	Kidderminster	275	324	Pershore	477	491
	Tenbury	329	337	Droitwich	495	507
	Martley	351	362	Bromsgrove	509	549
	Worcester	369	419	King's Norton	551	670
Volume 6d	Birmingham	1	294	Rugby	707	736
	Aston	299	545	Solihull	741	773
	Meriden	561		Warwick	775	835
	Atherstone	563	588	Stratford on Avon	841	857
	Nuneaton	591	609	Alcester	861	880
	Foleshill	611	633	Shipton on S	883	884
	Coventry	637	705	Southam	897	911
Volume 7a	Lutterworth	1	15	Bourn	577	605
	Mkt Harborough	25	27	Spalding	609	628
	Billesdon	45	53	Holbeach	633	645
	Blaby	55	103	Boston	657	690
	Hinckley	107	135	Sleaford	699	724
	Mkt Bosworth	137	161	Grantham	727	765
	Ashby de la Zouch	163	217	Lincoln	767	846
	Loughborough	219	265	Horncastle	851	860
	Barrow on Soar	267	316	Spilsby	881	919
	Leicester	319	492	Louth	917	979
	Melton Mowbray	499	513	Caistor	983	1069
	Oakham	523	531	Glanford Brigg	1071	1123
	Uppingham	535	539	Gainsborough	1127	1143
	Stamford	555	573			
Volume 7b	East Retford	1	27	Shardlow	617	672
	Worksop	39	77	Derby	675	778
	Mansfield	79	143	Belper	783	865
	Basford	147	320	Ashborne	877	915
	Nottingham	323	533	Chesterfield	917	1071
	Southwell	535	566	Bakewell	1073	1109
	Newark	567	596	Chapel en le Frith	1111	1142

Vol 7b ctd	Bingham	601	613	Hayfield	1145	1183
Volume 8a	Stockport	1	148	Congleton	435	486
	Macclesfield	151	237	Nantwich	487	573
	Altrincham	241	308	Chester	579	679
	Runcorn	319	365	Wirral	681	723
	Northwich	367	429	Birkenhead	727	831
Volume 8b	Liverpool	1	345	Prescot	839	972
	Toxteth Park	349	456	Ormskirk	977	1078
	West Derby	461	836			
Volume 8c	Wigan	1	216	Bury	677	837
	Warrington	219	316	Barton on Irwell	839	934
	Leigh	321	406	Chorlton	935	1268
	Bolton	409	672			
Volume 8d	Salford	1	224	Ashton	543	721
	Manchester	227	388	Oldham	725	947
	Prestwich	391	537			
Volume 8e	Rochdale	1	140	Fylde	939	999
	Haslingden	143	260	Garstang	1007	1018
	Burnley	261	433	Lancaster	1023	1083
	Clitheroe	439	468	Lunesdale	1089	1101
	Blackburn	477	714	Ulverston	1111	1157
	Chorley	715	771	Barrow in Furness	1159	1208
	Preston	775	937			
Volume 9a	Sedbergh	1		Wetherby	163	177
	Settle	7	29	Wharfedale	179	222
	Skipton	31	70	Keighley	223	290
	Pateley Bridge	79	83	Todmorden	297	320
	Ripon	85	102	Saddleworth	331	345
	Great Ouseburn	103	123	Huddersfield	351	528
	Knaresborough	129	159	Halifax	531	737
Volume 9b	Bradford Yorks	1	353	Bramley	477	522
	Hunslet	355	436	Leeds	523	802
	Holbeck	439	466	Dewsbury	803	996
Volume 9c	Wakefield	1	115	Rotherham	801	900
	Pontefract	117	175	Doncaster	909	969
	Hemsworth	179	186	Thorne	973	987
	Barnsley	193	306	Goole	991	1016
	Wortley	309	369	Selby	1017	1036
	Ecclesall	373	474	Tadcaster	1041	1071
	Sheffield	478	797			
Volume 9d	York	1	105	Thirsk	607	

Volume 9d continued	Pocklington	109	127	Helmsley	613	623
	Howden	137	149	Pickering	627	643
	Beverley	151	185	Whitby	653	669
	Sculcoates	189	320	Guisborough	683	715
	Hull	325	425	Middlesbrough	721	841
	Patrington	429	441	Stokesley	843	855
	Skirlaugh	453		Northallerton	857	858
	Driffield	467	479	Bedale	867	871
	Bridlington	485	504	Leyburn	877	887
	Scarborough	507	545	Askrigg	Not found	
	Malton	553	586	Reeth	Not found	
	Easingwold	587	595	Richmond	903	907
Volume 10a	Darlington	1	59	Durham	481	565
	Stockton	65	165	Easington	567	628
	Hartlepool	169	239	Houghton	635	681
	Auckland	241	348	Chester le Street	687	740
	Teesdale	353	372	Sunderland	741	929
	Weardale	377	393	South Shields	935	1082
	Lanchester	397	478	Gateshead	1083	1244
Volume 10b	Newcastle on Tyne	1	265	Penrith	653	692
	Tynemouth	271	431	Brampton	697	703
	Castle Ward	445	455	Longtown	705	712
	Hexham	465	494	Carlisle	713	770
	Haltwhistle	499	503	Wigton	775	803
	Bellingham	507		Cockermouth	805	883
	Morpeth	513	574	Whitehaven	885	952
	Alnwick	579	599	Bootle	957	969
	Berwick	609	628	East Ward	975	988
	Glendale	632	633	West Ward	989	1007
	Rothbury	641	642	Kendal	1015	1063
	Alston	645	653			
Volume 11a	Chepstow	1	36	Pontardawe	1095	1123
	Monmouth	41	81	Swansea	1129	1271
	Abergavenny	83	111	Gower	1275	1285
	Bedwelty	113	198	Llanelly	1293	1353
	Pontypool	203	251	Llandovery	1357	1367
	Newport Mon	253	375	Llandilofawr	1369	1394
	Cardiff	379	602	Carmarthen	1395	1433
	Pontypridd	603	820	Narberth	1438	1448
	Merthyr Tydfil	823	947	Pembroke	1461	1491
	Bridgend	951	1013	Haverfordwest	1505	1519
	Neath	1015	1090			
Volume 11b	Cardigan	1	17	Forden	229	248
	Newcastle Emlyn	19	31	Llanfyllin	251	273
	Lampeter	39	47	Holywell	275	320
	Aberayron	49	59	Wrexham	325	401

Volume 11b	Aberystwith	71	75	Ruthin	405	413
continued	Tregaron	87	89	St Asaph	423	450
	Builth	93	99	Llanrwst	453	458
	Brecknock	101	127	Corwen	467	480
	Crickhowell	129	149	Bala	Not found	
	Hay	155	161	Dolgelly	489	502
	Presteigne	Not found		Festiniog	505	529
	Knighton	163	179	Pwllheli	535	547
	Rhyader	187		Carnarvon	549	587
	Machynlleth	191	199	Bangor	589	622
	Newtown	203	226	Conway	625	652
	Montgomery	Not found		Anglesey	655	668
				Holyhead	673	695

Note : This is very much a working document based on less than 20% of the entries in the 1891/Q1 index.

(Referenced in chapter 12, page 149)

Seasonality - page range table for Essex/Suffolk 1844
(volume 12)

County	District	Q1	Q2	Q3	Q4
ESSEX	Billericay	1-13	1-15	1-31	1-29
	Braintree	-35	-41	-49	-62
	Chelmsford	-75	-87	-89	-118
	Colchester	-97	-117	-118	-145
	Dunmow	-124	-145	-135	-183
	Epping	-143	-165	-151	-205
	Halstead	-167	-193	-177	-240
	Lexden	-201	-229	-217	-289
	Maldon	-235	-259	-253	-337
	Ongar	-249	-271	-271	-365
	Orsett	-271	-297	-291	-387
	Rochford	-289	-319	-321	-426
	Romford	-303	-343	-337	-443
	Saffron				
	Walden	-329	-365	-361	-489
	Tendring	-361	-414	-403	-535
	West Ham	-371	-431	-423	-559
	Witham	-393	-455	-447	-585
SUFFOLK					
	Bosmere	-415	-477	-475	-628
	Cosford	-441	-509	-499	-661
	Ipswich	-476	-540	-529	-695
	Plomesgate	-505	-571	-565	-758
	Risbridge	-535	-603	-591	-802
	Samford	-557	-627	-617	-839
	Stow	-591	-659	-643	-898
	Sudbury	-625	-697	-687	-959
	Woodbridge	-653	-740	-719	-1021
Overall page range					
(Q1 = 100)		100	113	110	156
Number of index					
entries		1284	1495	1490	2875
Index entries					
(Q1 = 100)		100	116	116	224

Note that large increases in marriages in rural areas involve much smaller increases in the pages of data. Largely empty pages have plenty of room for additional marriages. This is much less true in urban areas.

Superintendent Registrar's District of

18   . Marriage solemnized at   in the   of   in the County of

Columns. No.	1 When Married.	2 Name and Surname.	3 Age.	4 Condition.	5 Rank or Profession.	6 Residence at the time of Marriage.	7 Father's Name and Surname.	8 Rank or Profession of Father.

18___

Married in the   according to the Rites and Ceremonies of the Established Church, by   or after   by me,

This Marriage } was solemnized { between us,   in the Presence of us, {

18   . Marriage solemnized at   in the   of   in the County of

Columns. No.	1 When Married.	2 Name and Surname.	3 Age.	4 Condition.	5 Rank or Profession.	6 Residence at the time of Marriage.	7 Father's Name and Surname.	8 Rank or Profession of Father.

18___

Married in the   according to the Rites and Ceremonies of the Established Church, by   or after   by me,

This Marriage } was solemnized { between us,   in the Presence of us, {

I,   Entr   numbered   is a true Copy of the Entr   so numbered, made in the Marriage Register Books of the   in the County of   do hereby certify that the forgoing,

comprising   of   day of   18

Witness my hand this

The sign-offs for the quarterly returns

Four different types of stationery were provided for this purpose,
for parishes, for registry offices, for Friends' meeting houses,
and for Jewish congregations.
Each type of stationery had it own special form of declaration at the foot of
each side for the clergyman or registrar or other congregation official
to attest the accuracy of the copies written on that side of the form.

The clergy's declaration

I --------- of ----------- in the County of ---------- do hereby certify that the
foregoing, comprising ----Entr--- numbered --------------, is a true Copy of
the Entr--- so numbered, made in the Marriage Register Books of the said -
-------------------,
              Witness my hand, this -------------- day of -------------- 18--.

The Registrar's declaration

I, ---------------------- Registrar of the District of ----------------- in the County
of ---------- do hereby certify, That this is a true Copy of the Entr----- of
Marriage registered in the said District, -------- the Entry of the Marriage of --
----------------- and -----------------, Number ---------- to the Entry of the
Marriage of -------------------- and -----------------, number ------------, Witness
my hand, this ----------- day of ------------ 18--.

                                        _____ Registrar

I have examined the above, and have compared it with the said Registration
Book, and hereby certify that it is a true Copy

    Witness my hand, this ------------ day of ---------- 18--

                                        _____ Superintendent Registrar

The synagogue declaration

I ----------------------- Secretary of a Synagogue of persons professing the Jewish Religion at ---------------------- in the County of --------------- do hereby certify, That the foregoing, comprising ------------ Entr---- numbered --------- -----------, is a true copy of the Entr----- so numbered, made in the Marriage Register Books of the said Synagogue. Winess my hand, this --------- day of - ------------- 18--.

                           _____ Secretary

The Quaker declaration

I James Hurnard Registering officer of the Society of Friends, commonly called Quakers, for the Monthly Meeting of Colchester in the County of Essex do hereby certify, That the foregoing, comprising two Entries numbered 6 and 7 is a true Copy of the Entries so numbered, made in the marriage Register Books of the said Monthly Meeting.

 Witness my hand, this twenty fifth day of the seventh month, commonly called July 1843.

                           _____ Registering Officer

In the case of the Quaker declaration, I have inserted the entries from one particular marriage film to illustrate the usage. All the forms of declaration were completed similarly.

I have not included the form of declaration used by a Superintendent Registrar for any marriages solemnised in his own district.

The Missing Jenkins clan in 1844/Q2

As noted in the body of this report (page 80), the GRO marriage index for the June quarter of 1844 has a gap in the Jenkin/Jenkins area. After a part-list of Jenkin names, Jenkins suddenly and impossibly begins with Thomas Jenkins. A comparison with other fiche for this part of the alphabet shows that about 80 names are missing from the 1844/Q2 index. It is a typed section of the index. The typist must have turned three sheets at once or resumed work at a wrong point. The index registers in the GRO basement have been checked and reflect the same position because they are the basis for the GRO fiche.

The following list of Jenkins references lost from the index was made by re-indexing from the GRO films for the Welsh volumes, 26 and 27. One name comes from volume 12, and two were found later in volume 10. One further Jenkins (Edward G) probably failed to reach the GRO at all. It is an ironic comment on the errors in the indexes that one Thomas Jenkins noticed in the films for vols 26 & 27 was one of the lucky ones in the index but was mis-indexed as Aberayron instead of Aberystwith.

Here are the Jenkin/Jenkins names from volumes 10, 12, 26 and 27 :

Jenkin and Jenkins in 1844 June Quarter

SURNAME	GIVEN	DISTRICT	VOL	PAGE	SPOUSE
Jenkin	Mary	Rhayader	26	457	Owen
Jenkins	Ann	Neath	26	719	Bevan
Jenkins	Ann	Neath	26	729	Owen
Jenkins	Ann	Llandilofawr	26	837	Jones
Jenkins	Ann	Bridgend	26	624	Short
Jenkins	Ann	Bridgend	26	667	Lewis
Jenkins	Anne	Llanelly	26	881	Phillip
Jenkins	David	Brecknock	26	497	Davies
Jenkins	David	Bridgend	26	599	Jenkins
Jenkins	David	Bridgend	26	605	Miles
Jenkins	Edward	Llanelly	26	884a	Morgan
Jenkins	Edward	Newport Mon	26	133	Williams
Jenkins	Edward G	Taunton	10		N.a.
Jenkins	Eleanor	Neath	26	725	Jenkins
Jenkins	Elenor	Merthyr T	26	710	Jenkins
Jenkins	Elinor	Haverfordwest	26	893	Morris
Jenkins	Elizabeth	Swansea	26	753	Morgan
Jenkins	Elizabeth	Abergavenny	26	37	Jenkins
Jenkins	Elizabeth	Bridgend	26	615	Thomas
Jenkins	Elizabeth	Bridgend	26	657	Harry

SURNAME	GIVEN	DISTRICT	VOL	PAGE	SPOUSE
Jenkins	Elizabeth	Aberystwith	27	41	Evans
Jenkins	Elizabeth	Taunton	10	811	Winchester
Jenkins	Emma	Ipswich	12	531	Cresswell
Jenkins	Evan	Cardigan	27	69	Peregrine
Jenkins	Hannah	Aberystwith	27	59	Isaac
Jenkins	Hannah	Newtown	27	193	Williams
Jenkins	Henry	Hereford	26	215	Watkins
Jenkins	James	Pontypool	26	157	Addams
Jenkins	Jane	Bridgend	26	595	Thomas
Jenkins	Jane	Bridgend	26	599	Jenkins
Jenkins	Jane	Tregaron	27	97	Davies
Jenkins	John	Merthyr T	26	673	Thomas
Jenkins	John	Chepstow	26	67	Darby
Jenkins	John	Aberystwith	27	20	Davis
Jenkins	Joseph	Abergavenny	26	37	Jenkins
Jenkins	Levi	Haverfordwest	26	939	Lewis
Jenkins	Lewis	Neath	26	725	Jenkins
Jenkins	Margaret	Merthyr T	26	677	Morgan
Jenkins	Margaret	Neath	26	721	Thomas
Jenkins	Margaret	Neath	26	732	Williams
Jenkins	Margaret	Newtown	27	195	Wilson
Jenkins	Mariah	Bridgend	26	581	Edwards
Jenkins	Mary	Merthyr T	26	711	Rees
Jenkins	Mary	Swansea	26	744	Richards
Jenkins	Mary	Aberystwith	27	19	Jones
Jenkins	Mary	Aberystwith	27	21	Davies
Jenkins	Rachel	Brecknock	26	493	Herring
Jenkins	Rees	Bridgend	26	616	Burnell
Jenkins	Robert	Taunton	10	831	Bull
Jenkins	Samuel	Wrexham	27	413	Smith
Jenkins	Sarah	Pontypool	26	179	Jones
Jenkins	Thomas	Merthyr T	26	710	Jenkins

Note : The entry for Edward G Jenkins is based on the index produced
by the Superintendent Registrar for Taunton. His bride was
Elizabeth Knight and the marriage was at St Mary's, West Buckland.
Neither Edward nor Elizabeth are in the GRO index, having been
either missed from the quarterly returns or missed in the GRO
indexing (see page 111). Therefore they cannot be positively
identified   by quarter within 1844 nor be given a GRO page reference.

Marriages from the Jewish congregation
of the Great Synagogue
in St James's Square in the City of London
in the March quarter of 1856

Secretary - James Oppenheim
(see chapter 7, page 96)

Marriage Register entry no.	Married parties	Location of the marriage	GRO index entry
173	Lewis Lyons, Rebecca Abrahams	The Great Synagogue 1/1	243
174	Lewis Salomons, Rachael Jacobs	The Great Synagogue 2/1	243
175	Aaron Levy, Cecilie Sacks	10 Finsbury Sq, St Lukes 2/1	244
176	Morris Abrahams, Clara Hyams	9 St George's Crescent, St George the Martyr 3/1	244
177	Lewis Benjamin, Rebecca Vince	The Great Synagogue 9/1	245
178	Gabriel Spera, Sarah Baker	The Great Synagogue 9/1	245
179	Jacob Lazarus, Eliza De Frece	166 Bishopsgate 9/1	246
180	Simon Moses, Hannah Simons	The Great Synagogue 9/1	246
181	Samuel Harris, Hannah Cohen	The Great Synagogue 9/1	247
182	Lyon Salomon Cohen, Rachel Hyman Plucker	The Great Synagogue 9/1	247
183	Benjamin Solomon, Fanny Nathan	The Great Synagogue 16/1	248
184	David Levy, Catherine Levy	The Great Synagogue 23/1	248
185	James Ochse, Elizabeth Hyams	21 Spencer St, Clerkenwell 23/1	249
186	Simon Price, Rachel Joseph	1 Fitzroy Sq, St Pancras 23/1	249
187	Abraham Simon Kupper, Lie Kabe	The Great Synagogue 23/1	250
188	Bernhard Hermann Seckendorf, Doris Brandt	The Great Synagogue 30/1	250
189	Isaac Morris, Rebecca Simons	The Great Synagogue 6/2	251
190	Ferdinand Nauhein, Doris Brandt	The Great Synagogue 6/2	251
191	David Philipp, Judith Mandelbaum	1 Church St, Stoke Newington 6/2	252
192	Judah Simmonds, Maria Solomon	34 York Rd, Lambeth 6/2	252
193	Abraham Isaacs, Julia Isaacs	Gt Synagogue Chambers 12/2	253

194	Harris Markis, Jessie Cohen	The Great Synagogue 13/2	253
195	Samuel Solomons, Rachel Friedman	The Great Synagogue 13/2	254
196	Morris Rouse, Hannah Magnus	The Great Synagogue 13/2	254
197	Davis Levy, Sarah Hart	Gt Synagogue Chambers 19/2	255
198	Barnet Lotheim, Rachel Arnheim	Hambro Synagogue, St Catherine Coleman 26/2	255
199	Eleazer Berclon, Hanna Pimentel	The Great Synagogue 27/2	256
200	Israel Freeman, Esther Joseph	The Great Synagogue 27/2	256

.... here the 2nd marriage register begins ....

1	Baron Isaacs, Julia Solomons	The Great Synagogue 27/2	257
2	Morris Hart, Ann Lazarus	12 Marlboro' Place, Walworth 27/2	257
3	Benjamin Julius Jonas, Julia Lawrance	10 Hester Villas, Paddington 28/2	258

.... here the Q1 return ended, omitting the March marriages ....

4	Hyam Simon, Jane Phillips	The Great Synagogue 5/3	258a
5	Marks Winestine, Kitty Faust	The Great Synagogue 5/3	258a
6	Michael Heymanson, Adelaide Jewell	20 Sydney Sq, Stepney 5/3	258b
7	Jacob Solomon, Georgiana Benjamin	7 Marylebone Street 5/3	258b
	Lewis Jacobs, Rachel Joshua	2 Claremont Villas, Canonbury 5/3	258c
	Bear? Myer, Fanny Grahman	The Great Synagogue 12/3	258c
	John Cohen, Jane Coleman	The Great Synagogue 12/3	258d
	John Moss Lawrence, Emily Asher	4 Gordon St, St Pancras 12/3	258d
	Benjamin Solomons, Sarah Mendoza	Gt Synagogue Chambers 12/3	258e
	Marcus van Raalte, Raman Mendes da Costa	35 Tavistock Sq. 12/3	258e
	Moss Lewis, Hannah Davis	King St, Hammersmith 19/3	258f
	Coleman Angel, Jane Samuels	The Great Synagogue 19/3	258f
	Hyam Joseph, Ann Hyman	The Great Synagogue 19/3	258g
	Lewis Levy, Jeanette Symons	Gt Synagogue Chambers 23/3	258g
	Isadore Bernard, Esther Clock	The Great Synagogue 26/3	258h
	Isaac Jacobs, Sarah Symons	The Great Synagogue 26/3	258h
	Israel Charles Marshall, Annie Friedeberg	The Great Synagogue 26/3	258i

| 22 | Lewis Levy, Julia Jacobs | 56 Mansell Street, Whitechapel 26/3 258i |

Notes   The details of dates and locations were noted from the film in haste and there is an apparent discontinuity in register book numbers between nos. 7 and 22.

Bernard Seckindorff in the GRO index looks like Seckendorff in the GRO film.
Eleazer Berclou in the index looks like Berclon in the film.
Ferdinand Nanheim in the index looks like Nauheim in the film.
Kitty Faust in the film is doubly indexed as Fanst and Faust.

Name patterns for 1844/Q1 marriages - bridegrooms

For groups of GRO volumes ...   ... and as percentages

	1-4	5-11	12-14	15-25	26-27	Total	1-4	5-11	12-14	15-25	26-27	Total
John	582	1004	345	2370	303	4604	14.2	16.4	15.8	18.9	18.1	17.3
William	677	1029	403	1902	245	4256	16.5	16.8	18.5	15.1	14.7	16.0
Thomas	389	527	157	1372	230	2675	9.5	8.6	7.2	10.9	13.8	10.1
James	365	572	216	1076	82	2311	8.9	9.3	9.9	8.6	4.9	8.7
George	333	488	154	734	49	1758	8.1	8.0	7.1	5.8	2.9	6.6
Joseph	127	203	67	715	43	1155	3.1	3.3	3.1	5.7	2.6	4.3
Henry	258	300	106	421	38	1123	6.3	4.9	4.9	3.3	2.3	4.2
Robert	157	180	129	440	51	957	3.8	2.9	5.9	3.5	3.1	3.6
Charles	189	273	86	301	21	870	4.6	4.4	3.9	2.4	1.3	3.3
Richard	123	229	49	378	54	833	3.0	3.7	2.2	3.0	3.2	3.1
Samuel	76	152	60	329	20	637	1.8	2.5	2.7	2.6	1.2	2.4
Edward	112	125	54	266	61	618	2.7	2.0	2.5	2.1	3.6	2.3
David	40	40	22	117	140	359	1.0	0.7	1.0	0.9	8.4	1.3
Benjamin	52	62	25	122	21	282	1.3	1.0	1.1	1.0	1.3	1.1
Frederick	65	61	25	55	5	211	1.6	1.0	1.1	0.4	0.3	0.8
Daniel	46	49	12	81	20	208	1.1	0.8	0.5	0.6	1.2	0.8
Francis	33	51	19	82	4	189	0.8	0.8	0.9	0.7	0.2	0.7
Isaac	23	53	19	82	7	184	0.6	0.9	0.9	0.7	0.4	0.7
Peter	9	28	6	116	4	163	0.2	0.5	0.3	0.9	0.2	0.6
Stephen	11	51	12	44	10	128	0.3	0.8	0.5	0.3	0.6	0.5
Abraham	10	20	11	76	5	122	0.2	0.3	0.5	0.6	0.3	0.5
Michael	20	17	4	72	3	116	0.5	0.3	0.2	0.6	0.2	0.4
Matthew	9	17	10	72	2	110	0.2	0.3	0.5	0.6	0.1	0.4
Alfred	33	36	2	28	1	100	0.8	0.6	0.1	0.2	0.1	0.4
Jonathan	9	14	15	57	1	96	0.2	0.2	0.7	0.5	0.1	0.4
Edwin	17	36	3	33	3	92	0.4	0.6	0.1	0.3	0.2	0.3
Edmund	8	23	12	48	1	92	0.2	0.4	0.5	0.4	0.1	0.3
Alexander	18	16	2	43	0	79	0.4	0.3	0.1	0.3	0.0	0.3
Joshua	4	8	5	47	4	68	0.1	0.1	0.2	0.4	0.2	0.3
Patrick	15	5	0	42	3	65	0.4	0.1	0.0	0.3	0.2	0.2
Hugh	7	4	0	31	21	63	0.2	0.1	0.0	0.2	1.3	0.2
Andrew	10	9	3	38	3	63	0.2	0.1	0.1	0.3	0.2	0.2
Evan	1	0	0	5	48	54	0.0	0.0	0.0	0.0	2.9	0.2
Jeremiah	4	5	8	28	1	46	0.1	0.1	0.4	0.2	0.1	0.2
Owen	0	0	0	9	22	31	0.0	0.0	0.0	0.1	1.3	0.1
Morgan	0	0	0	0	11	11	0.0	0.0	0.0	0.0	0.7	0.0
Griffith	0	1	0	0	10	11	0.0	0.0	0.0	0.0	0.6	0.0
Others	277	448	142	940	125	1932	6.7	7.3	6.5	7.5	7.5	7.2
Totals	4109	6136	2183	12572	1672	26672	100	100	100	100	100	100

Name patterns for 1844/Q1 marriages - brides

	For groups of GRO volumes ...						... and as percentages					
	1-4	5-11	12-14	15-25	26-27	Total	1-4	5-11	12-14	15-25	26-27	Total
Elizabeth	476	781	240	1416	229	3142	11.6	12.9	11.5	11.2	13.4	11.8
Mary	306	593	200	1741	295	3135	7.5	9.8	9.6	13.8	17.3	11.8
Ann	296	580	144	1328	133	2481	7.2	9.6	6.9	10.5	7.8	9.3
Sarah	375	515	234	1124	95	2343	9.2	8.5	11.2	8.9	5.6	8.8
Jane	191	395	56	809	127	1578	4.7	6.5	2.7	6.4	7.4	5.9
Mary Ann	316	400	201	552	26	1495	7.7	6.6	9.6	4.4	1.5	5.6
Hannah	78	143	77	656	52	1006	1.9	2.4	3.7	5.2	3.0	3.8
Eliza	198	259	100	327	31	915	4.8	4.3	4.8	2.6	1.8	3.4
Margaret	81	51	9	454	144	739	2.0	0.8	0.4	3.6	8.4	2.8
Harriet	131	211	80	243	21	686	3.2	3.5	3.8	1.9	1.2	2.6
Martha	84	125	47	354	36	646	2.1	2.1	2.2	2.8	2.1	2.4
Maria	112	117	75	174	14	492	2.7	1.9	3.6	1.4	0.8	1.9
Ellen	71	44	12	311	21	459	1.7	0.7	0.6	2.5	1.2	1.7
Catherine	82	66	14	216	55	433	2.0	1.1	0.7	1.7	3.2	1.6
Caroline	134	149	37	98	8	426	3.3	2.5	1.8	0.8	0.5	1.6
Anne	35	85	19	172	112	423	0.9	1.4	0.9	1.4	6.6	1.6
Charlotte	71	150	60	109	13	403	1.7	2.5	2.9	0.9	0.8	1.5
Emma	108	81	41	119	5	354	2.6	1.3	2.0	0.9	0.3	1.3
Susanna	60	78	38	131	8	315	1.5	1.3	1.8	1.0	0.5	1.2
Alice	0	21	8	241	10	280	0.0	0.3	0.4	1.9	0.6	1.1
Frances	54	54	26	121	15	270	1.3	0.9	1.2	1.0	0.9	1.0
Susan	39	65	72	40	8	224	1.0	1.1	3.4	0.3	0.5	0.8
Betsy etc	10	28	15	168	0	221	0.2	0.5	0.7	1.3	0.0	0.8
Rebecca	44	41	45	76	12	218	1.1	0.7	2.2	0.6	0.7	0.8
Esther	43	49	5	101	17	215	1.1	0.8	0.2	0.8	1.0	0.8
Eleanor	31	35	15	63	54	198	0.8	0.6	0.7	0.5	3.2	0.7
Mary other	56	56	14	64	7	197	1.4	0.9	0.7	0.5	0.4	0.7
Louisa	58	68	21	43	5	195	1.4	1.1	1.0	0.3	0.3	0.7
Isabella	24	12	3	139	0	178	0.6	0.2	0.1	1.1	0.0	0.7
Sophia	53	52	36	34	1	176	1.3	0.9	1.7	0.3	0.1	0.7
Rachel	22	26	11	63	26	148	0.5	0.4	0.5	0.5	1.5	0.6
Mary Anne	9	44	35	43	9	140	0.2	0.7	1.7	0.3	0.5	0.5
Fanny	24	43	9	59	1	136	0.6	0.7	0.4	0.5	0.1	0.5
Lucy	26	41	13	49	1	130	0.6	0.7	0.6	0.4	0.1	0.5
Amelia	33	33	9	34	5	114	0.8	0.5	0.4	0.3	0.3	0.4
Grace	9	53	1	38	8	109	0.2	0.9	0.0	0.3	0.5	0.4
Nancy etc	0	11	2	94	0	107	0.0	0.2	0.1	0.7	0.0	0.4
Matilda	27	33	8	24	1	93	0.7	0.5	0.4	0.2	0.1	0.3
Emily	28	30	13	11	0	82	0.7	0.5	0.6	0.1	0.0	0.3
Agnes	16	13	1	50	0	80	0.4	0.2	0.0	0.4	0.0	0.3
Julia	23	13	4	19	1	60	0.6	0.2	0.2	0.2	0.1	0.2
Others	252	429	43	712	102	1538	6.2	7.1	2.1	5.6	6.0	5.8
Totals	4086	6073	2093	12620	1708	26586	100	100	100	100	100	100

Some selected names in *each* GRO volume for the March quarters of 1844 and 1849

GRO vol no.	Caroline		David		George		Harriet		Margaret		Samuel	
	1844	1849	1844	1849	1844	1849	1844	1849	1844	1849	1844	1849
1	36	31	11	14	96	93	43	26	28	30	17	25
2	31	32	17	17	105	99	33	38	17	21	26	33
3	25	19	6	5	60	58	21	25	11	17	13	21
4	42	38	6	7	72	89	34	32	25	18	20	12
5	17	20	10	6	71	64	28	33	10	10	10	5
6	14	18	6	10	77	73	22	22	4	1	14	11
7	25	29	9	8	84	94	49	48	5	15	20	13
8	17	15	4	1	78	73	20	18	2	2	12	17
9	20	15	2	3	40	44	22	17	13	10	31	30
10	24	13	4	5	70	76	35	33	10	5	40	43
11	32	25	5	9	68	92	35	33	7	8	25	24
12	11	12	14	9	59	59	21	15	0	3	18	26
13	13	11	4	11	48	67	37	33	6	6	30	30
14	13	12	4	7	47	71	22	33	3	3	12	19
15	14	17	4	11	78	93	37	24	3	10	37	47
16	16	13	9	11	49	61	25	25	10	5	19	28
17	14	10	4	14	39	47	25	28	3	11	29	34
18	16	17	9	10	55	59	22	23	13	21	31	46
19	4	13	11	4	66	72	25	23	12	21	38	61
20	11	22	29	31	92	100	33	32	134	123	63	56
21	0	1	11	7	38	46	11	8	90	99	28	19
22	13	15	11	11	102	124	41	53	13	19	46	35
23	9	6	16	23	89	88	21	36	40	33	30	32
24	1	1	9	13	78	96	2	5	76	69	4	13
25	0	2	4	10	48	59	1	2	60	85	4	6
26	7	14	86	113	40	45	17	19	88	86	14	16
27	1	1	54	47	9	11	4	7	56	71	6	7
Totals	426	422	359	417	1758	1953	686	691	739	802	637	709

Note : Harriet includes variants such as Harriett, Harriot etc. Margaret includes variants

Two very localised names in 1844 and 1849 Grace and Isabel(la)

Grace		1844	1849	Isabella		1844	1849
	vol 9	30	31		vol 20	13	23
	vol 10	18	10		vol 21	25	17
	vol 20	2	10		vol 23	6	15
	vol 21	10	9		vol 24	44	48
	vol 22	8	7		vol 25	35	46
	vol 23	15	10				
All others		26	29			57	65
Totals		109	106			180	214

Some name frequencies in each volume in the
1844/Q1 and 1849/Q1 marriage indexes

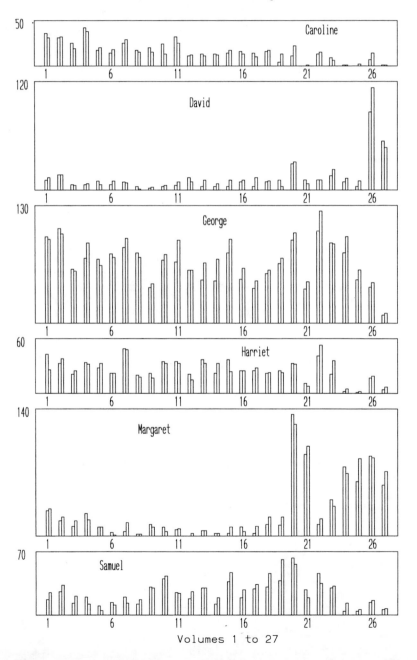

Volumes 1 to 27

Name patterns for 1891/Q1 marriages - bridegrooms

	For groups of GRO volumes ...						... and as percentages					
	1	2,3,5	4,7a	6,7b 8-10	11	Total	1	2,3,5	4,7a	6,7b 8-10	11	Total
William	205	253	76	605	87	1226	14.6	14.6	11.7	13.2	14.8	13.7
John	144	169	72	647	82	1114	10.2	9.7	11.0	14.1	14.0	12.4
Thomas	68	93	49	395	45	650	4.8	5.4	7.5	8.6	7.7	7.3
George	110	132	58	308	27	635	7.8	7.6	8.9	6.7	4.6	7.1
James	89	82	31	337	37	576	6.3	4.7	4.8	7.4	6.3	6.4
Charles	96	104	39	165	20	424	6.8	6.0	6.0	3.6	3.4	4.7
Henry	75	97	38	174	20	404	5.3	5.6	5.8	3.8	3.4	4.5
Joseph	36	53	15	221	12	337	2.6	3.1	2.3	4.8	2.0	3.8
Frederick	60	97	21	109	9	296	4.3	5.6	3.2	2.4	1.5	3.3
Robert	30	37	26	164	18	275	2.1	2.1	4.0	3.6	3.1	3.1
Edward	46	45	12	103	14	220	3.3	2.6	1.8	2.3	2.4	2.5
Arthur	48	46	28	85	6	213	3.4	2.7	4.3	1.9	1.0	2.4
Alfred	5	70	19	102	12	208	0.4	4.0	2.9	2.2	2.0	2.3
Richard	24	30	7	97	19	177	1.7	1.7	1.1	2.1	3.2	2.0
Samuel	23	26	5	113	7	174	1.6	1.5	0.8	2.5	1.2	1.9
Albert	31	40	12	71	5	159	2.2	2.3	1.8	1.6	0.9	1.8
Walter	35	45	20	55	3	158	2.5	2.6	3.1	1.2	0.5	1.8
Harry	30	40	11	59	1	141	2.1	2.3	1.7	1.3	.02	1.6
David	4	9	9	37	48	107	0.3	0.5	1.4	0.8	8.2	1.2
Herbert	15	16	13	38	3	85	1.1	0.9	2.0	0.8	0.5	0.9
Benjamin	11	14	10	41	9	85	0.8	0.8	1.5	0.9	1.5	0.9
Frank	20	17	3	35	2	77	1.4	1.0	0.5	0.8	0.3	0.9
Francis	11	19	3	33	3	69	0.8	1.1	0.5	0.7	0.5	0.8
Ernest	13	19	7	22	1	62	0.9	1.1	1.1	0.5	0.2	0.7
Edwin	14	15	3	22	5	59	1.0	0.9	0.5	0.5	0.9	0.7
Isaac	2	6	0	26	5	39	0.1	0.3	0.0	0.6	0.9	0.4
Daniel	6	9	2	17	3	37	0.4	0.5	0.3	0.4	0.5	0.4
Andrew	3	2	0	27	0	32	0.2	0.1	0.0	0.6	0.0	0.4
Alexander	10	3	3	12	1	29	0.7	0.2	0.5	0.3	0.2	0.3
Michael	5	4	1	17	2	29	0.4	0.2	0.2	0.4	0.3	0.3
Peter	3	2	0	16	1	22	0.2	0.1	0.0	0.3	0.2	0.2
Matthew	2	1	2	15	0	20	0.1	0.1	0.3	0.3	0.0	0.2
Edmund	3	2	1	10	2	18	0.2	0.1	0.2	0.2	0.3	0.2
Hugh	3	3	0	9	3	18	0.2	0.2	0.0	0.2	0.5	0.2
Stephen	5	5	0	5	2	17	0.4	0.3	0.0	0.1	0.3	0.2
Abraham	5	0	0	10	1	16	0.4	0.0	0.0	0.2	0.2	0.2
Jonathan	2	3	0	10	0	15	0.1	0.2	0.0	0.2	0.0	0.2
Patrick	2	1	0	10	0	13	0.1	0.1	0.0	0.2	0.0	0.1
Jeremiah	0	0	8	4	1	13	0.0	0.0	1.2	0.1	0.2	0.1
Evan	0	0	0	0	11	11	0.0	0.0	0.0	0.0	1.9	0.1
Others	111	125	48	350	59	693	7.9	7.2	7.4	7.6	9.1	7.7
Totals	1405	1734	652	4576	586	8953	100	100	100	100	100	100

Name patterns for 1891/Q1 marriages - brides

	1	2,3,5	4,7a	6,7b 8-10	11	Total	1	2,3,5	4,7a	6,7b 8-10	11	Total
		For groups of GRO volumes ...						... and as percentages				
Elizabeth	113	130	44	449	82	818	7.6	7.6	7.3	10.1	13.1	9.2
Sarah	80	117	32	379	57	665	5.4	6.8	5.3	8.5	9.1	7.5
Mary other	42	83	16	319	31	491	2.8	4.8	2.7	7.2	4.9	5.5
Annie	65	82	31	218	33	429	4.4	4.8	5.1	4.9	5.3	4.8
Mary Ann	76	69	36	189	28	398	5.1	4.0	6.0	4.2	4.5	4.5
Mary	20	43	11	244	45	363	1.3	2.5	1.8	5.5	7.2	4.1
Alice	82	64	27	147	13	333	5.5	3.7	4.5	3.3	2.1	3.7
Emma	58	63	25	157	7	310	3.9	3.7	4.2	3.5	1.1	3.5
Jane	48	40	14	170	33	305	3.2	2.3	2.3	3.8	5.3	3.4
Ellen	51	73	24	128	22	298	3.4	4.3	4.0	2.9	3.5	3.4
Margaret	25	13	1	157	52	248	1.7	0.8	0.2	3.5	8.3	2.8
Eliza	41	60	25	102	7	235	2.8	3.5	4.2	2.3	1.1	2.6
Emily	45	87	15	67	13	227	3.0	5.1	2.5	1.5	2.1	2.6
Ann	17	19	16	122	23	197	1.1	1.1	2.7	2.7	3.7	2.2
Hannah	8	17	10	130	11	176	0.5	1.0	1.7	2.9	1.8	2.0
Harriet	37	28	14	80	10	169	2.5	1.6	2.3	1.8	1.6	1.9
Martha	21	16	9	100	9	155	1.4	0.9	1.5	2.2	1.4	1.7
Louisa	35	35	8	53	8	139	2.4	2.0	1.3	1.2	1.3	1.6
Ada	23	27	11	74	0	135	1.5	1.6	1.8	1.7	0.0	1.5
Catherine	17	14	5	65	20	121	1.1	0.8	0.8	1.5	3.2	1.4
Fanny	12	45	8	44	5	114	0.8	2.6	1.3	1.0	0.8	1.3
Florence	27	33	9	38	3	110	1.8	1.9	1.5	0.9	0.5	1.2
Clara	19	24	7	48	1	99	1.3	1.4	1.2	1.1	0.2	1.1
Charlotte	12	19	14	45	0	90	0.8	1.1	2.3	1.0	0.0	1.0
Maria	18	14	7	46	2	87	1.2	0.8	1.2	1.0	0.3	1.0
Edith	19	23	4	34	2	82	1.3	1.3	0.7	0.8	0.3	0.9
Lucy	15	24	8	30	2	79	1.0	1.4	1.3	0.7	0.3	0.9
Agnes	6	19	7	44	1	77	0.4	1.1	1.2	1.0	0.2	0.9
Kate	24	20	12	20	1	77	1.6	1.2	2.0	0.4	0.2	0.9
Rose	25	19	4	24	3	75	1.7	1.1	0.7	0.5	0.5	0.8
Caroline	14	22	8	24	3	71	0.9	1.3	1.3	0.5	0.5	0.8
Frances	24	8	4	26	2	64	1.6	0.5	0.7	0.6	0.3	0.7
Isabella	6	4	4	50	0	64	0.4	0.2	0.7	1.1	0.0	0.7
Eleanor	18	6	4	30	2	60	1.2	0.3	0.7	0.7	0.3	0.7
Esther	7	5	5	36	4	57	0.5	0.3	0.8	0.8	0.6	0.6
Amelia	13	11	11	18	2	55	0.9	0.6	1.8	0.4	0.3	0.6
Susan	13	18	1	19	3	54	0.9	1.0	0.2	0.4	0.5	0.6
Susanna	9	7	7	29	1	53	0.6	0.4	1.2	0.7	0.2	0.6
Betsy etc	4	14	4	25	2	49	0.3	0.8	0.7	0.6	0.3	0.6
Minnie	10	14	1	24	0	49	0.7	0.8	0.2	0.5	0.0	0.6
Julia	11	11	5	20	0	47	0.7	0.6	0.8	0.4	0.0	0.5

-    continued   -

Name patterns for 1891/Q1 marriages - brides
(continued)

| | For groups of GRO volumes ... | | | | | ... and as percentages | | | | | |
	1	2,3,5	4,7a	6,7b 8-10	11	Total	1	2,3,5	4,7a	6,7b 8-10	11	Total
Matilda	13	10	4	17	1	45	0.9	0.6	0.7	0.4	0.2	0.5
Rebecca	8	6	4	14	3	35	0.5	0.3	0.7	0.3	0.5	0.4
Sophia	9	6	4	11	0	30	0.6	0.3	0.7	0.2	0.0	0.3
Rachel	6	1	0	18	1	26	0.4	0.1	0.0	0.4	0.2	0.3
Anne	0	3	1	9	9	22	0.0	0.2	0.2	0.2	1.4	0.2
Grace	4	5	2	3	1	15	0.3	0.3	0.3	0.1	0.2	0.2
Mary Ann	3	1	0	1	2	7	0.2	0.1	0.0	0.0	0.3	0.1
Others	233	243	79	361	68	984	15.7	14.2	13.1	8.1	10.8	11.1
Totals	1486	1715	602	4458	628	8889	100	100	100	100	100	100

Notes :Because of the greater diversity of names in 1891 compared with 1844, the list of
women's names is longer and the proportion of names in the "others" category
has also approximately doubled.